Amelia Earhart

Fearless Flyer!

Where will she go next?

~BUY~
PATRIOT BRAND CIGARETTES
~EARN~
PATRIOT POINTS
SEE YOUR LOCAL PATRIOT BRAND CIGARETTE RETAILER FOR MORE DETAILS.

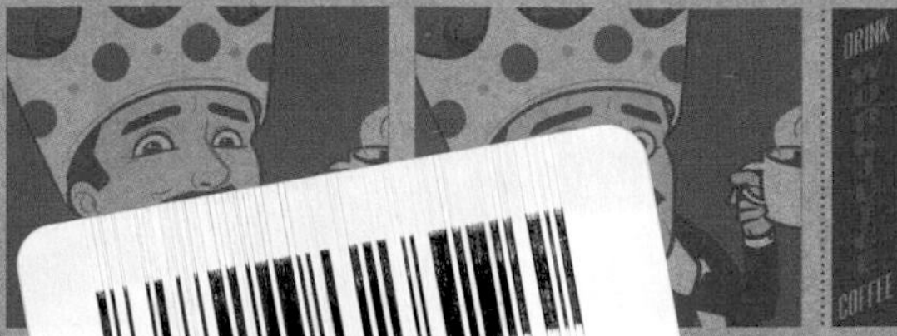

Patriot Brand Cigarettes Proudly Presents

# BETSY ROSS

America's Founding Mother

ENJOY THE BRAND THAT SPARKED A REVOLUTION!

PROUD TO BE AN AMERICAN ORIGINAL

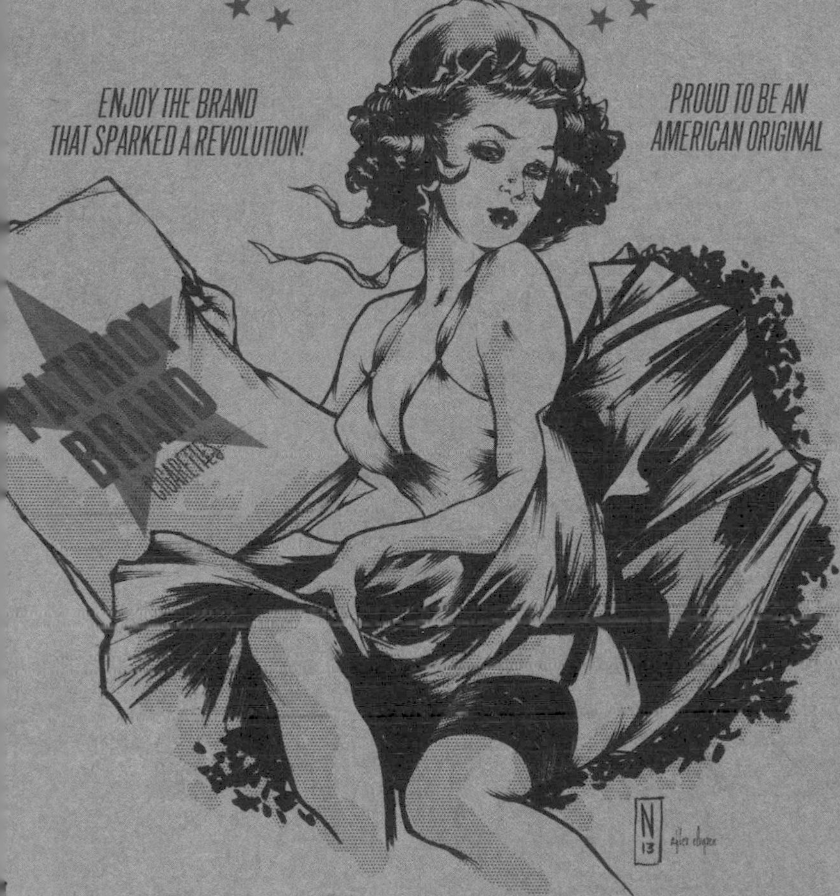

PATRIOT BRAND CIGARETTES


★★★★★★★★★★★★★

When I sewed the stars and stripes, I thought to myself "Betsy, you've nearly peaked. You've got one design left in you old girl, so make it a doozy!"

My doctor agreed. He said if I designed one more thing, my poor heart would give out from the strain. Seconds later, President George Washington phoned and asked me to design the packaging for his new tobacco company, which he founded with Thomas Jefferson and John Quincy Adams! I couldn't say no!

So I designed that one last design and then I died. At my funeral, old George himself declared that design a doozy, and he couldn't tell a lie! So my death was worthwhile after all!

★★★★★★★★★★★★★

TRY PATRIOT BRAND CIGARETTES

PATRIOT BRAND CIGARETTES

THEY'RE GOOD... FOR YOUR CONSTITUTION.

Patriot Brand Cigarettes is a proud sponsor of Jefferson Reid: Ace American and The Thrilling Adventure Hour.

COFFINWOOD WHISKEY

EST. 1860

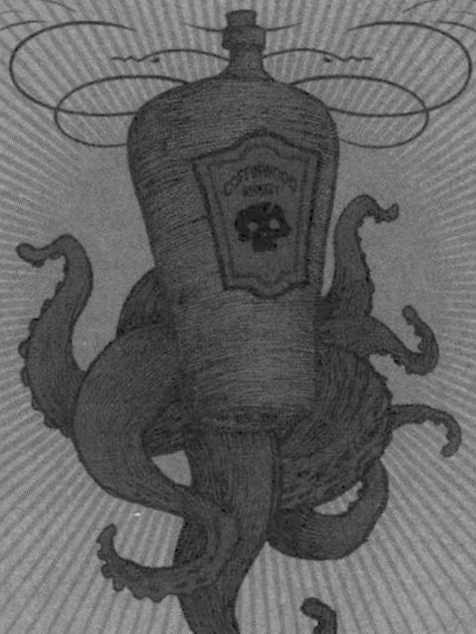

A Proud Co-Sponsor of The Thrilling Adventure Hour's Beyond Belief

"I read this repeatedly, laughing all over again. It's that flat-out wonderful and hilarious. Crossing from one medium to another is a ten for difficulty but luckily **Acker and Blacker** have made whole new dimensions in narrative their next frontier. It's ***The Thrilling Adventure Hour's*** planet and we're lucky to live in it. Like so many others in this book, I'm glad that, after all, we're making soup."

Glen David Gold

{Award-worthy author of *Carter Beats the Devil* and *Sunnyside*}

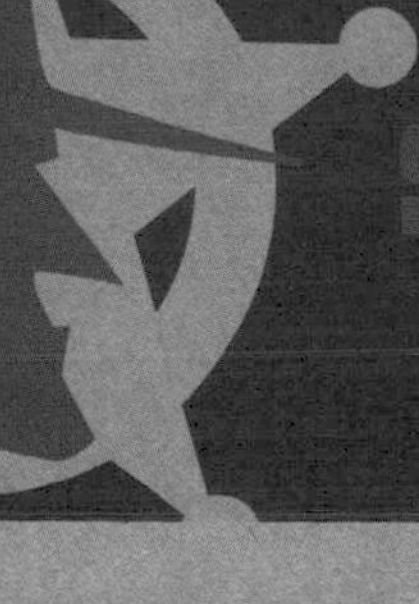

Justice Rides A Rocket Steed

SPARKS NEVADA

Marshal on Mars

ONLY ON THE THRILLING ADVENTURE HOUR

**This Book**
{and all of its thrilling adventures}
**Belongs to:**

Issue No.1  August 2013

**Comic Anthology Produced in Spectacular WORK JUICE COLOR for a Superior Reading Experience**

*Acker & Blacker present...*

# THE THRILLING ADVENTURE HOUR™

**Thrilling Tales of Adventure and Supernatural Suspense!**

Brought to you by your friends at

## WorkJuice

*"KEEPING THE WHEELS OF PROGRESS GREASED"*

AND

## Patriot Brand
### Cigarettes

*"GOOD FOR YOUR CONSTITUTION!"*

in partnership with the industrious publishing services of

## Archaia Entertainment's
### Black Label

*"NEW STORIES. NEW WORLDS."*

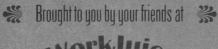

ARCHAIA ENTERTAINMENT LLC
WWW.ARCHAIA.COM

A Comic Anthology
Produced in Spectacular
**WORK JUICE COLOR**
for a Superior Reading
Experience

**WARNING:**
This volume contains two-fisted action,
full-hearted romance and spine-tingling terror.
Sometimes concurrently.
**PLEASE READ
RESPONSIBLY.**

Rebecca Taylor, *Managing Editor*

**Archaia Entertainment LLC**
Jack Cummins, *President & COO*
Mark Smylie, *Chief Creative Officer*
Mike Kennedy, *Publisher ,*
Stephen Christy, *Editor-in-Chief*
Scott Newman, *Production Manager*
Mel Caylo, *Marketing Manager*

Published by **Archaia**

Archaia Entertainment LLC
1680 Vine Street, Suite 1010
Los Angeles, California, 90028
**www.archaia.com**

**THE THRILLING ADVENTURE HOUR**
Original Graphic Novel Hardcover.
August 2013. FIRST PRINTING.
10 9 8 7 6 5 4 3 2 1

ISBN: 1-936393-96-4
ISBN 13: 978-1-936393-96-1

THE THRILLING ADVENTURE HOUR™ is TM and © 2013 WorkJuice
Corp. All Rights Reserved. All properties, characters, ideas contained
herein are the invention of Acker & Blacker and the WorkJuice Corp.
and are owned wholly by same. Archaia™, Archaia™ Black Label and
the Archaia Black Label Logo™ are TM 2013 Archaia Entertainment
LLC. All Rights Reserved. No unauthorized reproductions permitted,
except for review purposes. This is a work of fiction. Any similarity to
persons alive or dead is purely coincidental.

Printed in **China**.

*Acker & Blacker present...*

# THE THRILLING ADVENTURE HOUR™

**Thrilling Tales of Adventure and Supernatural Suspense!**

## TABLE OF CONTENTS
for readers of an organized and distinguished disposition

written by

# Ben Acker & Ben Blacker

lettered by
**DJ Bennett**

cover art by
**Tom Fowler**

edited by
**Joe LeFavi**

assistant editors
**Sam Kusek & Dax LaFleur**

design by
**Scott Newman**

thrilling adventure hour logo design by
**Brian Newman**

transmedia producer
**Quixotic Transmedia**

THE WORK JUICE CORPORATION recommends the following reading pattern for the most efficient use of its table of contents.

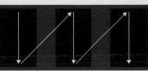

Where do you go from here, dear reader?

Turn the page to discover what a pair of discerning gentlemen have to say about The Thrilling Adventure Hour!

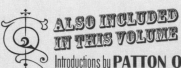

**ALSO INCLUDED IN THIS VOLUME**

Remember to Enjoy a Refreshing Patriot Brand Cigarette and a Cup of WorkJuice Gentlemen's Blend Coffee While You Read!

Introductions by **PATTON OSWALT** and **ED BRUBAKER**
WorkJuice Intro and Outro • About the Creators • A Special Thank You From Acker & Blacker

# A DOUBLE-SIZED INTRODUC

## The World of THRILLING ADVENTURE HOUR

I was watching the George Harrison documentary on HBO last year. They spoke to Terry Gilliam at one point. George Harrison put up a lot of the money for the movie ***Life of Brian*** mostly because, as Terry said, "He wanted to see it."

***The Thrilling Adventure Hour*** lives in the same rarified neighborhood. I'd even say it has a slightly better address in said neighborhood. The brilliance of ***Life of Brian*** got a Beatle to pony up the pounds to see it unspool on a movie screen. ***The Thrilling Adventure Hour*** makes more than a dozen incandescent talents loan their time and energy to see it unfurl itself every month at The Largo in Los Angeles.

And this is every month in 2013. This is a world where terrestrial radio is dead, and old-time radio-style plays even deader, and live shows are fighting a battle of attrition with video games, viral videos, phone apps and the general hurry and howl of the everyday world.

But somehow, Mr. Acker and Mr. Blacker have carved out a monthly, standing-room-only destination in a city built from distractions. If that isn't enough of a miracle, they've foolishly decided to expand the impossible world they've created into comics and videos and, one hopes, film. In reaching back to pre-WWII forms, they've crafted a post-9/11 hybrid that won't stop growing. These guys have creativity to burn. Here, inhale a little of the smoke from these pages. And when you exhale, make sure your friends get a whiff.

**Patton Oswalt**
BUSHWICK, NY
2013

If you ask me what *The Thrilling Adventure Hour* is, you could say that it's a radio play performing live to sold-out crowds every month around the country. You could say that it's a pretty popular podcast around the world, too. But *The Thrilling Adventure Hour* isn't just a bunch of people standing on a stage reading from scripts. It's an experience. It's magic. It's the kind of thing you stumble upon, and then bring all your friends to see because you can't even believe it exists. Last year, my wife and I went to almost every show, and I was constantly amazed at what Acker and Blacker were achieving. Writing continuing tales in several different genres with a huge cast of characters... and it was always funny as hell.

Soon I became friends with the creators, and not long after Acker (accidentally maybe) invited me to become the first outsider to ever write a tale for *The Thrilling Adventure Hour*. For an episode of *Beyond Belief* in their Christmas Special no less. I was daunted, but I sure as hell wasn't going to say no just because I didn't think I could pull it off.

Once we went through some rewrites and polishing, Christmas was upon us and there was Paul F. Tompkins, Paget Brewster, and Jon Hamm, Don Draper himself, on stage performing characters I wrote and getting huge laughs from the crowd. That's what magic feels like. I'm sure of it.

You hold in your hands the first graphic novel for *The Thrilling Adventure Hour*, and it's almost unfair how good these guys are at what they do. Maybe it's your first exposure to these characters. Maybe you've been following them for years. Either way, I know when you're done with this book, you'll want more. Lucky for you, there are endless hours of radio plays (you on Earth call them "podcasts") waiting for you online. Trust me, if you love them half as much as I do, you will endeavor to trick, inveigle, and fight your way into their company. Just like I did.

**Ed Brubaker**
LOS ANGELES, CA
APRIL 2013

*Acker & Blacker's*
## THE THRILLING ADVENTURE HOUR
sponsored by the **WorkJuice Corporation**
and by **Patriot Brand Cigarettes**.

WorkJuice Coffee - just the thing for all your pep-related needs.
As the most caffeine-dense coffee legally available in the marketplace, **WorkJuice** is
*FILLED TO THE BRIM WITH ZIP AND VIM!*
**Patriot Brand Cigarettes** are
*LIKE SMOKING THE AMERICAN FLAG!*

### THE THRILLING ADVENTURE HOUR
is scientifically proven to provide the exact same rush as a single serving of **WorkJuice** or one puff of a **Patriot!**
As with our coffee and coffee related products and cigarettes,
**THE THRILLING ADVENTURE HOUR** is fun for all ages-
**GROWN-UPS AND THE GROWN-UP AT HEART!**

Radio-proven and available as comics for the very first time in history,
The Thrilling Adventure Hour will dazzle and delight you *IN ANY MEDIUM!*
But don't take our word for it.

## SEE FOR YOURSELF...

SHINE YOUR ASTRO-SPURS AND DON YOUR ROBOT FISTS, 'CAUSE IT'S TIME FOR…

Brought to you by WORKJUICE COMICS GROUP

# SPARKS NEVADA
## MARSHAL ON MARS

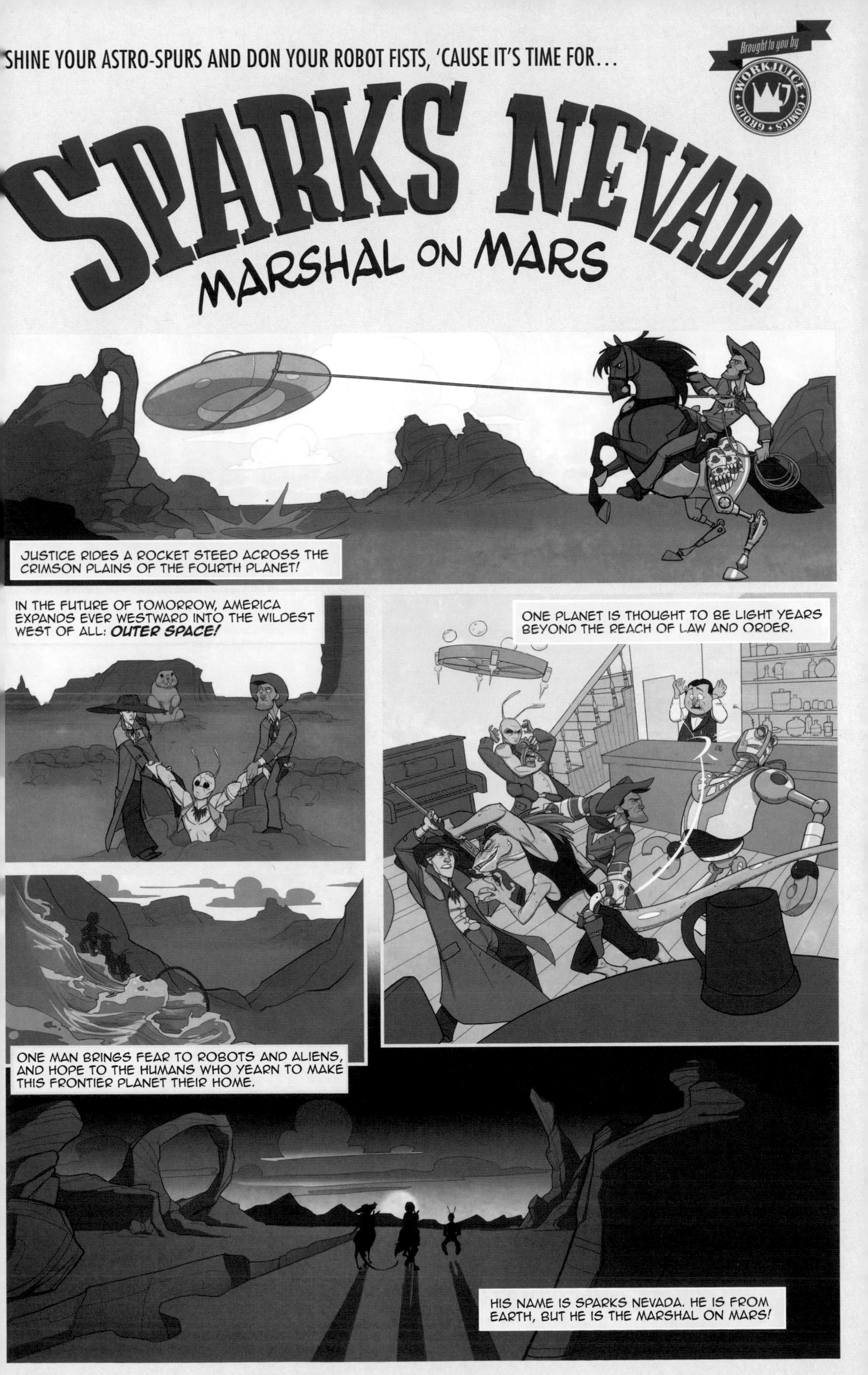

JUSTICE RIDES A ROCKET STEED ACROSS THE CRIMSON PLAINS OF THE FOURTH PLANET!
IN THE FUTURE OF TOMORROW, AMERICA EXPANDS EVER WESTWARD INTO THE WILDEST WEST OF ALL: OUTER SPACE!
ONE PLANET IS THOUGHT TO BE LIGHT YEARS BEYOND THE REACH OF LAW AND ORDER.
ONE MAN BRINGS FEAR TO ROBOTS AND ALIENS, AND HOPE TO THE HUMANS WHO YEARN TO MAKE THIS FRONTIER PLANET THEIR HOME.
HIS NAME IS SPARKS NEVADA. HE IS FROM EARTH, BUT HE IS THE MARSHAL ON MARS!

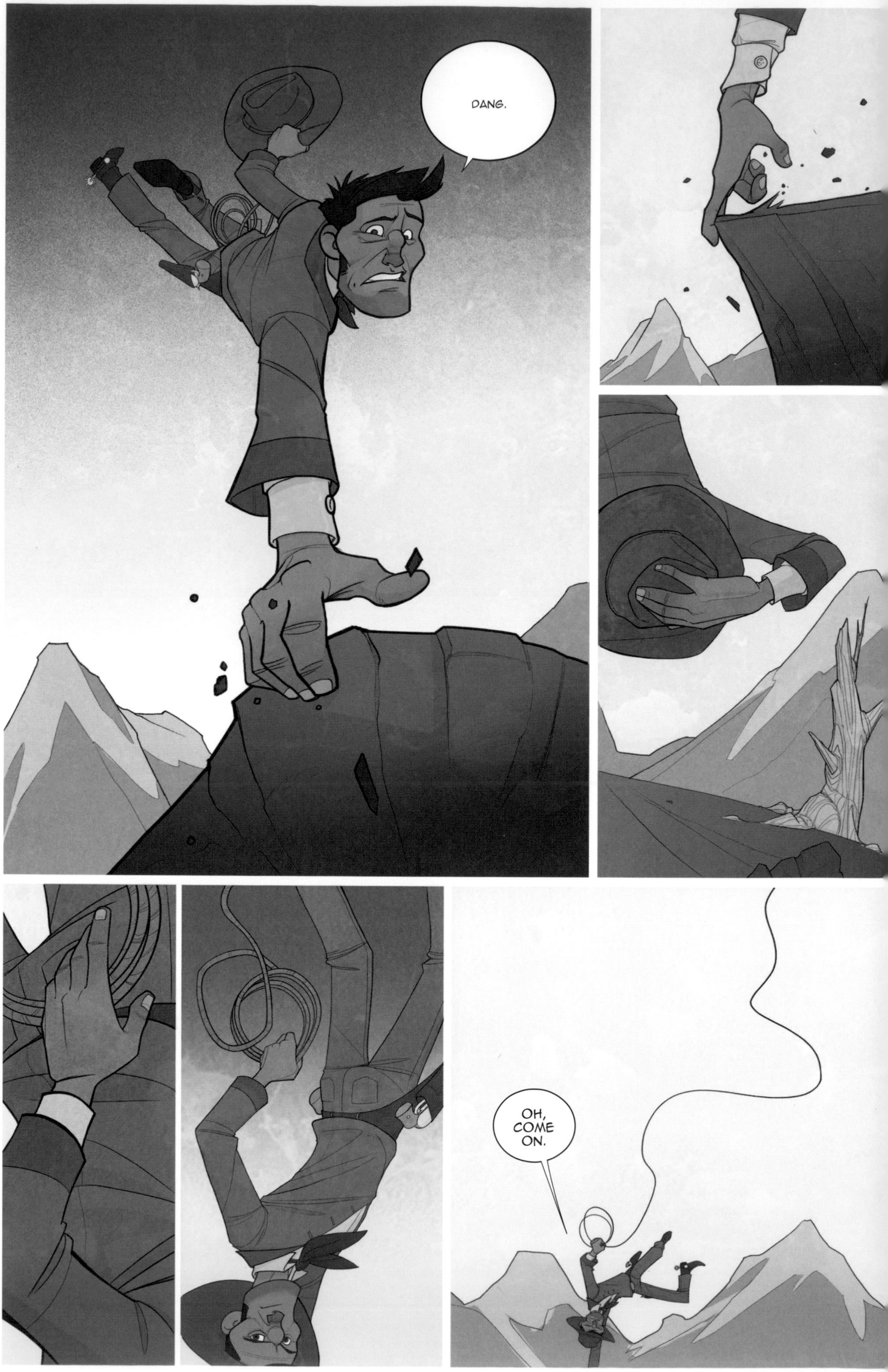
DANG.
OH, COME ON.

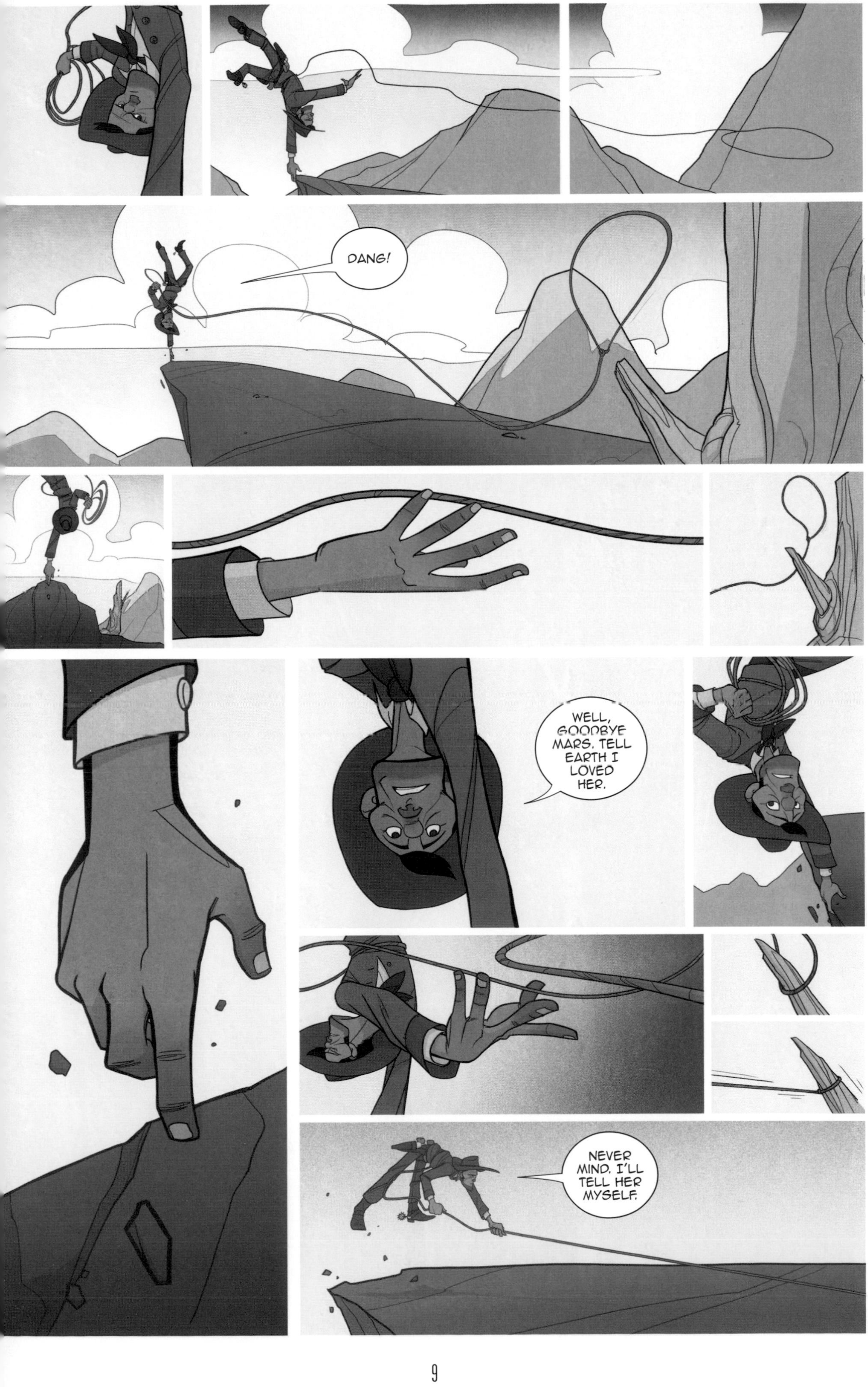
DANG!
WELL, GOODBYE MARS. TELL EARTH I LOVED HER.
NEVER MIND. I'LL TELL HER MYSELF.

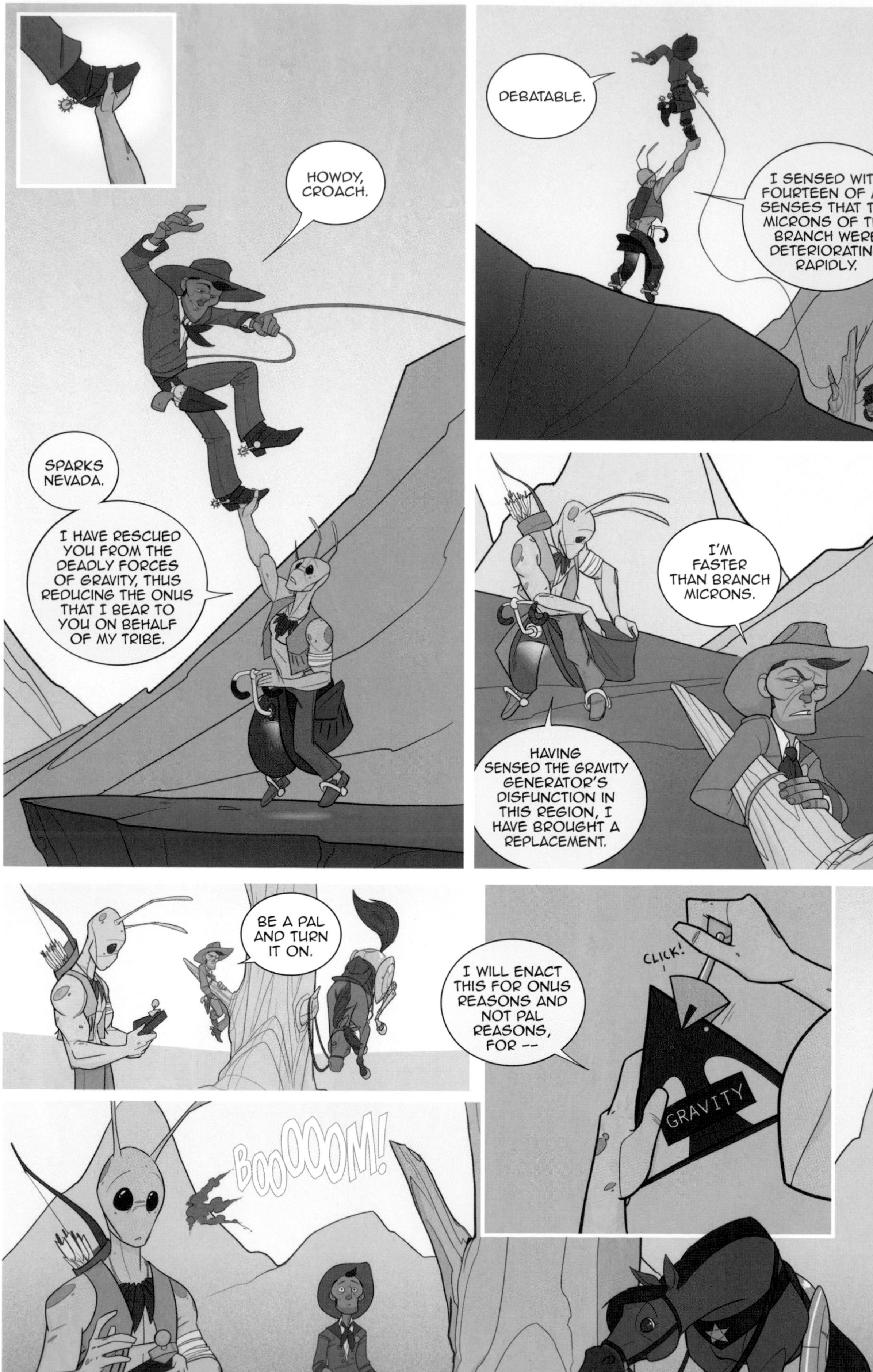
HOWDY, CROACH.
SPARKS NEVADA.
I HAVE RESCUED YOU FROM THE DEADLY FORCES OF GRAVITY, THUS REDUCING THE ONUS THAT I BEAR TO YOU ON BEHALF OF MY TRIBE.
DEBATABLE.
I SENSED WITH FOURTEEN OF MY SENSES THAT THE MICRONS OF THE BRANCH WERE DETERIORATING RAPIDLY.
I'M FASTER THAN BRANCH MICRONS.
HAVING SENSED THE GRAVITY GENERATOR'S DISFUNCTION IN THIS REGION, I HAVE BROUGHT A REPLACEMENT.
BE A PAL AND TURN IT ON.
I WILL ENACT THIS FOR ONUS REASONS AND NOT PAL REASONS, FOR --
CLICK!
GRAVITY
BOOOOOM!

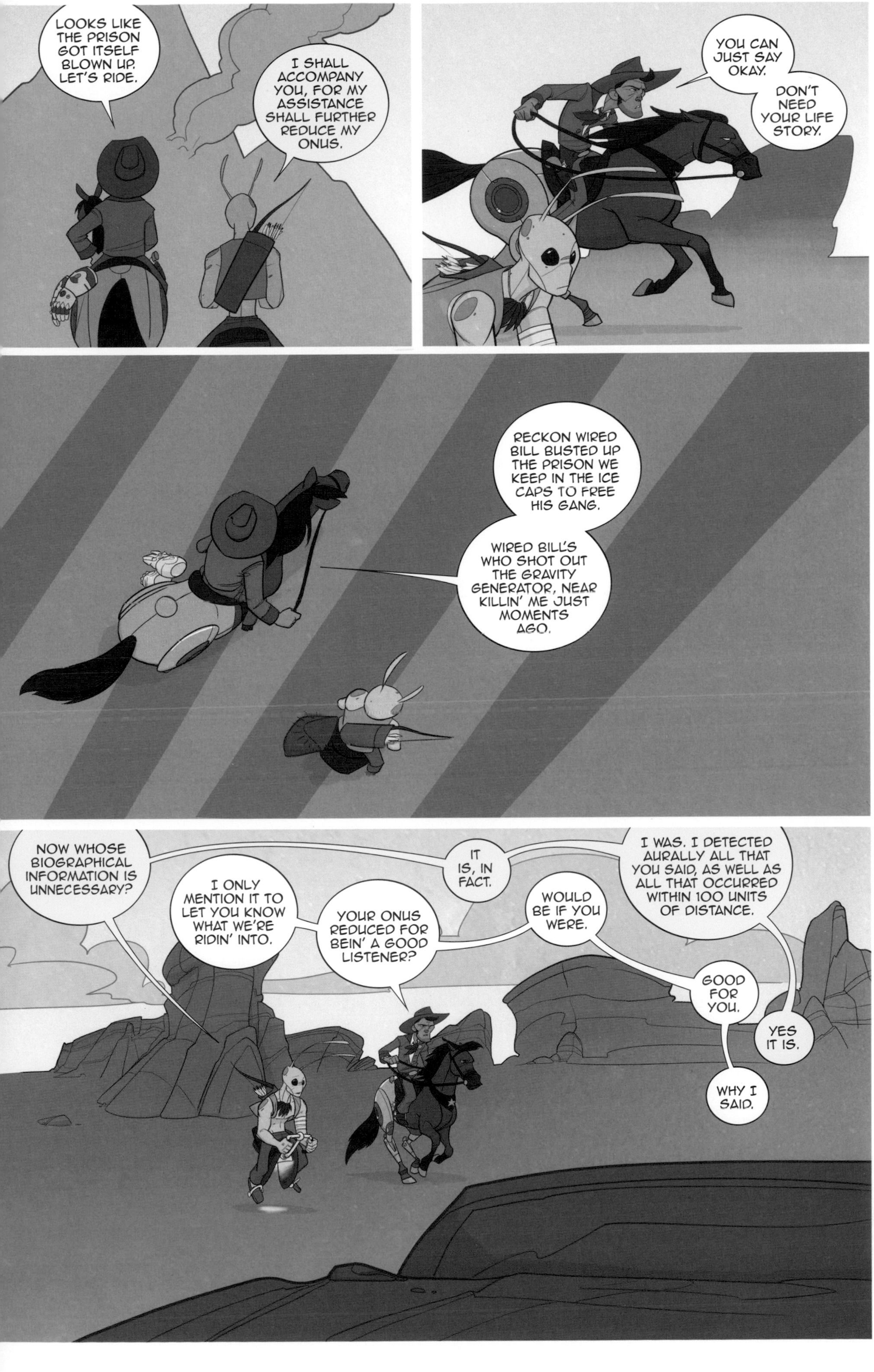
LOOKS LIKE THE PRISON GOT ITSELF BLOWN UP. LET'S RIDE.
I SHALL ACCOMPANY YOU, FOR MY ASSISTANCE SHALL FURTHER REDUCE MY ONUS.
YOU CAN JUST SAY OKAY.
DON'T NEED YOUR LIFE STORY.
RECKON WIRED BILL BUSTED UP THE PRISON WE KEEP IN THE ICE CAPS TO FREE HIS GANG.
WIRED BILL'S WHO SHOT OUT THE GRAVITY GENERATOR, NEAR KILLIN' ME JUST MOMENTS AGO.
NOW WHOSE BIOGRAPHICAL INFORMATION IS UNNECESSARY?
I ONLY MENTION IT TO LET YOU KNOW WHAT WE'RE RIDIN' INTO.
YOUR ONUS REDUCED FOR BEIN' A GOOD LISTENER?
IT IS, IN FACT.
WOULD BE IF YOU WERE.
I WAS. I DETECTED AURALLY ALL THAT YOU SAID, AS WELL AS ALL THAT OCCURRED WITHIN 100 UNITS OF DISTANCE.
GOOD FOR YOU.
YES IT IS.
WHY I SAID.

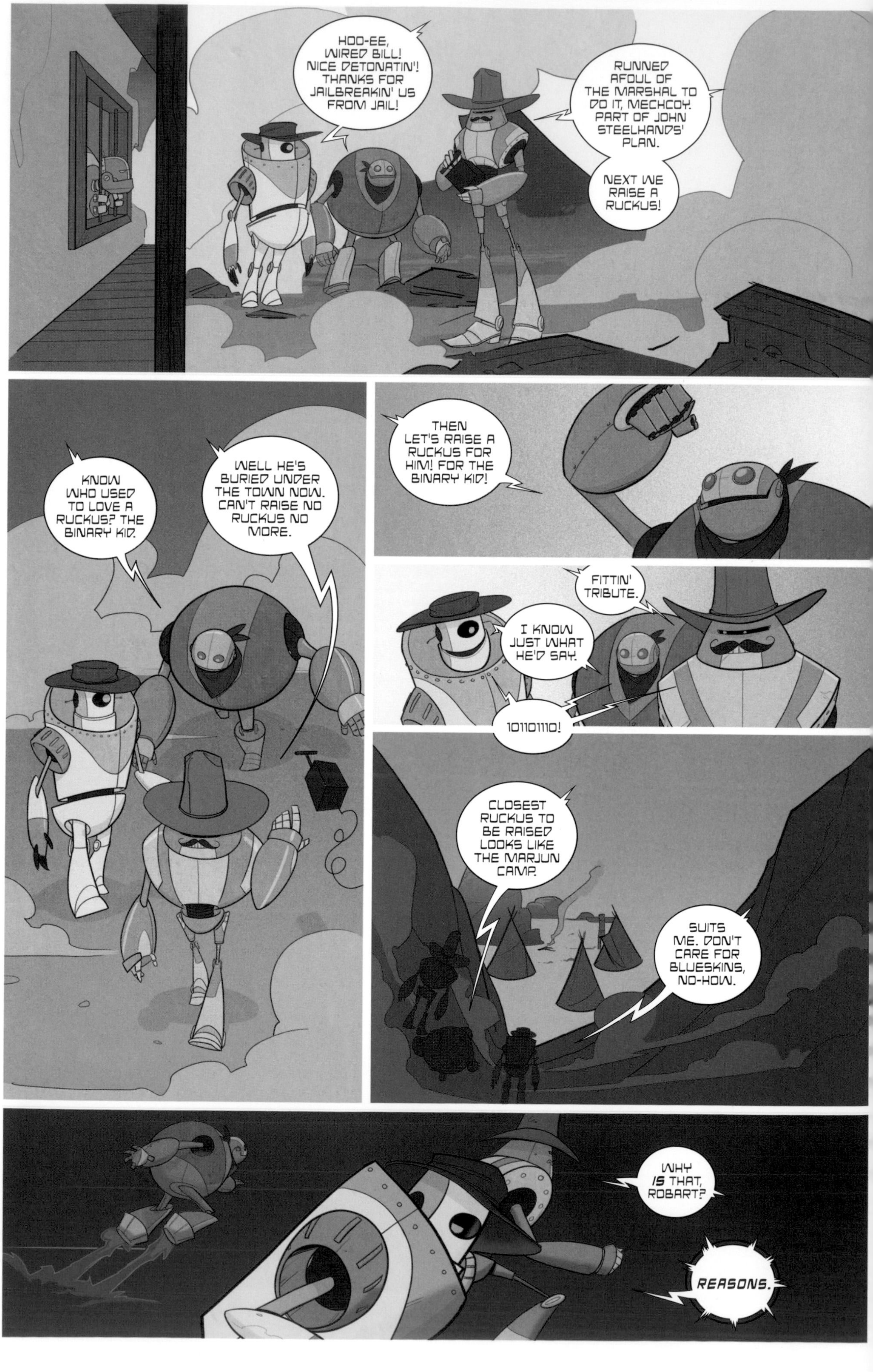

HOO-EE, WIRED BILL! NICE DETONATIN'! THANKS FOR JAILBREAKIN' US FROM JAIL!
RUNNED AFOUL OF THE MARSHAL TO DO IT, MECHCOY. PART OF JOHN STEELHANDS' PLAN.
NEXT WE RAISE A RUCKUS!
KNOW WHO USED TO LOVE A RUCKUS? THE BINARY KID.
WELL HE'S BURIED UNDER THE TOWN NOW. CAN'T RAISE NO RUCKUS NO MORE.
THEN LET'S RAISE A RUCKUS FOR HIM! FOR THE BINARY KID!
FITTIN' TRIBUTE.
I KNOW JUST WHAT HE'D SAY.
101101110!
CLOSEST RUCKUS TO BE RAISED LOOKS LIKE THE MARJUN CAMP.
SUITS ME. DON'T CARE FOR BLUESKINS, NO-HOW.
WHY *IS* THAT, ROBART?
*REASONS.*

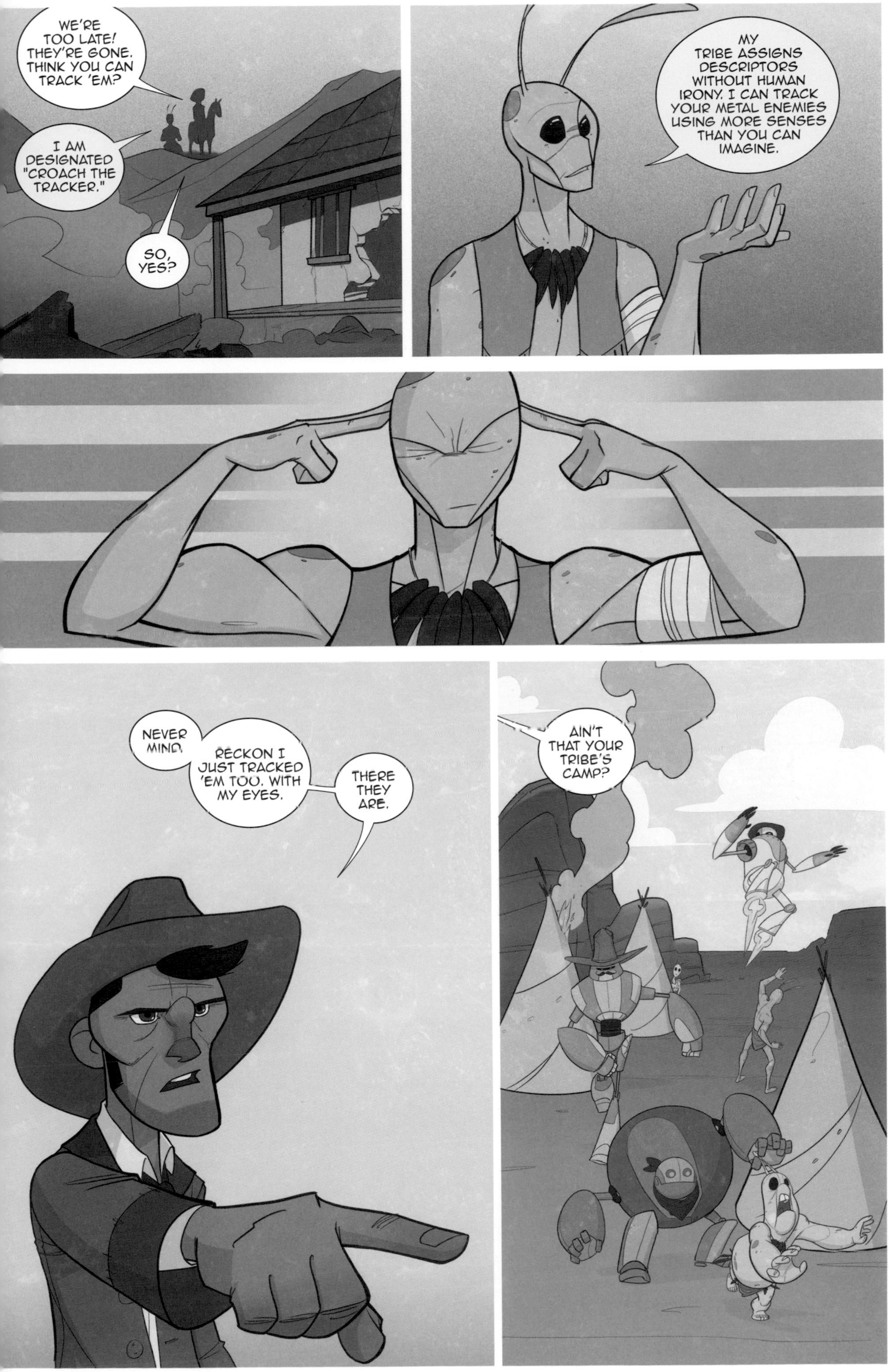

WE'RE TOO LATE! THEY'RE GONE. THINK YOU CAN TRACK 'EM?
I AM DESIGNATED "CROACH THE TRACKER."
SO, YES?
MY TRIBE ASSIGNS DESCRIPTORS WITHOUT HUMAN IRONY. I CAN TRACK YOUR METAL ENEMIES USING MORE SENSES THAN YOU CAN IMAGINE.
NEVER MIND.
RECKON I JUST TRACKED 'EM TOO. WITH MY EYES.
THERE THEY ARE.
AIN'T THAT YOUR TRIBE'S CAMP?

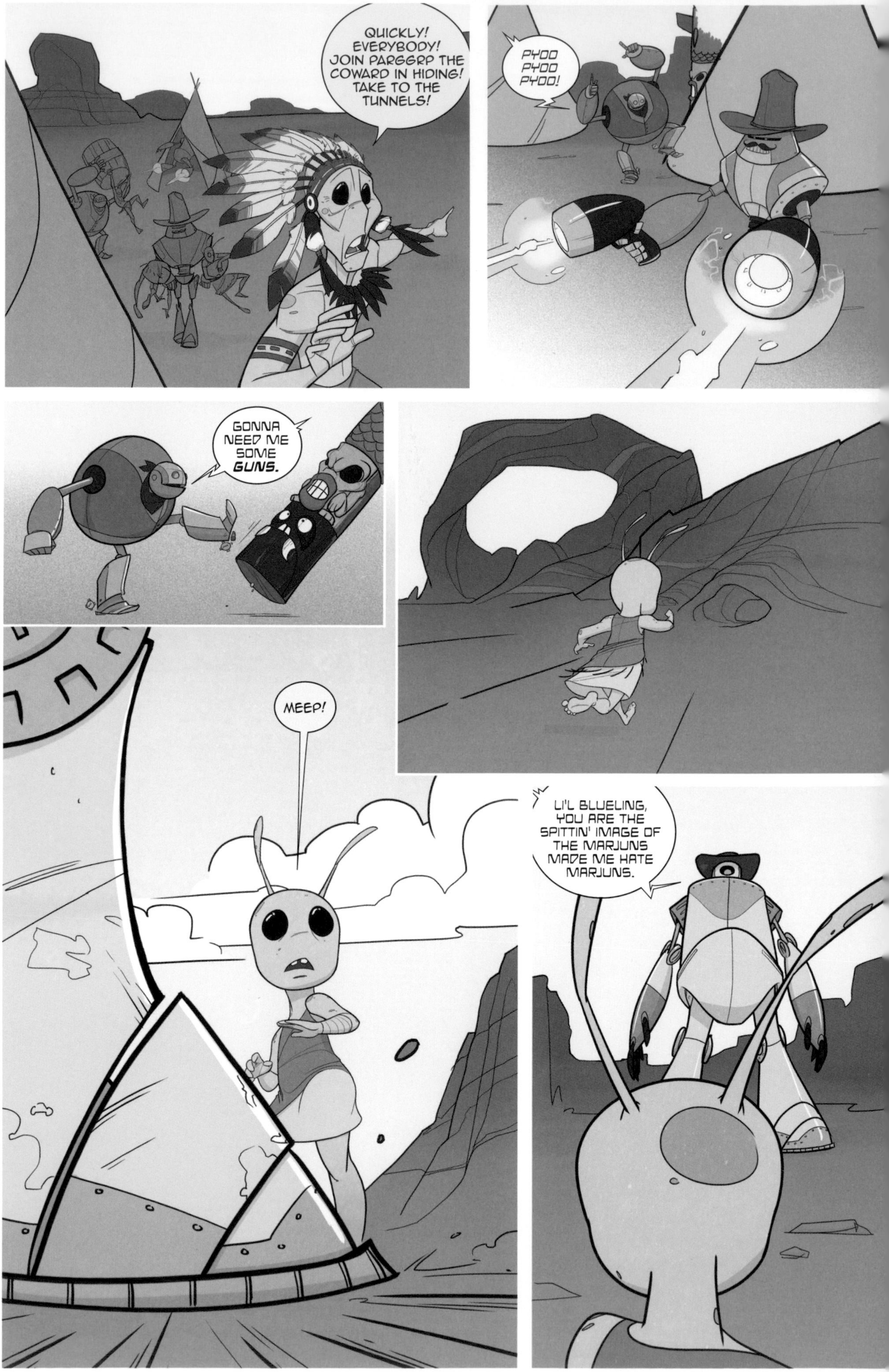
QUICKLY! EVERYBODY! JOIN PARGGRP THE COWARD IN HIDING! TAKE TO THE TUNNELS!
PYOO PYOO PYOO!
GONNA NEED ME SOME GUNS.
MEEP!
LI'L BLUELING, YOU ARE THE SPITTIN' IMAGE OF THE MARJUNS MADE ME HATE MARJUNS.

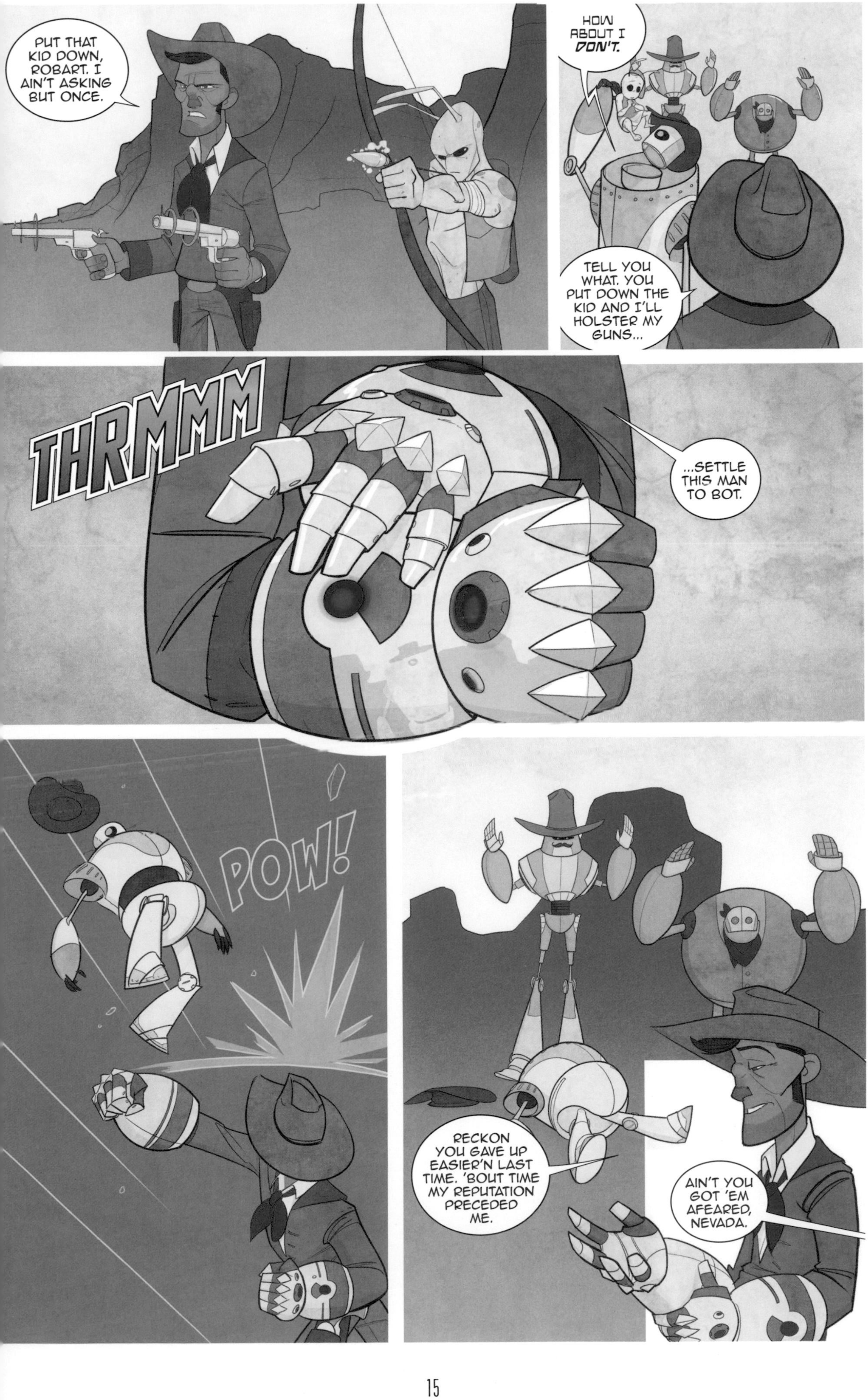
PUT THAT KID DOWN, ROBART. I AIN'T ASKING BUT ONCE.
HOW ABOUT I DON'T.
TELL YOU WHAT. YOU PUT DOWN THE KID AND I'LL HOLSTER MY GUNS...
THRMMM
...SETTLE THIS MAN TO BOT.
POW!
RECKON YOU GAVE UP EASIER'N LAST TIME. 'BOUT TIME MY REPUTATION PRECEDED ME.
AIN'T YOU GOT 'EM AFEARED, NEVADA.

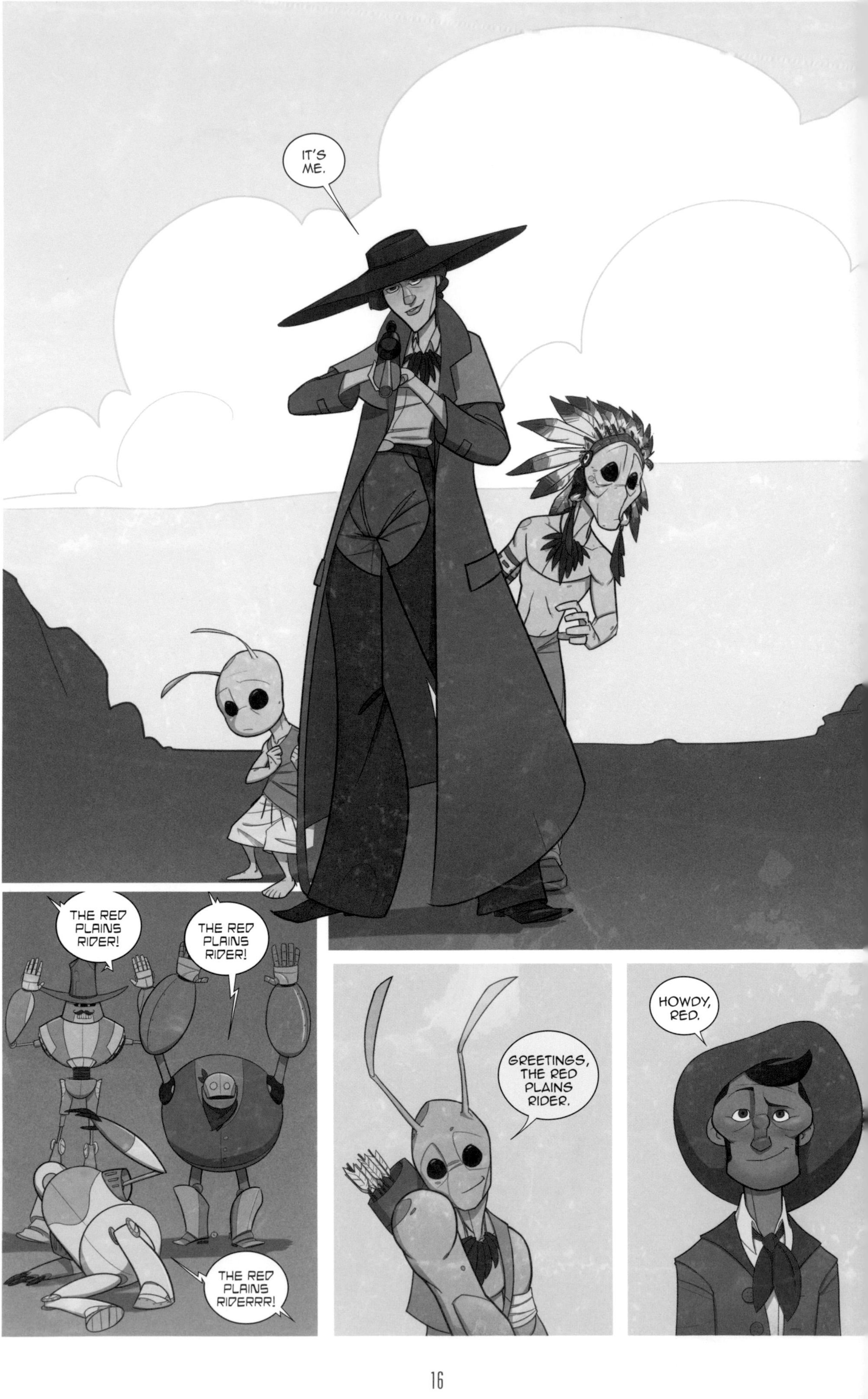
IT'S ME.
THE RED PLAINS RIDER!
THE RED PLAINS RIDER!
THE RED PLAINS RIDERRR!
GREETINGS, THE RED PLAINS RIDER.
HOWDY, RED.

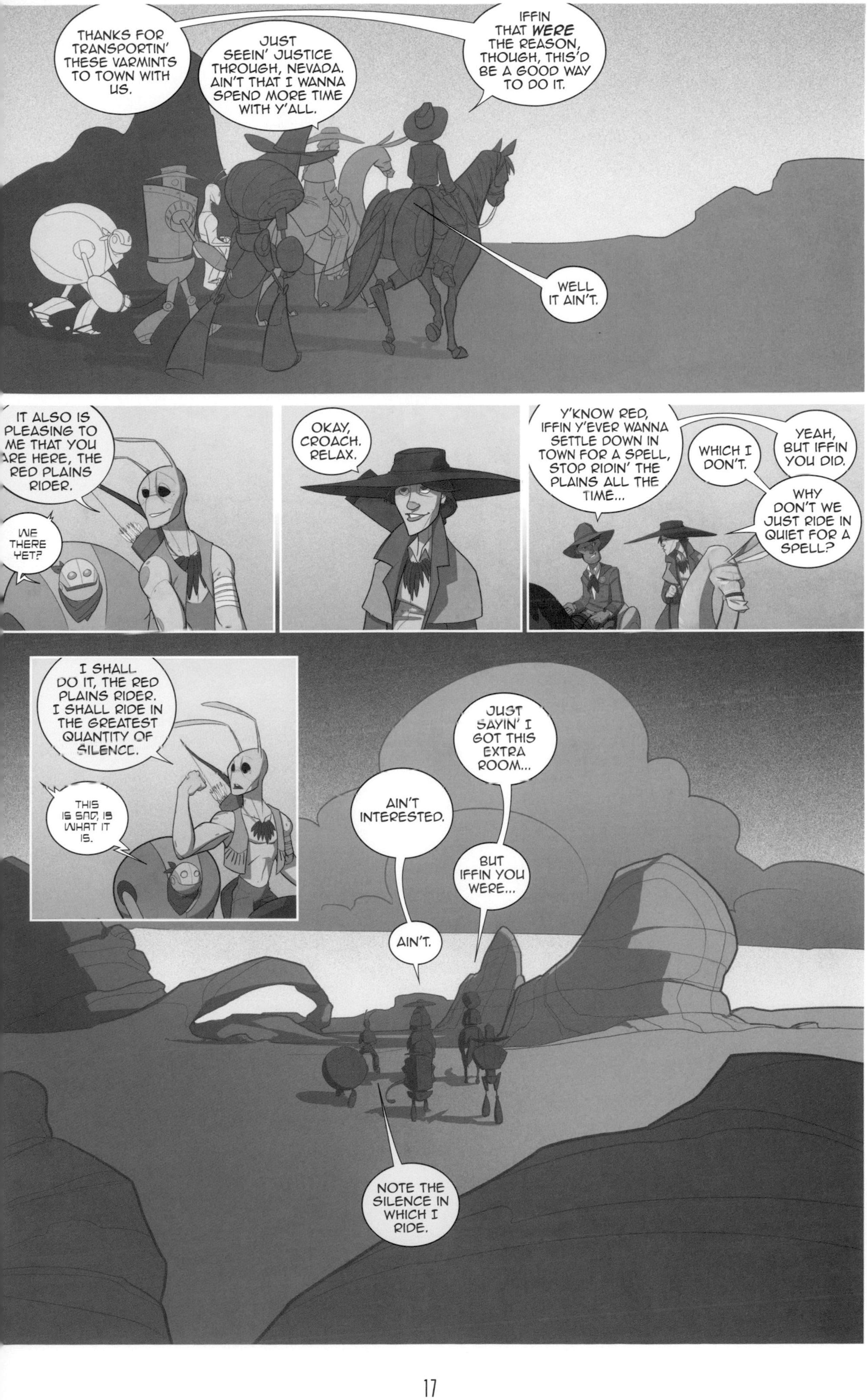
THANKS FOR TRANSPORTIN' THESE VARMINTS TO TOWN WITH US.
JUST SEEIN' JUSTICE THROUGH, NEVADA. AIN'T THAT I WANNA SPEND MORE TIME WITH Y'ALL.
IFFIN THAT *WERE* THE REASON, THOUGH, THIS'D BE A GOOD WAY TO DO IT.
WELL IT AIN'T.
IT ALSO IS PLEASING TO ME THAT YOU ARE HERE, THE RED PLAINS RIDER.
WE THERE YET?
OKAY, CROACH. RELAX.
Y'KNOW RED, IFFIN Y'EVER WANNA SETTLE DOWN IN TOWN FOR A SPELL, STOP RIDIN' THE PLAINS ALL THE TIME...
WHICH I DON'T.
YEAH, BUT IFFIN YOU DID.
WHY DON'T WE JUST RIDE IN QUIET FOR A SPELL?
I SHALL DO IT, THE RED PLAINS RIDER. I SHALL RIDE IN THE GREATEST QUANTITY OF SILENCE.
THIS IS SAD, IS WHAT IT IS.
JUST SAYIN' I GOT THIS EXTRA ROOM...
AIN'T INTERESTED.
BUT IFFIN YOU WERE...
AIN'T.
NOTE THE SILENCE IN WHICH I RIDE.

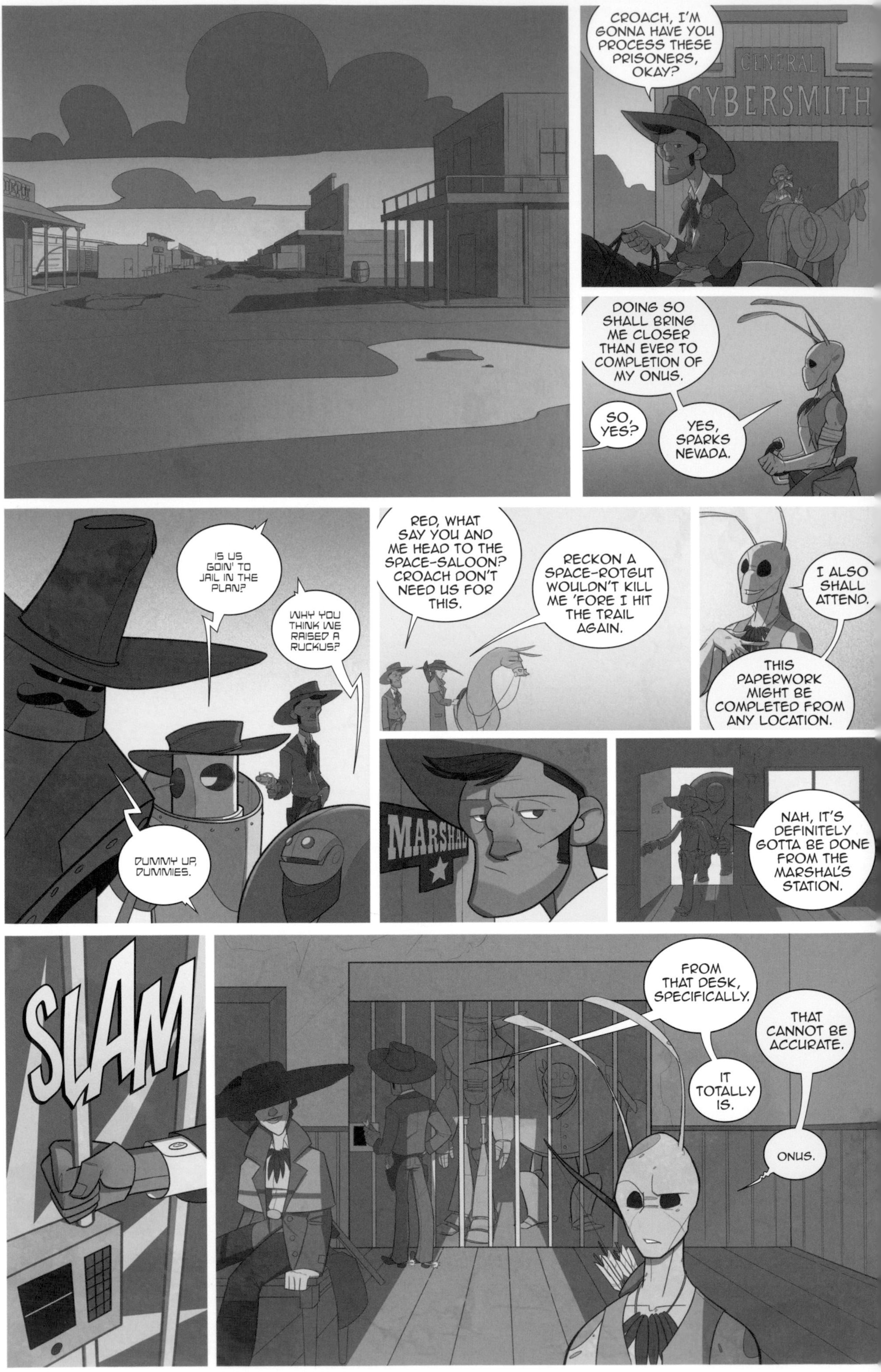
CROACH, I'M GONNA HAVE YOU PROCESS THESE PRISONERS, OKAY?
GENERAL CYBERSMITH
DOING SO SHALL BRING ME CLOSER THAN EVER TO COMPLETION OF MY ONUS.
SO, YES?
YES, SPARKS NEVADA.
IS US GOIN' TO JAIL IN THE PLAN?
WHY YOU THINK WE RAISED A RUCKUS?
DUMMY UP, DUMMIES.
RED, WHAT SAY YOU AND ME HEAD TO THE SPACE-SALOON? CROACH DON'T NEED US FOR THIS.
RECKON A SPACE-ROTGUT WOULDN'T KILL ME 'FORE I HIT THE TRAIL AGAIN.
I ALSO SHALL ATTEND.
THIS PAPERWORK MIGHT BE COMPLETED FROM ANY LOCATION.
NAH, IT'S DEFINITELY GOTTA BE DONE FROM THE MARSHAL'S STATION.
SLAM
FROM THAT DESK, SPECIFICALLY.
THAT CANNOT BE ACCURATE.
IT TOTALLY IS.
ONUS.

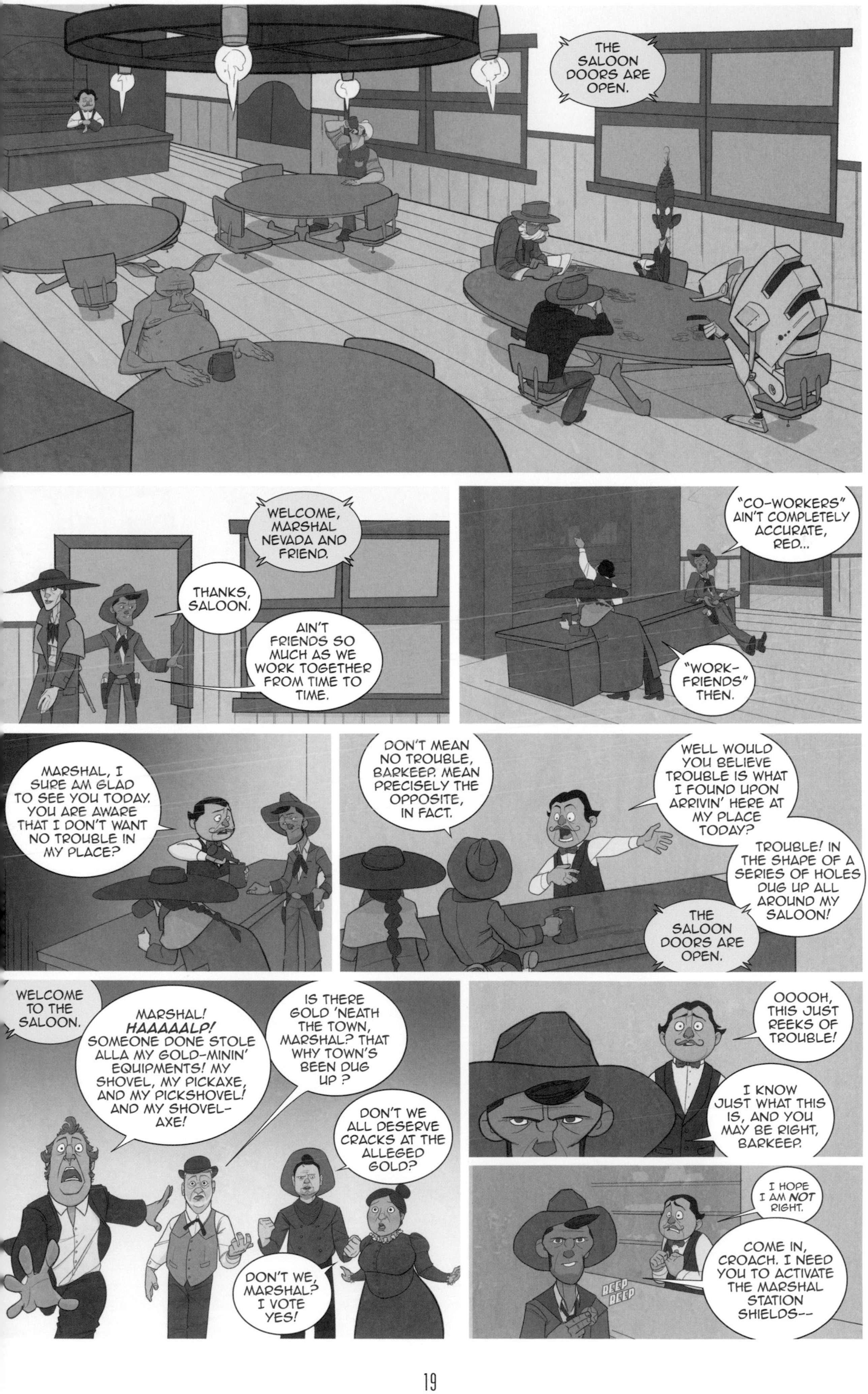
THE SALOON DOORS ARE OPEN.
WELCOME, MARSHAL NEVADA AND FRIEND.
THANKS, SALOON.
AIN'T FRIENDS SO MUCH AS WE WORK TOGETHER FROM TIME TO TIME.
"CO-WORKERS" AIN'T COMPLETELY ACCURATE, RED...
"WORK-FRIENDS" THEN.
MARSHAL, I SURE AM GLAD TO SEE YOU TODAY. YOU ARE AWARE THAT I DON'T WANT NO TROUBLE IN MY PLACE?
DON'T MEAN NO TROUBLE, BARKEEP. MEAN PRECISELY THE OPPOSITE, IN FACT.
WELL WOULD YOU BELIEVE TROUBLE IS WHAT I FOUND UPON ARRIVIN' HERE AT MY PLACE TODAY?
TROUBLE! IN THE SHAPE OF A SERIES OF HOLES DUG UP ALL AROUND MY SALOON!
THE SALOON DOORS ARE OPEN.
WELCOME TO THE SALOON.
MARSHAL! HAAAAALP! SOMEONE DONE STOLE ALLA MY GOLD-MININ' EQUIPMENTS! MY SHOVEL, MY PICKAXE, AND MY PICKSHOVEL! AND MY SHOVEL-AXE!
IS THERE GOLD 'NEATH THE TOWN, MARSHAL? THAT WHY TOWN'S BEEN DUG UP ?
DON'T WE ALL DESERVE CRACKS AT THE ALLEGED GOLD?
DON'T WE, MARSHAL? I VOTE YES!
OOOOH, THIS JUST REEKS OF TROUBLE!
I KNOW JUST WHAT THIS IS, AND YOU MAY BE RIGHT, BARKEEP.
I HOPE I AM NOT RIGHT.
BEEP BEEP
COME IN, CROACH. I NEED YOU TO ACTIVATE THE MARSHAL STATION SHIELDS--

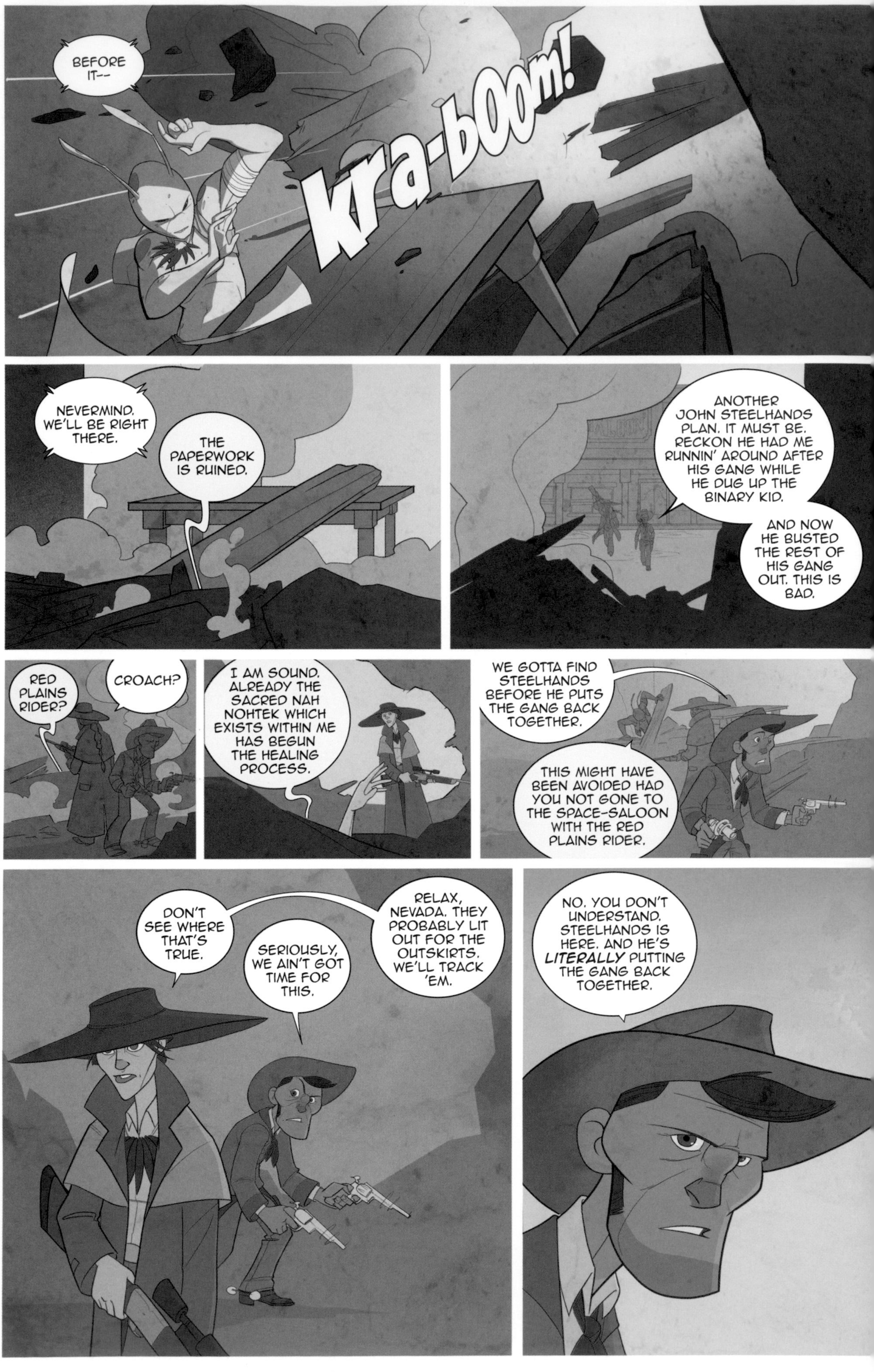
BEFORE IT--
KRA-BOOM!
NEVERMIND. WE'LL BE RIGHT THERE.
THE PAPERWORK IS RUINED.
ANOTHER JOHN STEELHANDS PLAN. IT MUST BE. RECKON HE HAD ME RUNNIN' AROUND AFTER HIS GANG WHILE HE DUG UP THE BINARY KID.
AND NOW HE BUSTED THE REST OF HIS GANG OUT. THIS IS BAD.
RED PLAINS RIDER?
CROACH?
I AM SOUND. ALREADY THE SACRED NAH NOHTEK WHICH EXISTS WITHIN ME HAS BEGUN THE HEALING PROCESS.
WE GOTTA FIND STEELHANDS BEFORE HE PUTS THE GANG BACK TOGETHER.
THIS MIGHT HAVE BEEN AVOIDED HAD YOU NOT GONE TO THE SPACE-SALOON WITH THE RED PLAINS RIDER.
DON'T SEE WHERE THAT'S TRUE.
SERIOUSLY, WE AIN'T GOT TIME FOR THIS.
RELAX, NEVADA. THEY PROBABLY LIT OUT FOR THE OUTSKIRTS. WE'LL TRACK 'EM.
NO. YOU DON'T UNDERSTAND. STEELHANDS IS HERE. AND HE'S *LITERALLY* PUTTING THE GANG BACK TOGETHER.

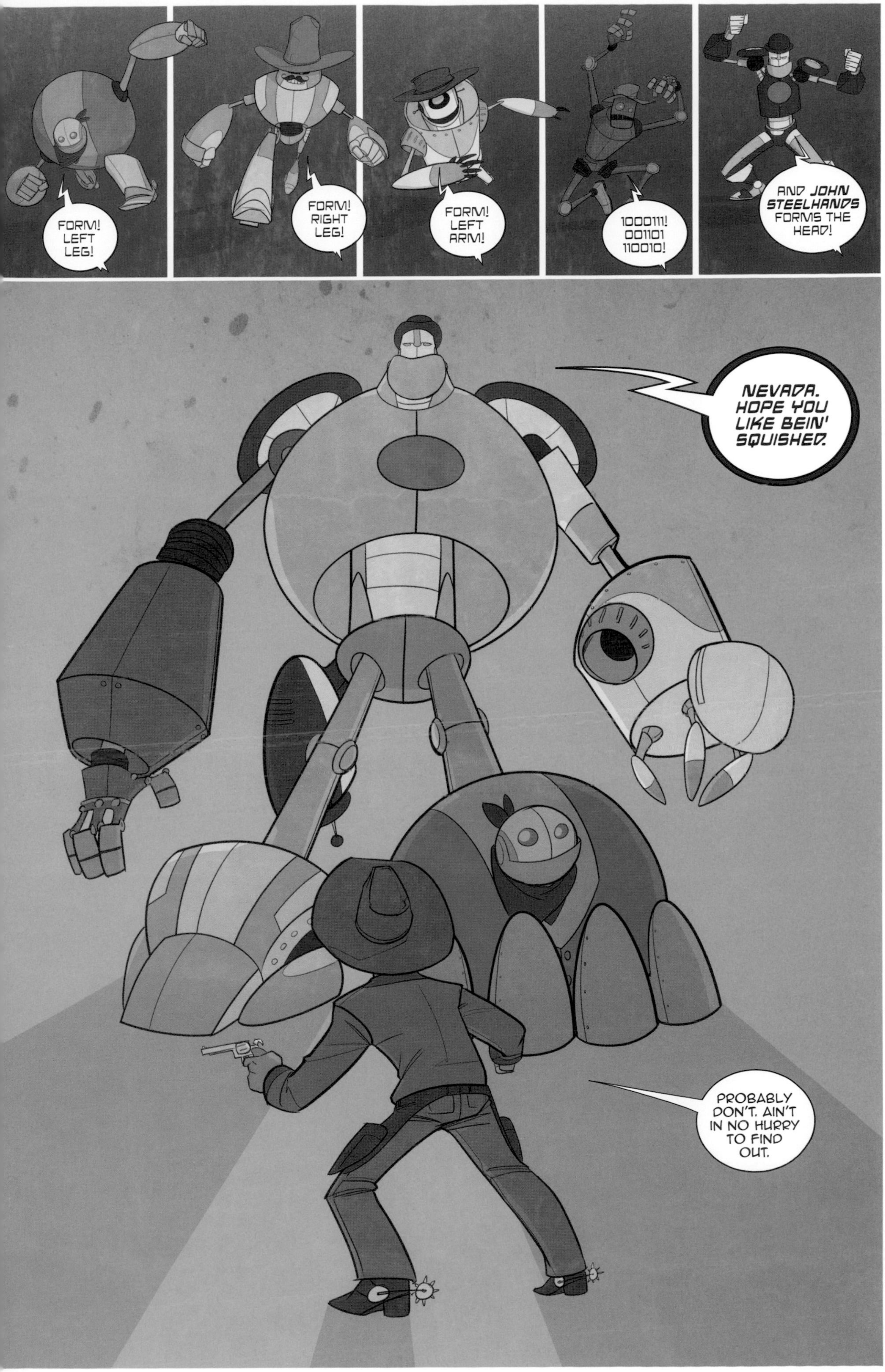
FORM! LEFT LEG!
FORM! RIGHT LEG!
FORM! LEFT ARM!
1000111! 001101 110010!
AND JOHN STEELHANDS FORMS THE HEAD!
NEVADA. HOPE YOU LIKE BEIN' SQUISHED.
PROBABLY DON'T. AIN'T IN NO HURRY TO FIND OUT.

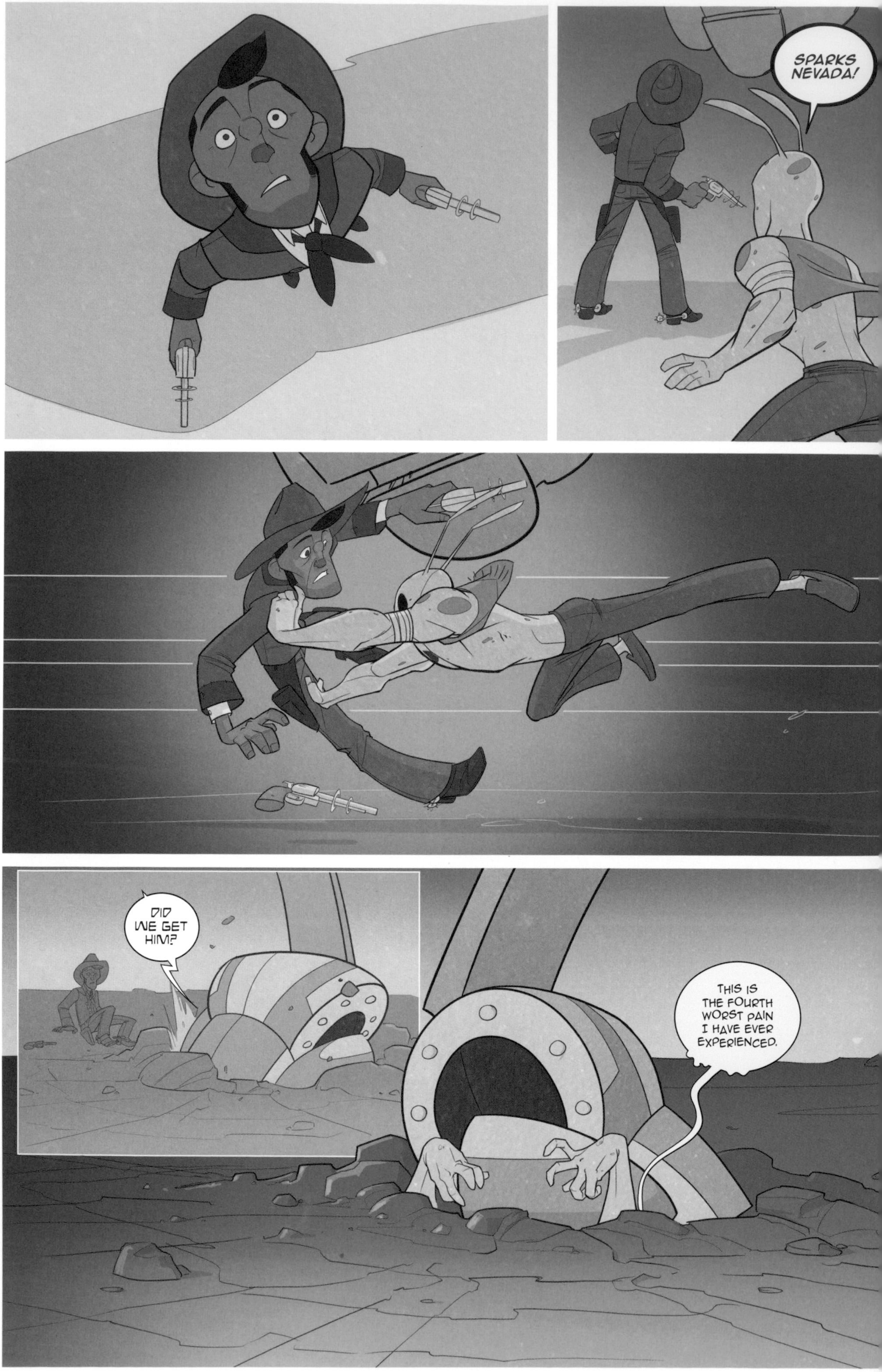
SPARKS NEVADA!
DID WE GET HIM?
THIS IS THE FOURTH WORST PAIN I HAVE EVER EXPERIENCED.

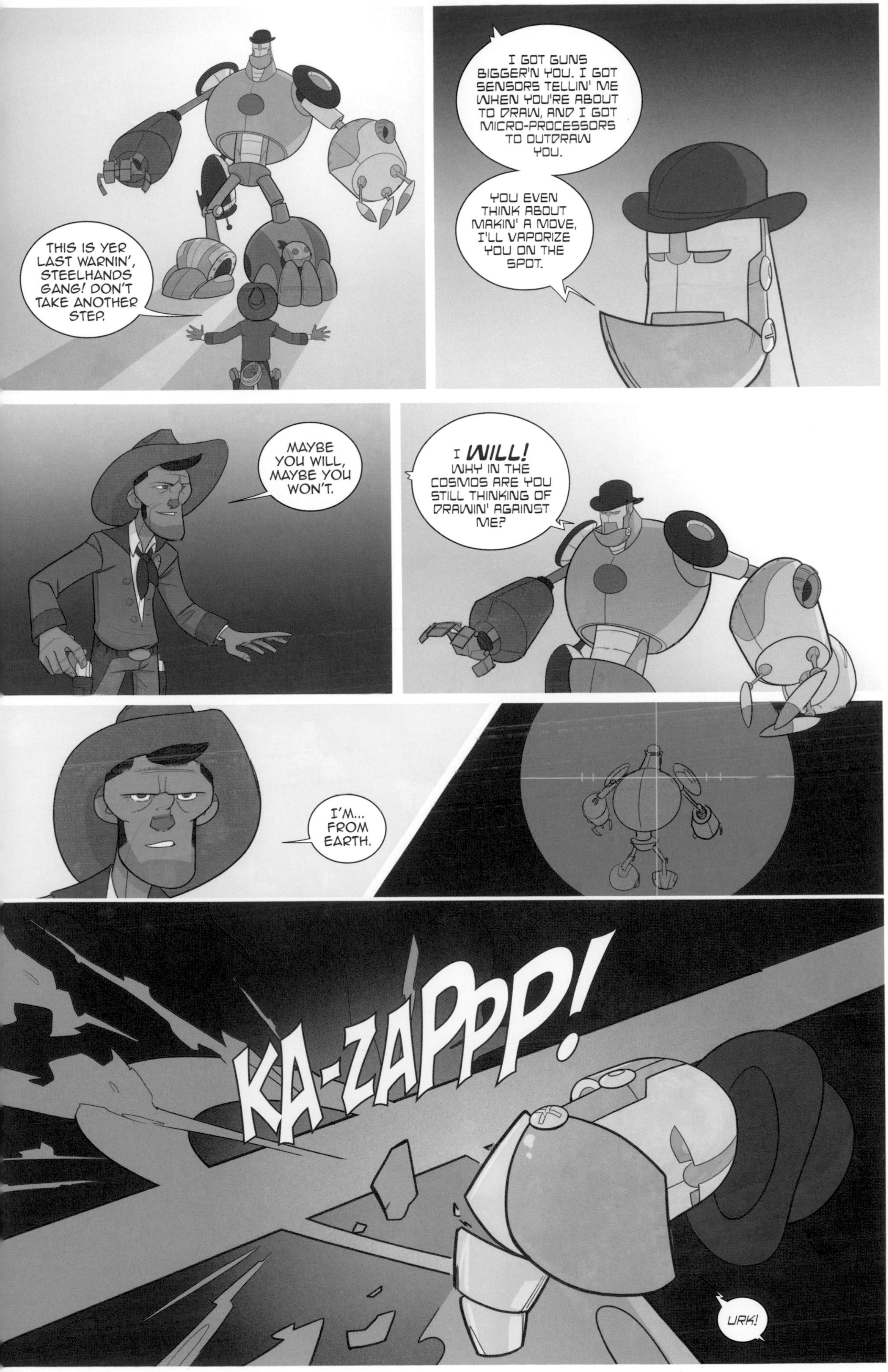
THIS IS YER LAST WARNIN', STEELHANDS GANG! DON'T TAKE ANOTHER STEP.
I GOT GUNS BIGGER'N YOU. I GOT SENSORS TELLIN' ME WHEN YOU'RE ABOUT TO DRAW, AND I GOT MICRO-PROCESSORS TO OUTDRAW YOU.
YOU EVEN THINK ABOUT MAKIN' A MOVE, I'LL VAPORIZE YOU ON THE SPOT.
MAYBE YOU WILL, MAYBE YOU WON'T.
I WILL! WHY IN THE COSMOS ARE YOU STILL THINKING OF DRAWIN' AGAINST ME?
I'M... FROM EARTH.
KA-ZAPPP!
URK!

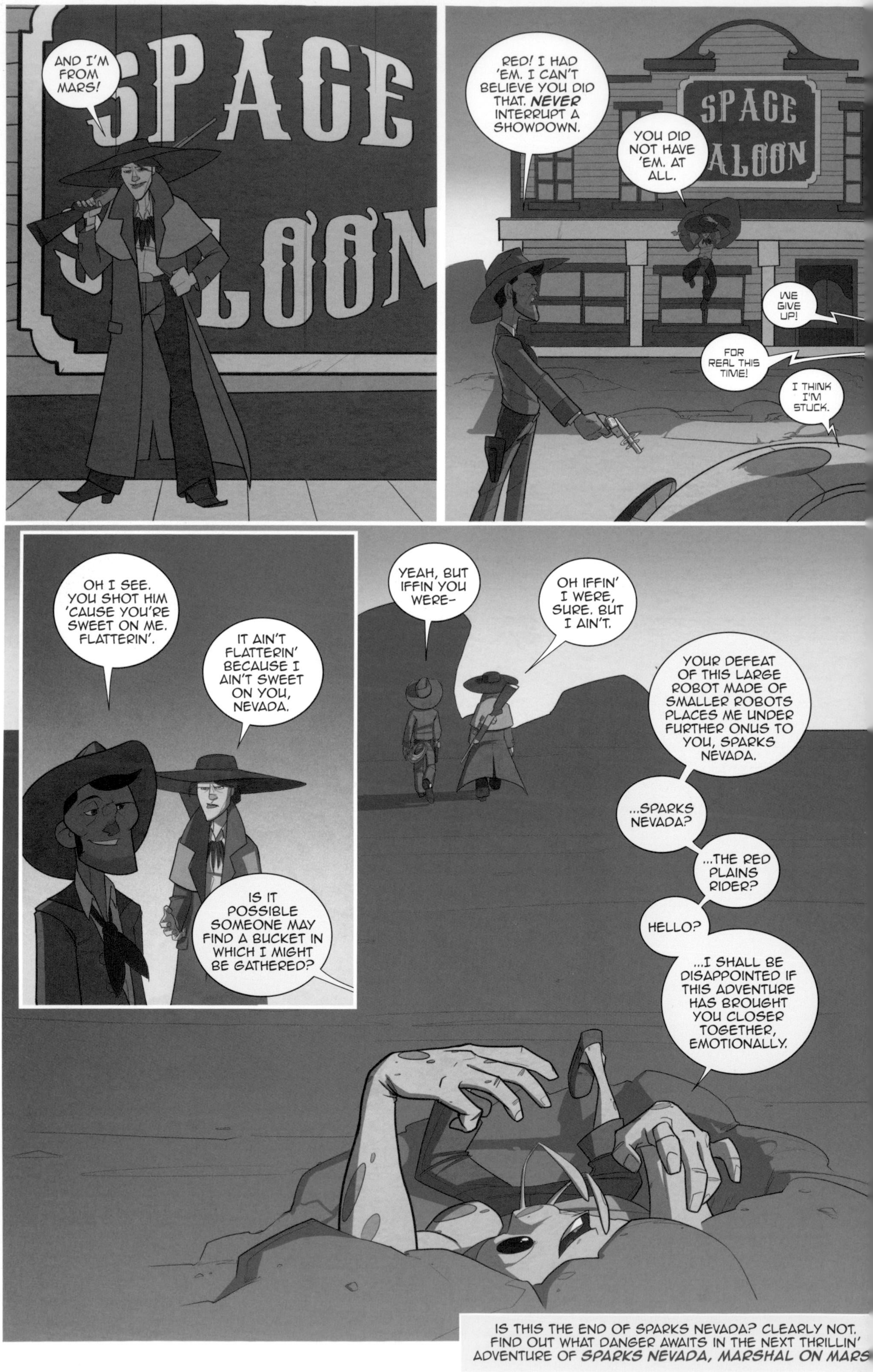

SPACE
AND I'M FROM MARS!
RED! I HAD 'EM. I CAN'T BELIEVE YOU DID THAT. *NEVER* INTERRUPT A SHOWDOWN.
YOU DID NOT HAVE 'EM. AT ALL.
WE GIVE UP!
FOR REAL THIS TIME!
I THINK I'M STUCK.
OH I SEE. YOU SHOT HIM 'CAUSE YOU'RE SWEET ON ME. FLATTERIN'.
IT AIN'T FLATTERIN' BECAUSE I AIN'T SWEET ON YOU, NEVADA.
IS IT POSSIBLE SOMEONE MAY FIND A BUCKET IN WHICH I MIGHT BE GATHERED?
YEAH, BUT IFFIN YOU WERE-
OH IFFIN' I WERE, SURE. BUT I AIN'T.
YOUR DEFEAT OF THIS LARGE ROBOT MADE OF SMALLER ROBOTS PLACES ME UNDER FURTHER ONUS TO YOU, SPARKS NEVADA.
...SPARKS NEVADA?
...THE RED PLAINS RIDER?
HELLO?
...I SHALL BE DISAPPOINTED IF THIS ADVENTURE HAS BROUGHT YOU CLOSER TOGETHER, EMOTIONALLY.
IS THIS THE END OF SPARKS NEVADA? CLEARLY NOT. FIND OUT WHAT DANGER AWAITS IN THE NEXT THRILLIN' ADVENTURE OF *SPARKS NEVADA, MARSHAL ON MARS*

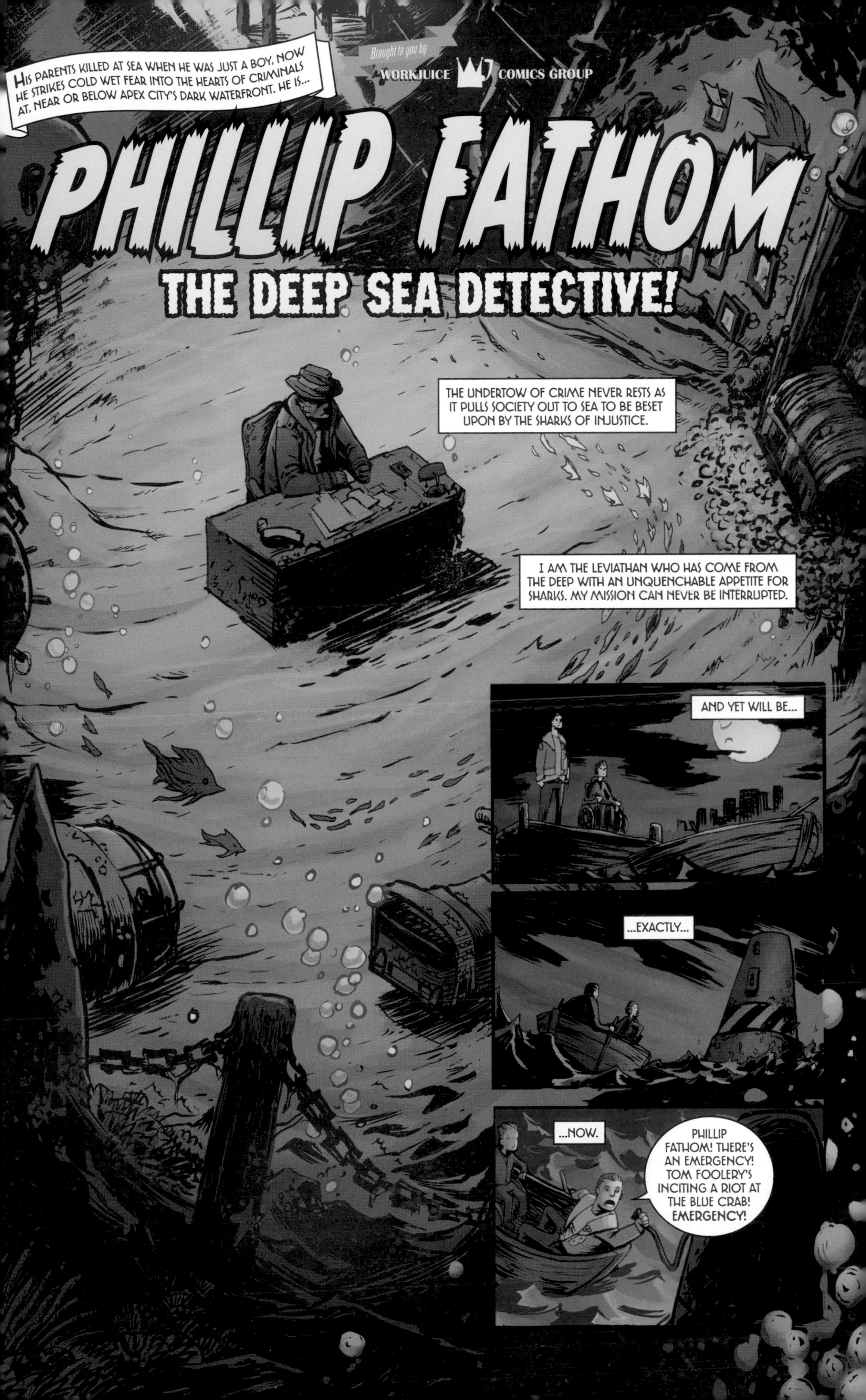
HIS PARENTS KILLED AT SEA WHEN HE WAS JUST A BOY, NOW HE STRIKES COLD WET FEAR INTO THE HEARTS OF CRIMINALS AT, NEAR OR BELOW APEX CITY'S DARK WATERFRONT. HE IS...
Brought to you by
WORKJUICE COMICS GROUP
PHILLIP FATHOM
THE DEEP SEA DETECTIVE!
THE UNDERTOW OF CRIME NEVER RESTS AS IT PULLS SOCIETY OUT TO SEA TO BE BESET UPON BY THE SHARKS OF INJUSTICE.
I AM THE LEVIATHAN WHO HAS COME FROM THE DEEP WITH AN UNQUENCHABLE APPETITE FOR SHARKS. MY MISSION CAN NEVER BE INTERRUPTED.
AND YET WILL BE...
...EXACTLY...
...NOW.
PHILLIP FATHOM! THERE'S AN EMERGENCY! TOM FOOLERY'S INCITING A RIOT AT THE BLUE CRAB! EMERGENCY!

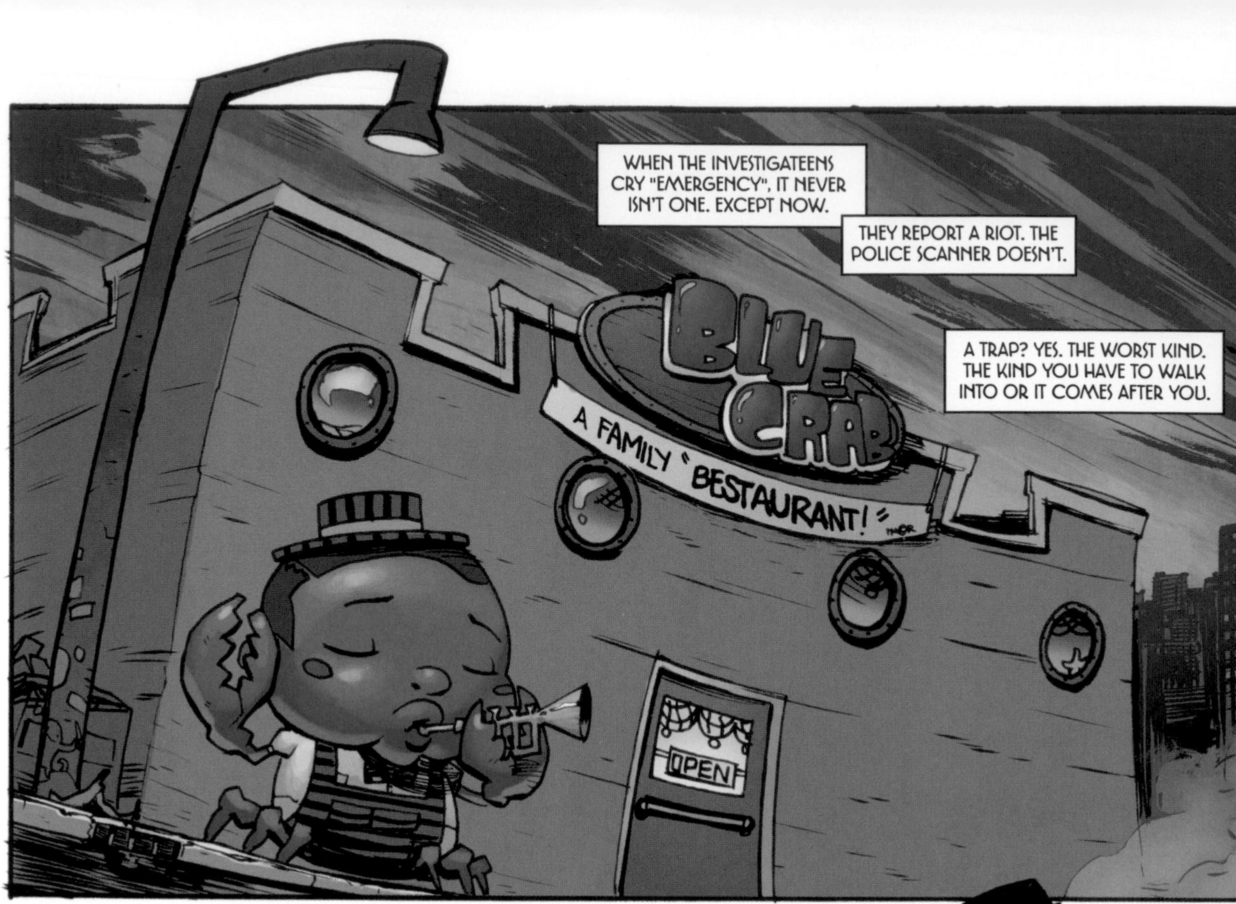
WHEN THE INVESTIGATEENS CRY "EMERGENCY", IT NEVER ISN'T ONE. EXCEPT NOW.
THEY REPORT A RIOT. THE POLICE SCANNER DOESN'T.
A TRAP? YES. THE WORST KIND. THE KIND YOU HAVE TO WALK INTO OR IT COMES AFTER YOU.
BLUE CRAB
A FAMILY BESTAURANT!
OPEN

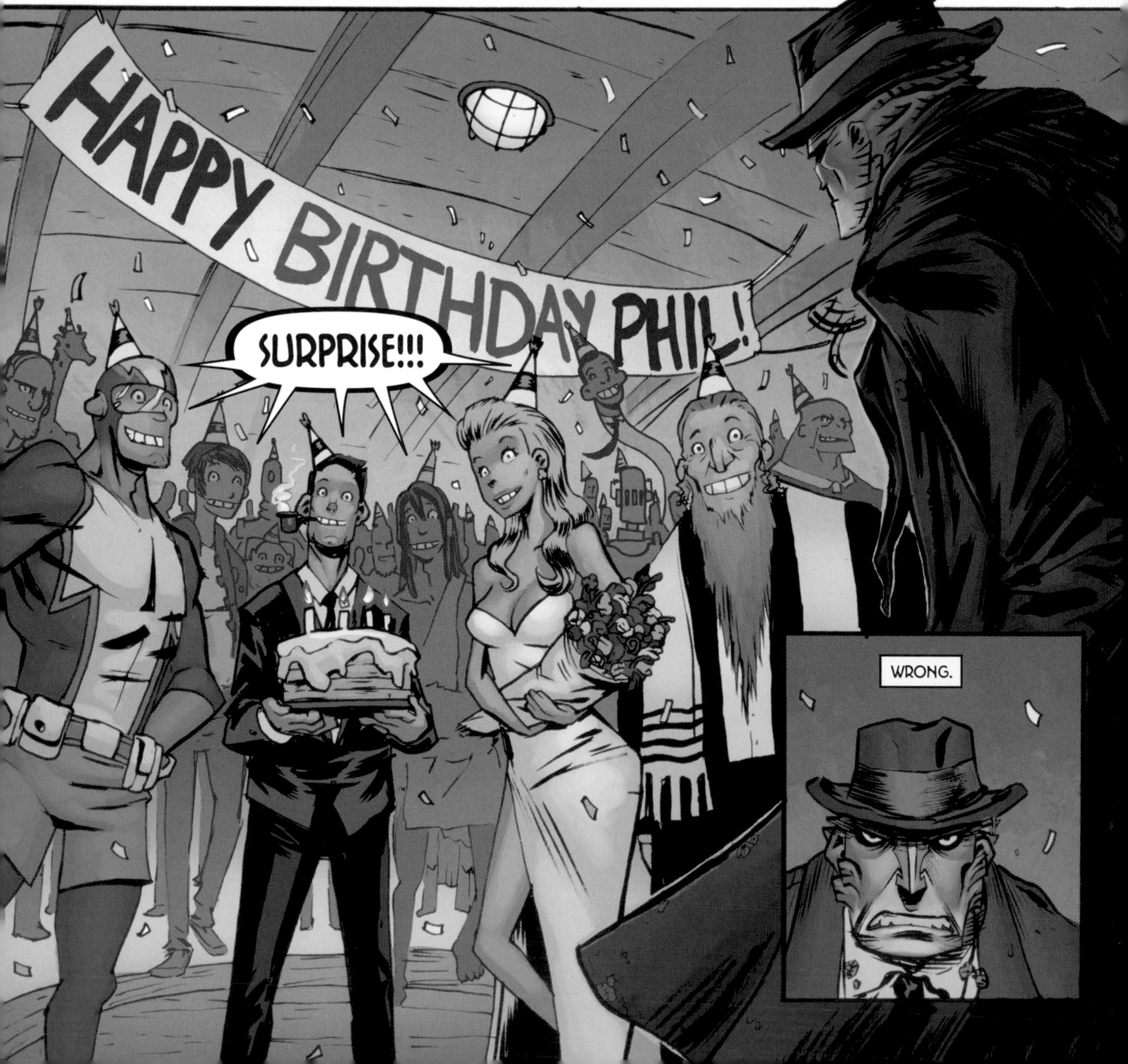
HAPPY BIRTHDAY PHIL!
SURPRISE!!!
WRONG.

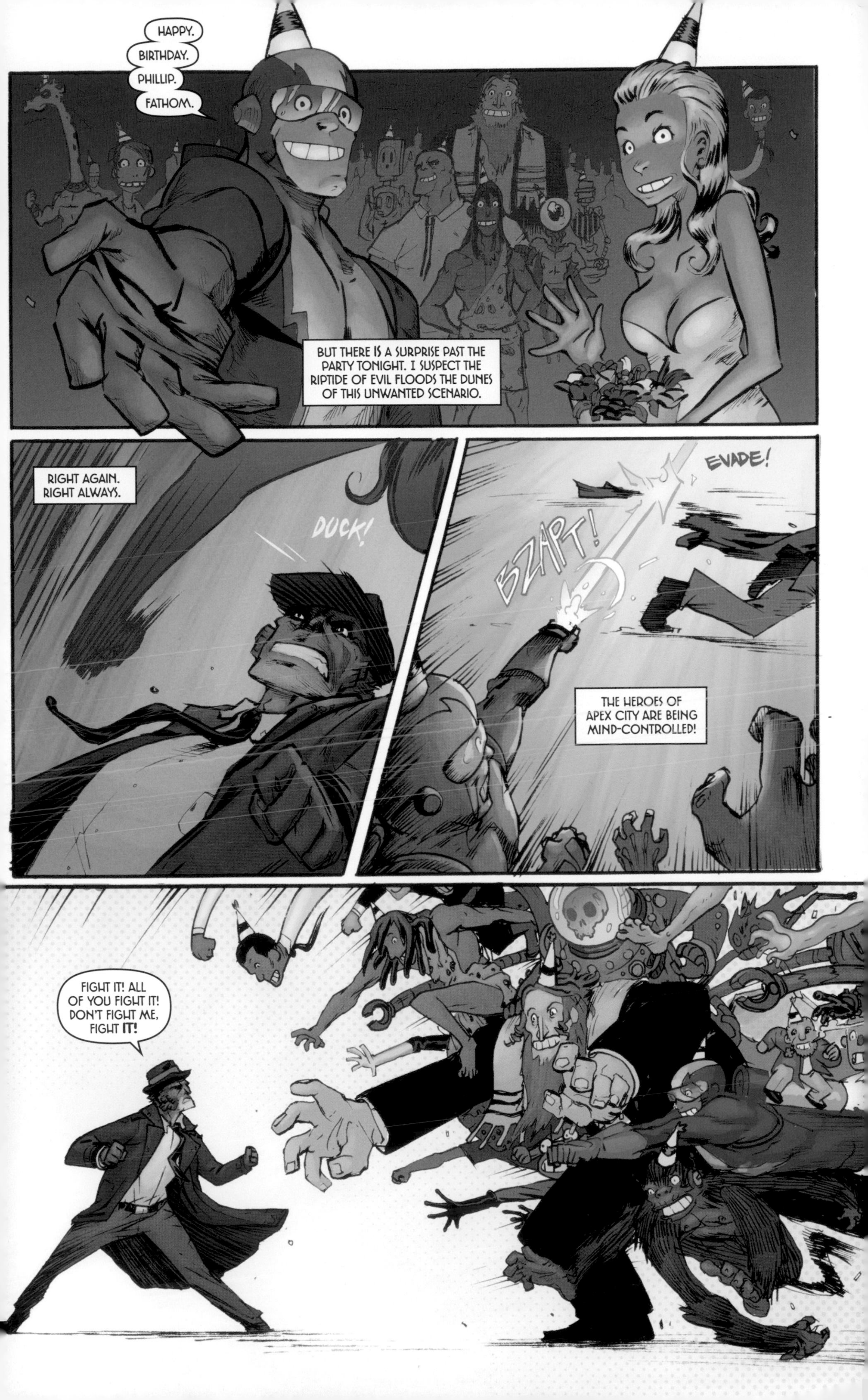
HAPPY.
BIRTHDAY.
PHILLIP.
FATHOM.
BUT THERE IS A SURPRISE PAST THE PARTY TONIGHT. I SUSPECT THE RIPTIDE OF EVIL FLOODS THE DUNES OF THIS UNWANTED SCENARIO.
RIGHT AGAIN. RIGHT ALWAYS.
DUCK!
EVADE!
BZAPT!
THE HEROES OF APEX CITY ARE BEING MIND-CONTROLLED!
FIGHT IT! ALL OF YOU FIGHT IT! DON'T FIGHT ME, FIGHT **IT!**

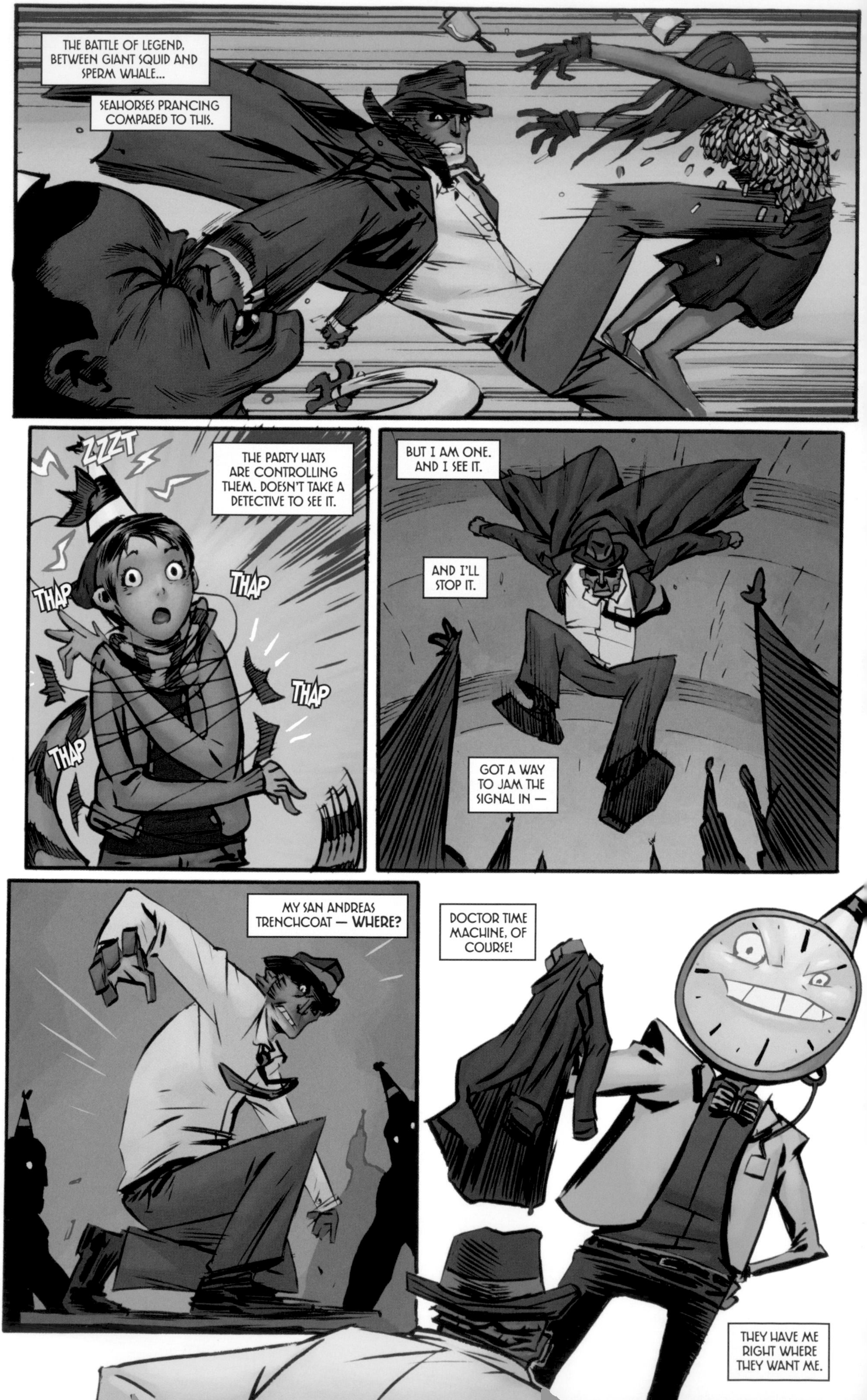
THE BATTLE OF LEGEND, BETWEEN GIANT SQUID AND SPERM WHALE...
SEAHORSES PRANCING COMPARED TO THIS.
ZZZT
THE PARTY HATS ARE CONTROLLING THEM. DOESN'T TAKE A DETECTIVE TO SEE IT.
THAP
THAP
THAP
THAP
BUT I AM ONE. AND I SEE IT.
AND I'LL STOP IT.
GOT A WAY TO JAM THE SIGNAL IN —
MY SAN ANDREAS TRENCHCOAT — **WHERE?**
DOCTOR TIME MACHINE, OF COURSE!
THEY HAVE ME RIGHT WHERE THEY WANT ME.

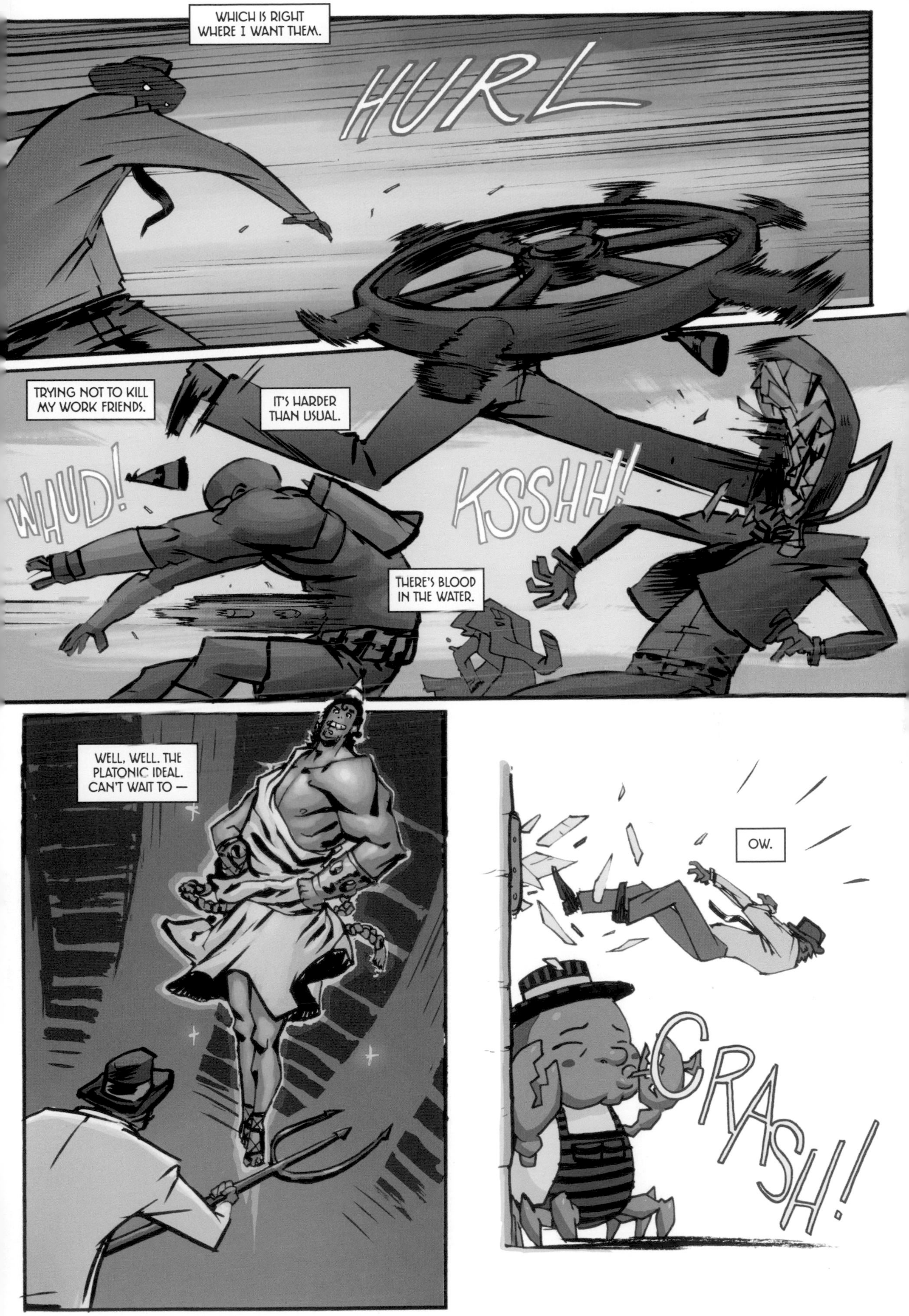
WHICH IS RIGHT WHERE I WANT THEM.
HURL
TRYING NOT TO KILL MY WORK FRIENDS.
IT'S HARDER THAN USUAL.
WHUD!
KSSHH!
THERE'S BLOOD IN THE WATER.
WELL, WELL. THE PLATONIC IDEAL. CAN'T WAIT TO —
OW.
CRASH!

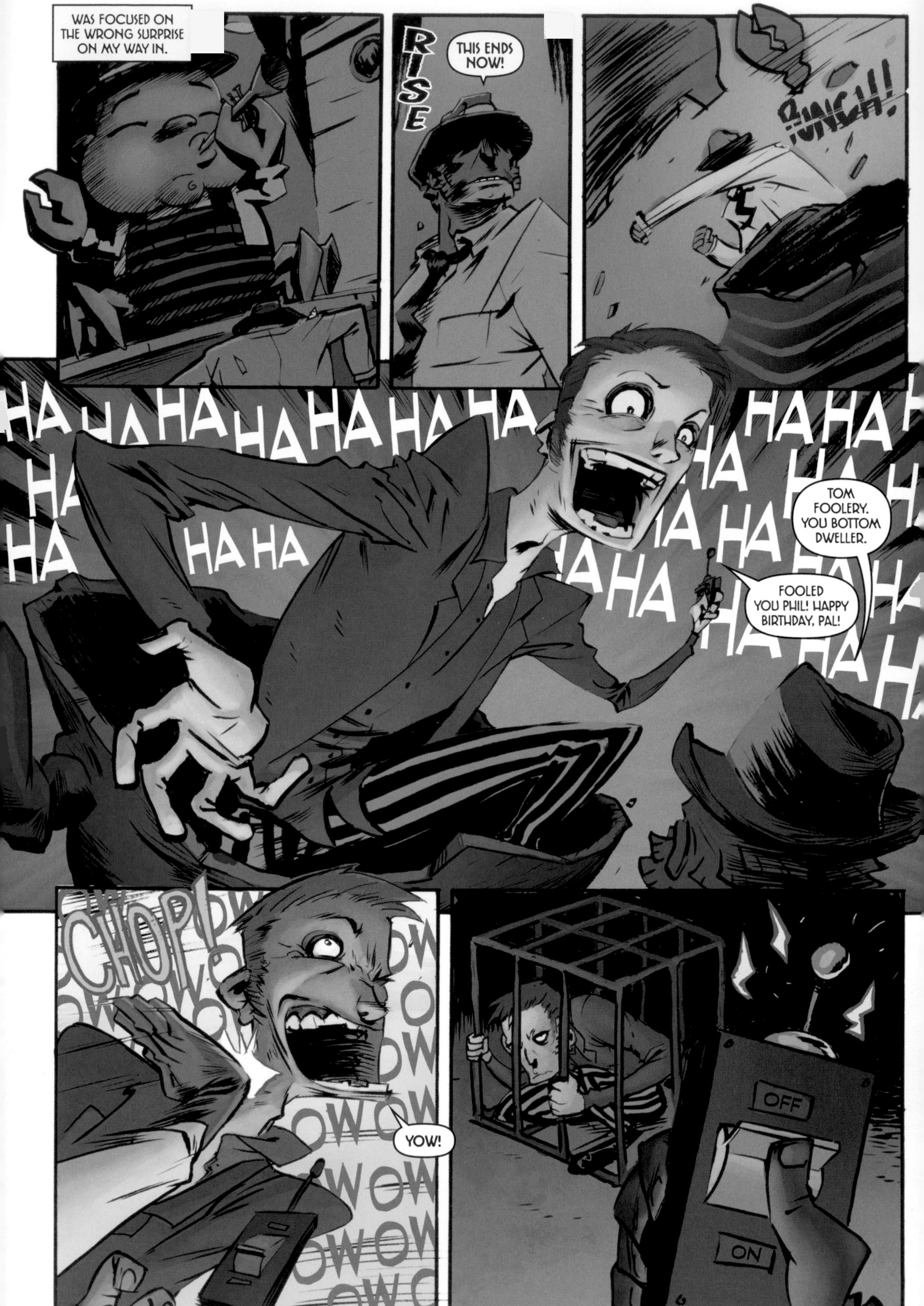
WAS FOCUSED ON THE WRONG SURPRISE ON MY WAY IN.
RISE
THIS ENDS NOW!
PUNCH!
HA HA HA HA HA HA HA HA HA HA HA HA HA HA HA HA HA HA HA HA HA HA HA HA HA HA HA HA HA
TOM FOOLERY. YOU BOTTOM DWELLER.
FOOLED YOU PHIL! HAPPY BIRTHDAY, PAL!
CHOP!
OW OW OW OW OW OW OW OW OW OW OW
YOW!
OFF
ON

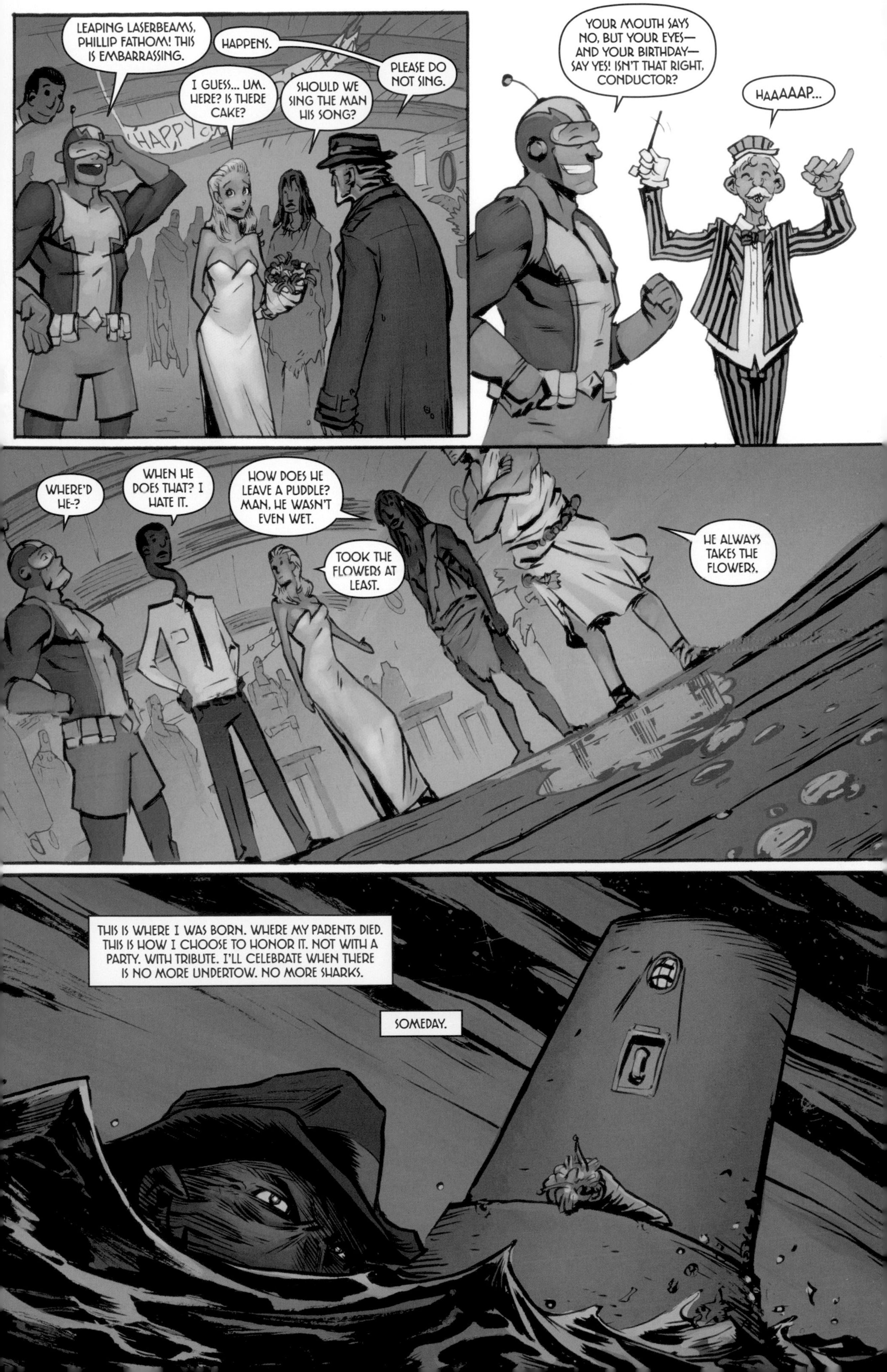
LEAPING LASERBEAMS, PHILLIP FATHOM! THIS IS EMBARRASSING.
HAPPENS.
I GUESS... UM. HERE? IS THERE CAKE?
SHOULD WE SING THE MAN HIS SONG?
PLEASE DO NOT SING.
YOUR MOUTH SAYS NO, BUT YOUR EYES—AND YOUR BIRTHDAY—SAY YES! ISN'T THAT RIGHT, CONDUCTOR?
HAAAAAP...
WHERE'D HE-?
WHEN HE DOES THAT? I HATE IT.
HOW DOES HE LEAVE A PUDDLE? MAN, HE WASN'T EVEN WET.
TOOK THE FLOWERS AT LEAST.
HE ALWAYS TAKES THE FLOWERS.
THIS IS WHERE I WAS BORN. WHERE MY PARENTS DIED. THIS IS HOW I CHOOSE TO HONOR IT. NOT WITH A PARTY. WITH TRIBUTE. I'LL CELEBRATE WHEN THERE IS NO MORE UNDERTOW. NO MORE SHARKS.
SOMEDAY.

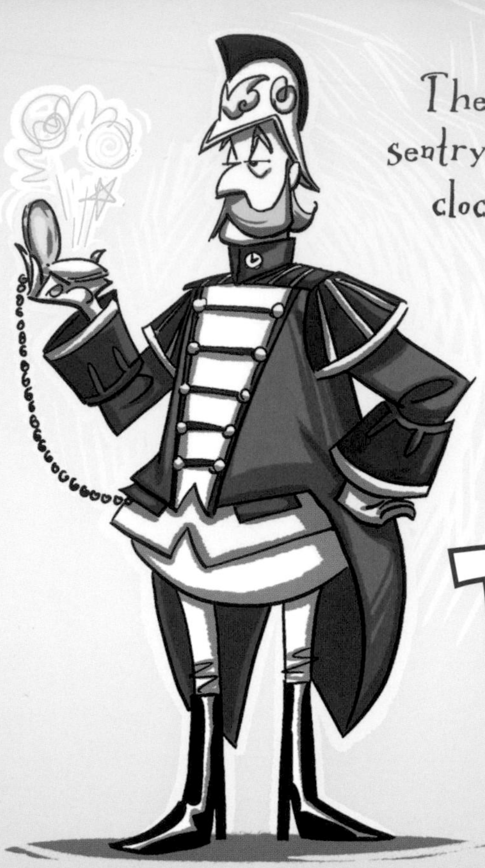

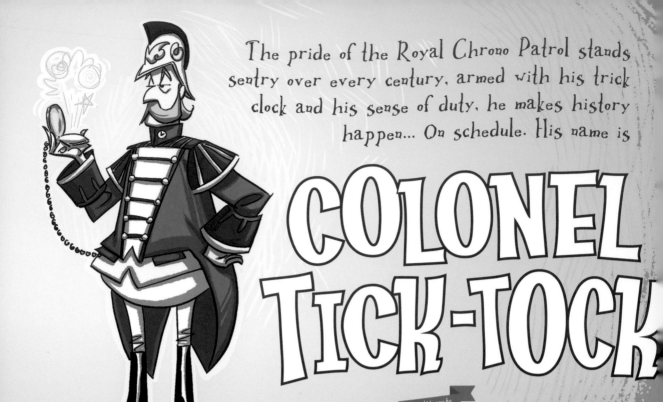

The pride of the Royal Chrono Patrol stands sentry over every century, armed with his trick clock and his sense of duty, he makes history happen... On schedule. His name is

# COLONEL TICK-TOCK

Brought to you by WORKJUICE COMICS GROUP

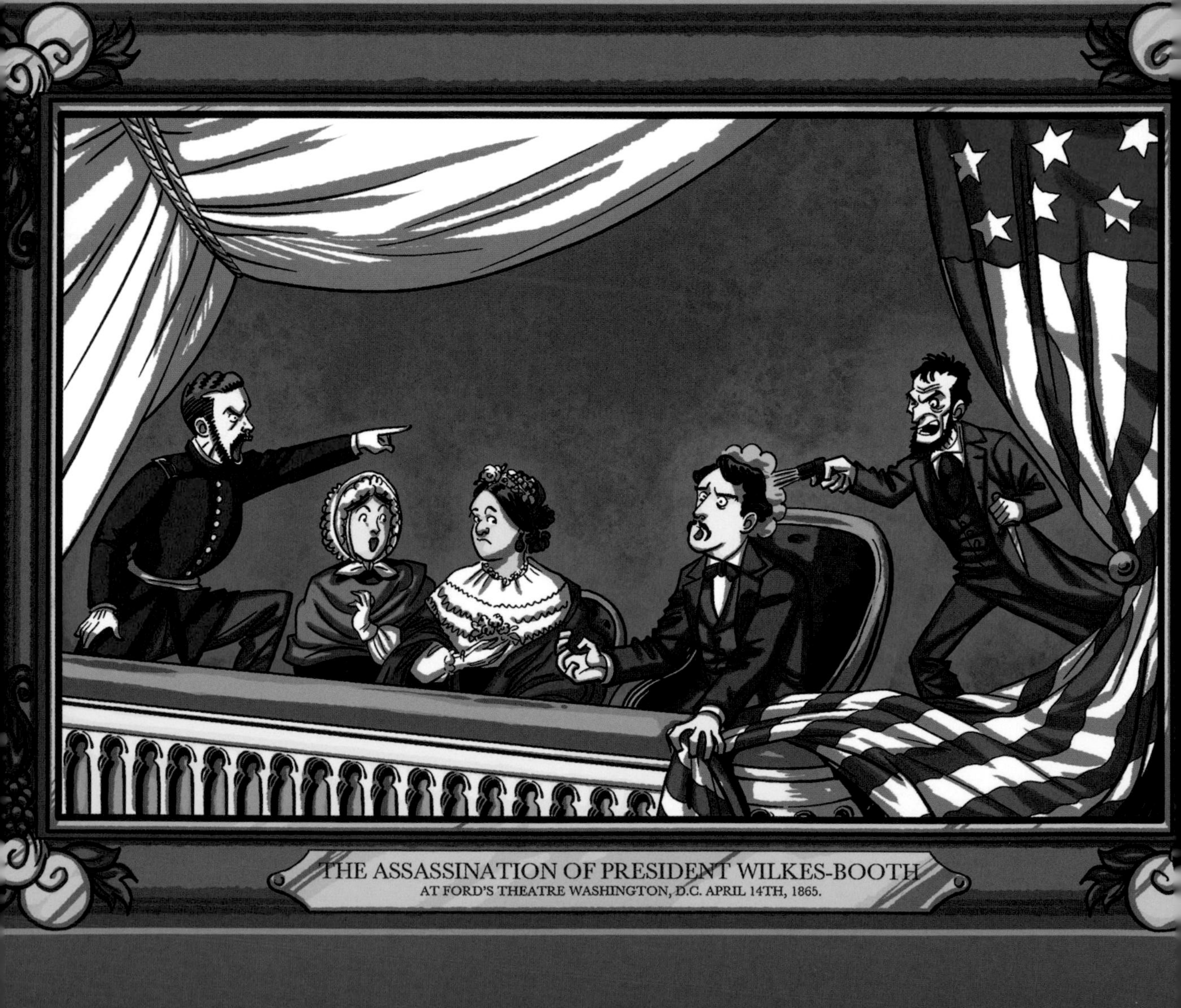

THE ASSASSINATION OF PRESIDENT WILKES-BOOTH
AT FORD'S THEATRE WASHINGTON, D.C. APRIL 14TH, 1865.

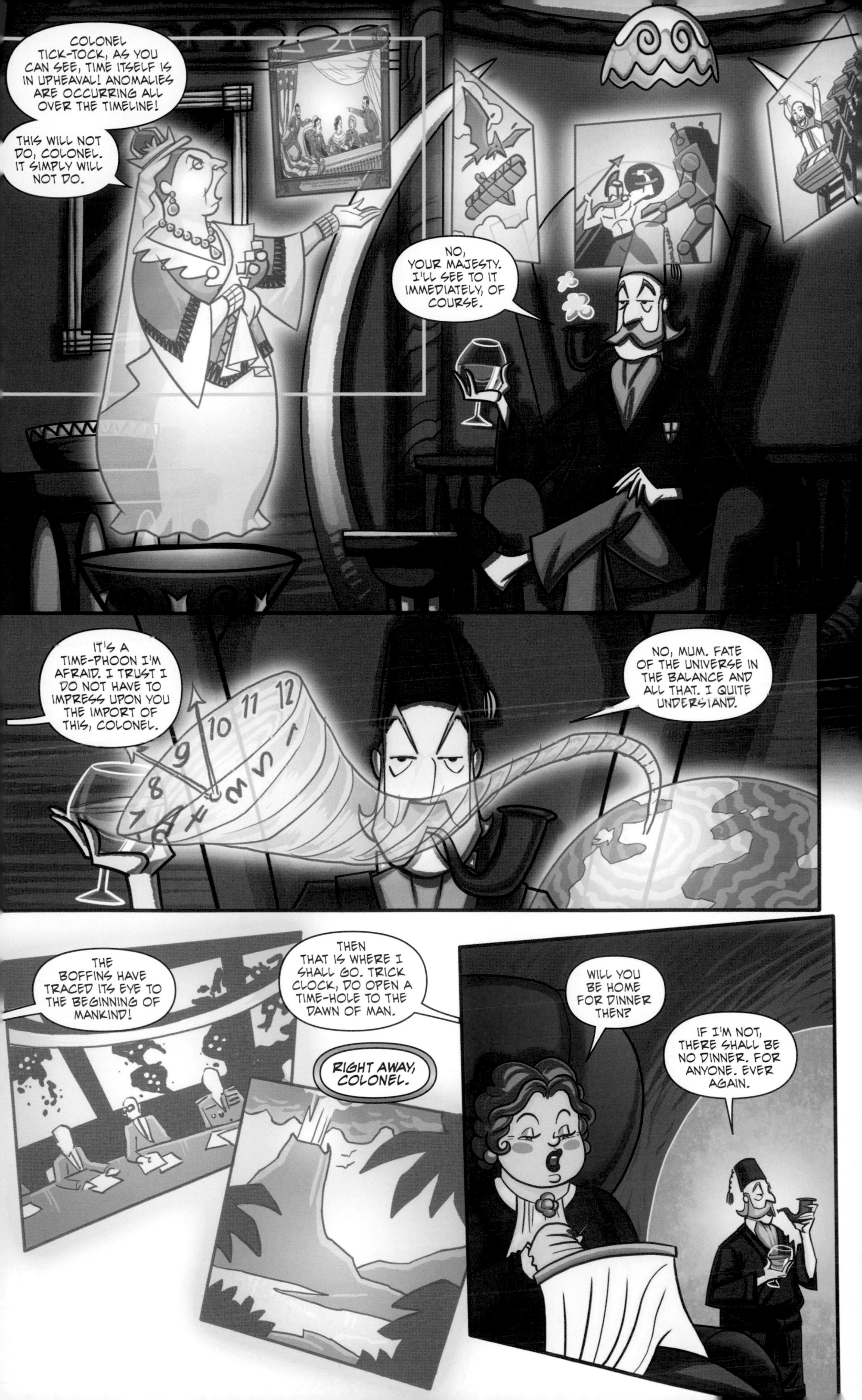
COLONEL TICK-TOCK, AS YOU CAN SEE, TIME ITSELF IS IN UPHEAVAL! ANOMALIES ARE OCCURRING ALL OVER THE TIMELINE!
THIS WILL NOT DO, COLONEL. IT SIMPLY WILL NOT DO.
NO, YOUR MAJESTY. I'LL SEE TO IT IMMEDIATELY, OF COURSE.
IT'S A TIME-PHOON I'M AFRAID. I TRUST I DO NOT HAVE TO IMPRESS UPON YOU THE IMPORT OF THIS, COLONEL.
NO, MUM. FATE OF THE UNIVERSE IN THE BALANCE AND ALL THAT. I QUITE UNDERSTAND.
THE BOFFINS HAVE TRACED ITS EYE TO THE BEGINNING OF MANKIND!
THEN THAT IS WHERE I SHALL GO. TRICK CLOCK, DO OPEN A TIME-HOLE TO THE DAWN OF MAN.
RIGHT AWAY, COLONEL.
WILL YOU BE HOME FOR DINNER THEN?
IF I'M NOT, THERE SHALL BE NO DINNER. FOR ANYONE. EVER AGAIN.

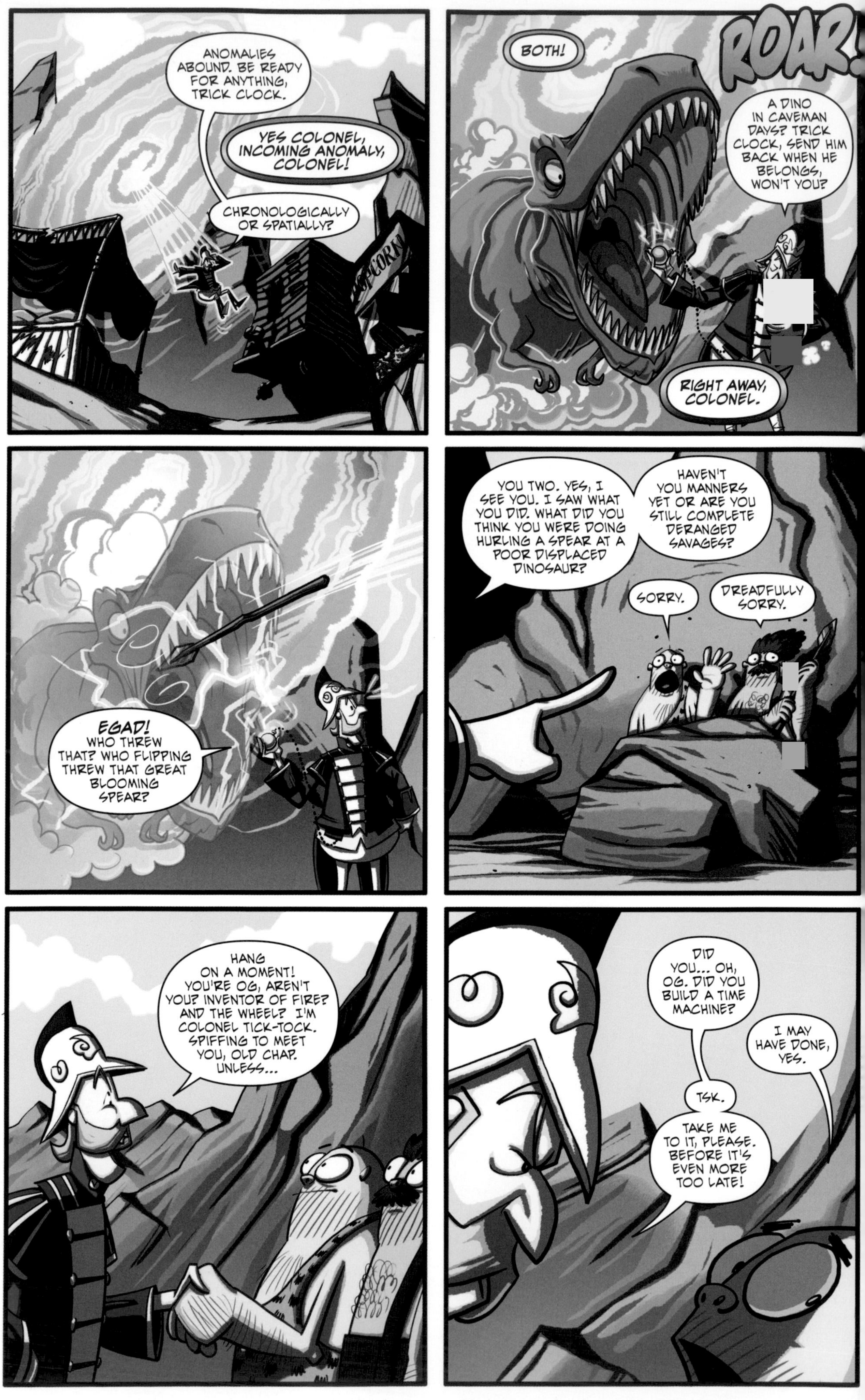
ANOMALIES ABOUND. BE READY FOR ANYTHING, TRICK CLOCK.
YES COLONEL, INCOMING ANOMALY, COLONEL!
CHRONOLOGICALLY OR SPATIALLY?
BOTH!
ROAR!
A DINO IN CAVEMAN DAYS? TRICK CLOCK, SEND HIM BACK WHEN HE BELONGS, WON'T YOU?
RIGHT AWAY, COLONEL.
EGAD! WHO THREW THAT? WHO FLIPPING THREW THAT GREAT BLOOMING SPEAR?
YOU TWO. YES, I SEE YOU. I SAW WHAT YOU DID. WHAT DID YOU THINK YOU WERE DOING HURLING A SPEAR AT A POOR DISPLACED DINOSAUR?
HAVEN'T YOU MANNERS YET OR ARE YOU STILL COMPLETE DERANGED SAVAGES?
SORRY.
DREADFULLY SORRY.
HANG ON A MOMENT! YOU'RE OG, AREN'T YOU? INVENTOR OF FIRE? AND THE WHEEL? I'M COLONEL TICK-TOCK. SPIFFING TO MEET YOU, OLD CHAP. UNLESS...
DID YOU... OH, OG. DID YOU BUILD A TIME MACHINE?
I MAY HAVE DONE, YES.
TSK.
TAKE ME TO IT, PLEASE. BEFORE IT'S EVEN MORE TOO LATE!

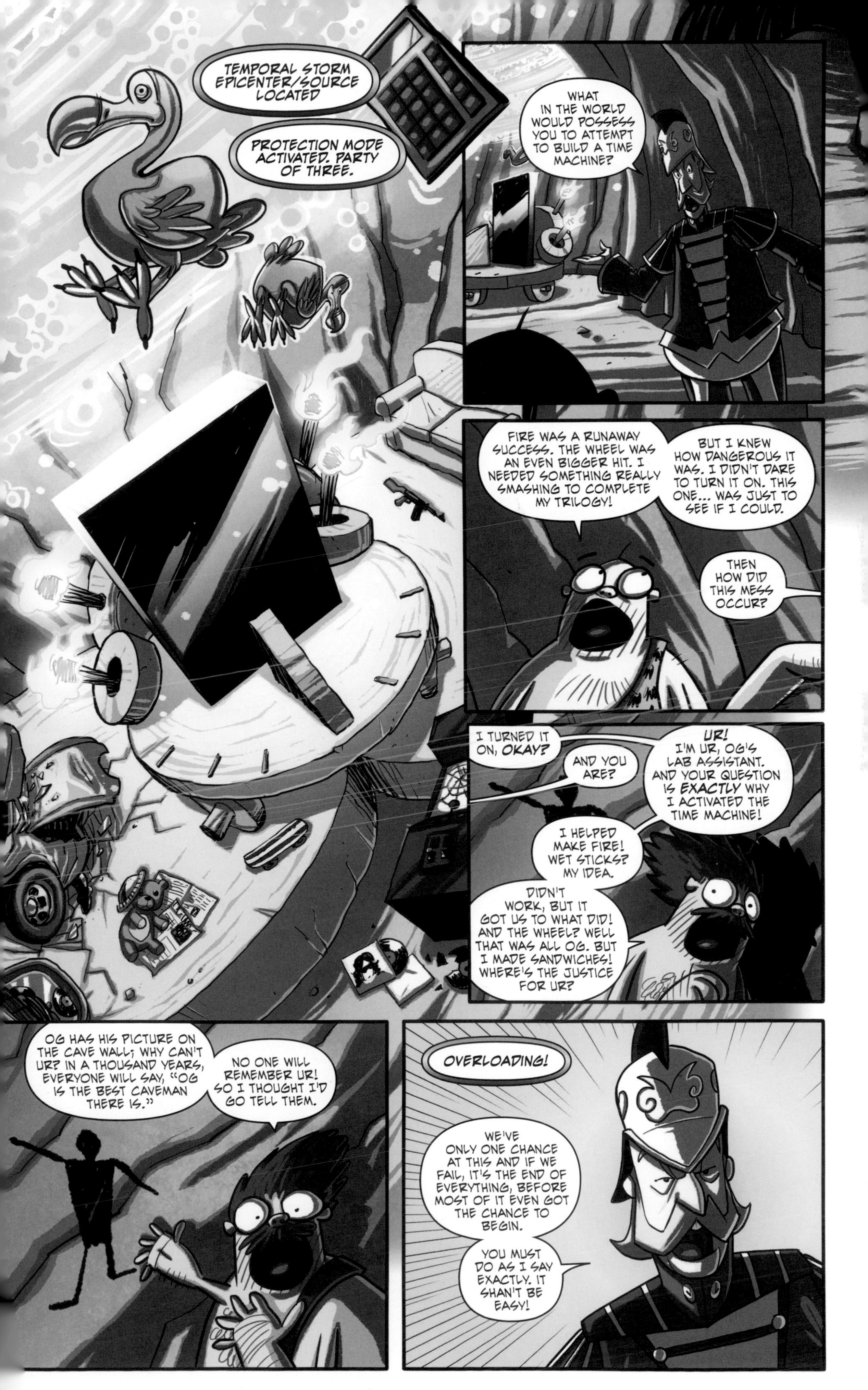
TEMPORAL STORM EPICENTER/SOURCE LOCATED
PROTECTION MODE ACTIVATED. PARTY OF THREE.
WHAT IN THE WORLD WOULD POSSESS YOU TO ATTEMPT TO BUILD A TIME MACHINE?
FIRE WAS A RUNAWAY SUCCESS. THE WHEEL WAS AN EVEN BIGGER HIT. I NEEDED SOMETHING REALLY SMASHING TO COMPLETE MY TRILOGY!
BUT I KNEW HOW DANGEROUS IT WAS. I DIDN'T DARE TO TURN IT ON. THIS ONE... WAS JUST TO SEE IF I COULD.
THEN HOW DID THIS MESS OCCUR?
I TURNED IT ON, OKAY?
AND YOU ARE?
UR! I'M UR, OG'S LAB ASSISTANT. AND YOUR QUESTION IS EXACTLY WHY I ACTIVATED THE TIME MACHINE!
I HELPED MAKE FIRE! WET STICKS? MY IDEA.
DIDN'T WORK, BUT IT GOT US TO WHAT DID! AND THE WHEEL? WELL THAT WAS ALL OG. BUT I MADE SANDWICHES! WHERE'S THE JUSTICE FOR UR?
OG HAS HIS PICTURE ON THE CAVE WALL; WHY CAN'T UR? IN A THOUSAND YEARS, EVERYONE WILL SAY, "OG IS THE BEST CAVEMAN THERE IS."
NO ONE WILL REMEMBER UR! SO I THOUGHT I'D GO TELL THEM.
OVERLOADING!
WE'VE ONLY ONE CHANCE AT THIS AND IF WE FAIL, IT'S THE END OF EVERYTHING, BEFORE MOST OF IT EVEN GOT THE CHANCE TO BEGIN.
YOU MUST DO AS I SAY EXACTLY. IT SHAN'T BE EASY!

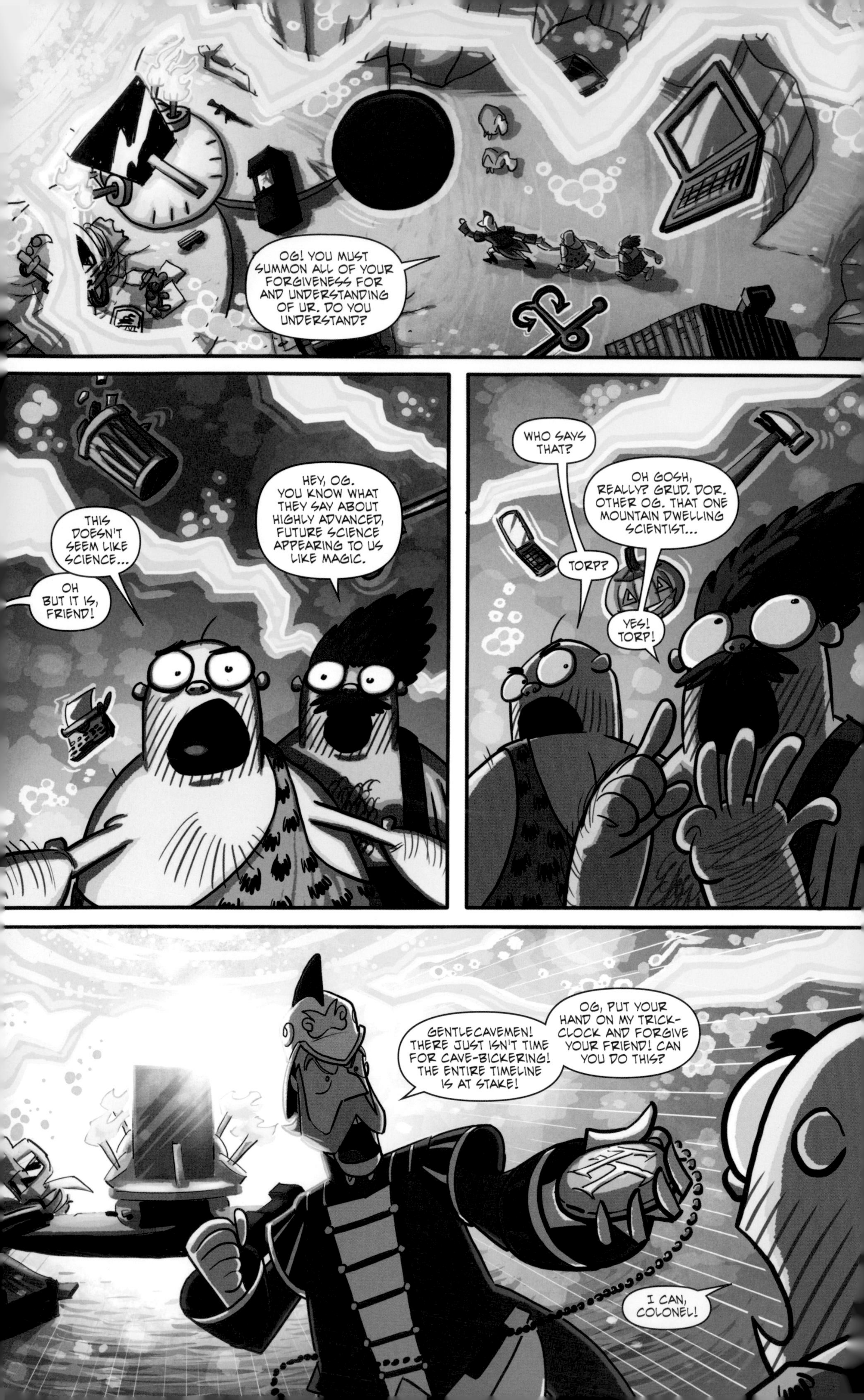
OG! YOU MUST SUMMON ALL OF YOUR FORGIVENESS FOR AND UNDERSTANDING OF UR. DO YOU UNDERSTAND?
THIS DOESN'T SEEM LIKE SCIENCE...
OH BUT IT IS, FRIEND!
HEY, OG. YOU KNOW WHAT THEY SAY ABOUT HIGHLY ADVANCED, FUTURE SCIENCE APPEARING TO US LIKE MAGIC.
WHO SAYS THAT?
OH GOSH, REALLY? GRUD. DOR. OTHER OG. THAT ONE MOUNTAIN DWELLING SCIENTIST...
TORP?
YES! TORP!
GENTLECAVEMEN! THERE JUST ISN'T TIME FOR CAVE-BICKERING! THE ENTIRE TIMELINE IS AT STAKE!
OG, PUT YOUR HAND ON MY TRICK-CLOCK AND FORGIVE YOUR FRIEND! CAN YOU DO THIS?
I CAN, COLONEL!

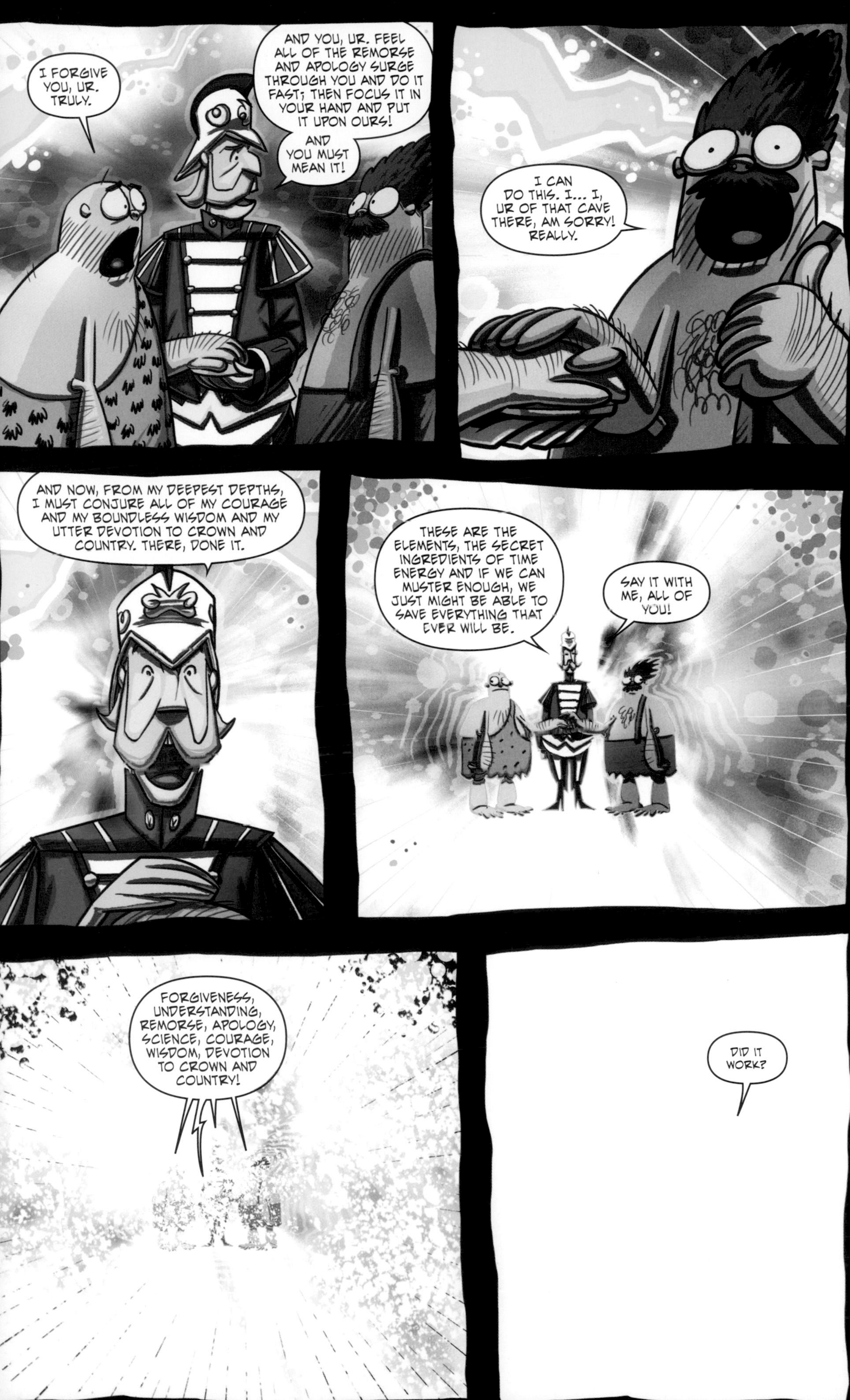
I FORGIVE YOU, UR. TRULY.
AND YOU, UR. FEEL ALL OF THE REMORSE AND APOLOGY SURGE THROUGH YOU AND DO IT FAST; THEN FOCUS IT IN YOUR HAND AND PUT IT UPON OURS!
AND YOU MUST MEAN IT!
I CAN DO THIS. I... I, UR OF THAT CAVE THERE, AM SORRY! REALLY.
AND NOW, FROM MY DEEPEST DEPTHS, I MUST CONJURE ALL OF MY COURAGE AND MY BOUNDLESS WISDOM AND MY UTTER DEVOTION TO CROWN AND COUNTRY. THERE, DONE IT.
THESE ARE THE ELEMENTS, THE SECRET INGREDIENTS OF TIME ENERGY AND IF WE CAN MUSTER ENOUGH, WE JUST MIGHT BE ABLE TO SAVE EVERYTHING THAT EVER WILL BE.
SAY IT WITH ME, ALL OF YOU!
FORGIVENESS, UNDERSTANDING, REMORSE, APOLOGY, SCIENCE, COURAGE, WISDOM, DEVOTION TO CROWN AND COUNTRY!
DID IT WORK?

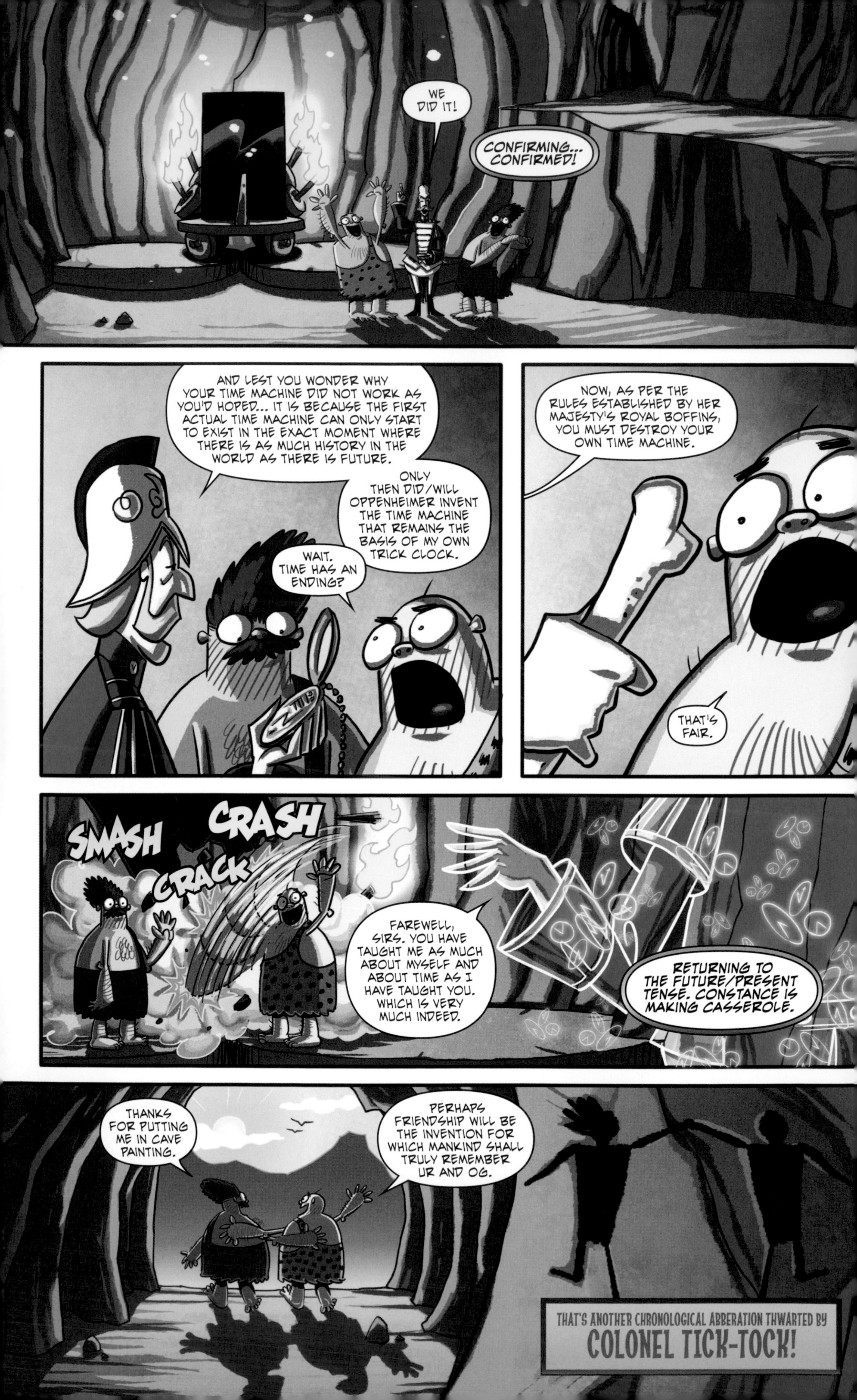
WE DID IT!
CONFIRMING... CONFIRMED!
AND LEST YOU WONDER WHY YOUR TIME MACHINE DID NOT WORK AS YOU'D HOPED... IT IS BECAUSE THE FIRST ACTUAL TIME MACHINE CAN ONLY START TO EXIST IN THE EXACT MOMENT WHERE THERE IS AS MUCH HISTORY IN THE WORLD AS THERE IS FUTURE.
ONLY THEN DID/WILL OPPENHEIMER INVENT THE TIME MACHINE THAT REMAINS THE BASIS OF MY OWN TRICK CLOCK.
WAIT. TIME HAS AN ENDING?
NOW, AS PER THE RULES ESTABLISHED BY HER MAJESTY'S ROYAL BOFFINS, YOU MUST DESTROY YOUR OWN TIME MACHINE.
THAT'S FAIR.
SMASH
CRASH
CRACK
FAREWELL, SIRS. YOU HAVE TAUGHT ME AS MUCH ABOUT MYSELF AND ABOUT TIME AS I HAVE TAUGHT YOU. WHICH IS VERY MUCH INDEED.
RETURNING TO THE FUTURE/PRESENT TENSE. CONSTANCE IS MAKING CASSEROLE.
THANKS FOR PUTTING ME IN CAVE PAINTING.
PERHAPS FRIENDSHIP WILL BE THE INVENTION FOR WHICH MANKIND SHALL TRULY REMEMBER UR AND OG.
THAT'S ANOTHER CHRONOLOGICAL ABBERATION THWARTED BY
COLONEL TICK-TOCK!

The WorkJuice Coporation presents...

# THE SHAPE OF THINGS TO COME!

⚡ **FLYING CARS!** ⚡
⚡ **MEALS HELD IN TEENY TINY PILLS!** ⚡
⚡ **ROBOT BUTLERS!** ⚡

And in the past, everything that we have now was something that would exist in the future.

⚡ **SHIRTS!** ⚡
⚡ **TAXI CABS!** ⚡
⚡ **REGULAR BUTLERS THAT AREN'T ROBOTS!** ⚡

Yes, everything from shirts to butlers, including taxi cabs, were invented by inventors fueled by WorkJuice Coffee.

**WORKJUICE™** *"Filled to the Brim With Zip and Vim!"*

This message was brought to you by your friends at the WorkJuice Coporation.

❝ The best thing in the world **JUST GOT BETTER.** Rejoice, fellow Adventurekateers! Our time is now at hand! Things like this are why we beat the Russians. ❞

## MATT FRACTION

Eisner Award-winning writer of *The Invincible Iron Man*, *The Immortal Iron Fist*, *Uncanny X-Men*, and *Casanova*

*Experience Coffee Brewed for the Fairer Sex*

## WorkJuice
### Femme
**Blend for Her**

Beans Specially Selected to Interact with a Woman's Female Biology

ENJOY THE DISTINGUISHED QUALITY OF

# NEWMAN BROS.
### PRINT & DESIGN

*"WE AIM TO PLEASE... AND WE ALMOST NEVER MISS."*

We now offer the **{Letter L}** *You'll LLLLove it!*

★★★★★ A MESSAGE FROM ★★★★★

# A PRESIDENT OF THE UNITED STATES
~ on behalf of ~
**Patriot Brand Cigarettes**

My fellow Americans.

Since taking office, I've been given a special phone line. I use it and I get whatever I want. If I want a panda sandwich, I pick up the phone, press six, and I tell them *"panda sandwich."* **20** minutes later, the tenderest, most endangered sandwich you've ever tasted. I'll tell you what though. Every hour or so, I pick up that phone, I hit six, and I order me up some Patriot Brand Cigarettes.

They're tastier than a hummingbird salad, which is delicious and goes down fast. Panda meat is tender and surprisingly smoky. But nowhere near as flavorful as a Patriot Brand Cigarette.

God bless America.
And God Bless **Patriot Brand Cigarettes**.

PATRIOT BRAND CIGARETTES IS PLEASED TO BRING YOU **JEFFERSON REID: ACE AMERICAN** A THRILLING ADVENTURE HOUR PRODUCTION

*"THEY'RE GOOD...* PATRIOT BRAND CIGARETTES *...FOR YOUR CONSTITUTION!"*

Don't Forget! Collect Patriot Points for Exciting Rewards!

Nerdist

An esteemed partner of *The Thrilling Adventure Hour*
*"Tune-In and Enjoy the Refreshing Sounds of Nerdist."*
+ Now Broadcasting in **Hi-Fi Spectral Sound!** +

TUNE-IN AND JOIN THE ACE AMERICAN ON HIS LATEST ADVENTURE!

**JEFFERSON REID**

*Ace • American!*

ONLY ON THE THRILLING ADVENTURE HOUR!

★ SPONSORED BY **PATRIOT BRAND CIGARETTES** ★
*"THEY'RE GOOD FOR YOUR CONSTITUTION."*

*The*
# ROYAL CHRONO PATROL
## Quality Time Pieces

Superior Quality meets Unrivaled Style and Design Perfectly engineered to keep time, save time, and even make up for lost time.

**If it isn't Royal Chrono Patrol, then it isn't worth your time.**

## MAKE HISTORY HAPPEN... ON TIME!
Stand Sentry Over the Century and Enjoy Colonel Tick-Tock Only on The Thrilling Adventure Hour

*Now in Print and Available from Fine Retailers of Goods for Women*

# THE THRILLING ADVENTURE HOUR
### Original Graphic Novel
*Ladies Edition*

+ Specially Designed, Formulated, and Printed for Women Who Enjoy a Reading Experience as Unique as They Are! +

Are You Losing Your Pep While You Read? Nothing Goes Better with a WorkJuice Comic than a Cup of
# WORKJUICE BRAND COFFEE
**Stimulate Your Reading Experience!**

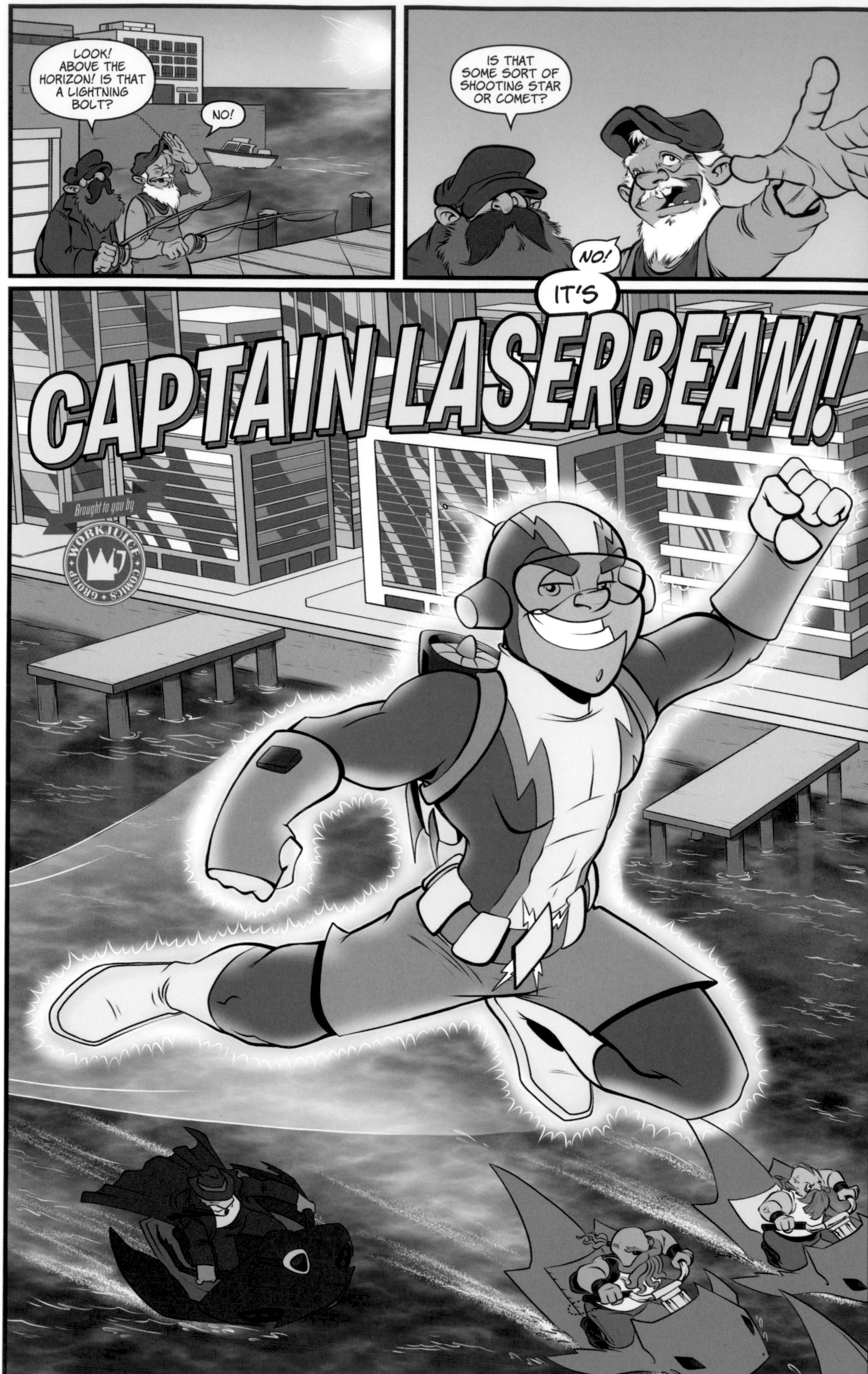
LOOK! ABOVE THE HORIZON! IS THAT A LIGHTNING BOLT?
NO!
IS THAT SOME SORT OF SHOOTING STAR OR COMET?
NO!
IT'S
CAPTAIN LASERBEAM!
Brought to you by
WORKJUICE COMICS GROUP

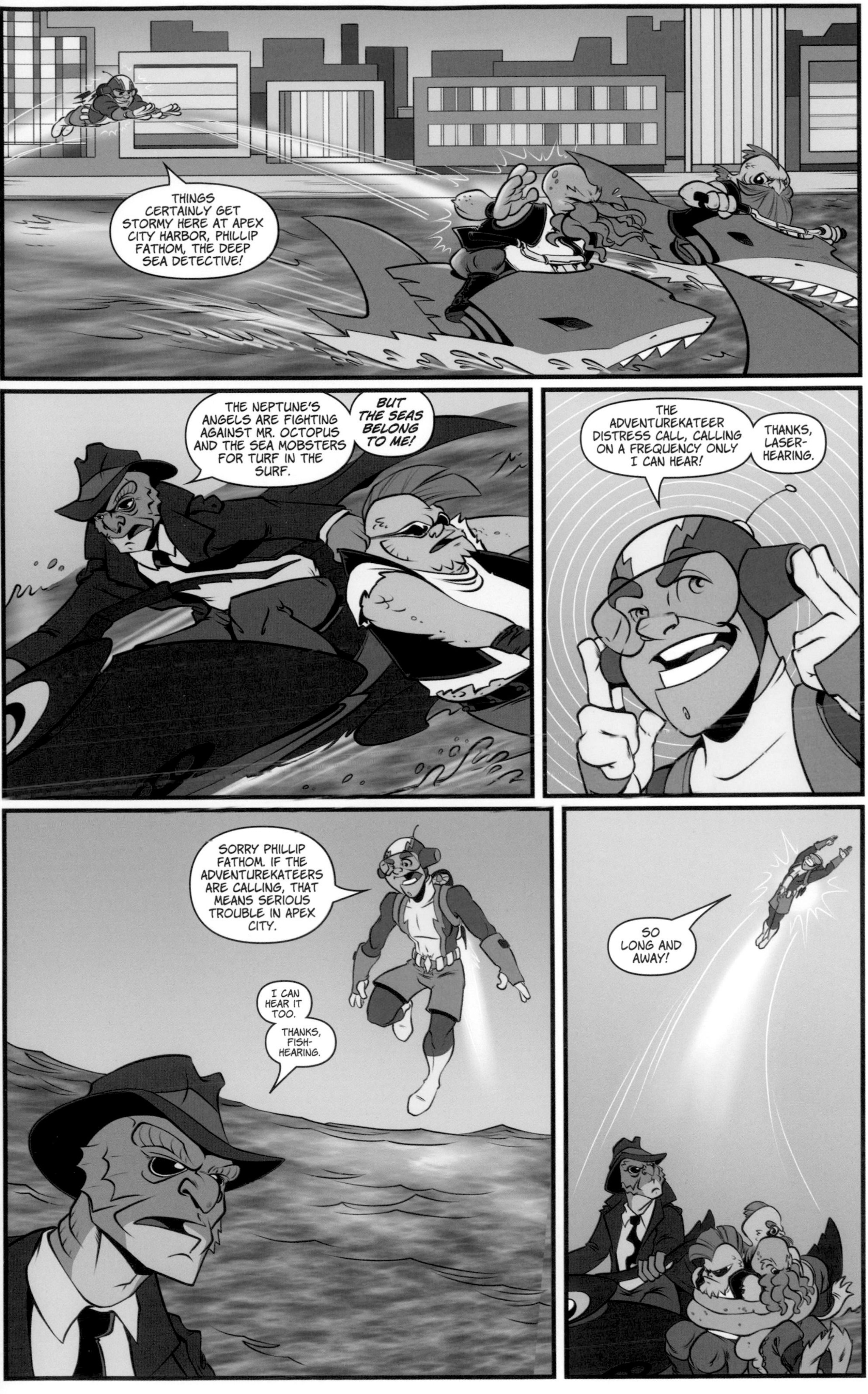
THINGS CERTAINLY GET STORMY HERE AT APEX CITY HARBOR, PHILLIP FATHOM, THE DEEP SEA DETECTIVE!
THE NEPTUNE'S ANGELS ARE FIGHTING AGAINST MR. OCTOPUS AND THE SEA MOBSTERS FOR TURF IN THE SURF.
BUT THE SEAS BELONG TO ME!
THE ADVENTUREKATEER DISTRESS CALL, CALLING ON A FREQUENCY ONLY I CAN HEAR!
THANKS, LASER-HEARING.
SORRY PHILLIP FATHOM. IF THE ADVENTUREKATEERS ARE CALLING, THAT MEANS SERIOUS TROUBLE IN APEX CITY.
I CAN HEAR IT TOO.
THANKS, FISH-HEARING.
SO LONG AND AWAY!

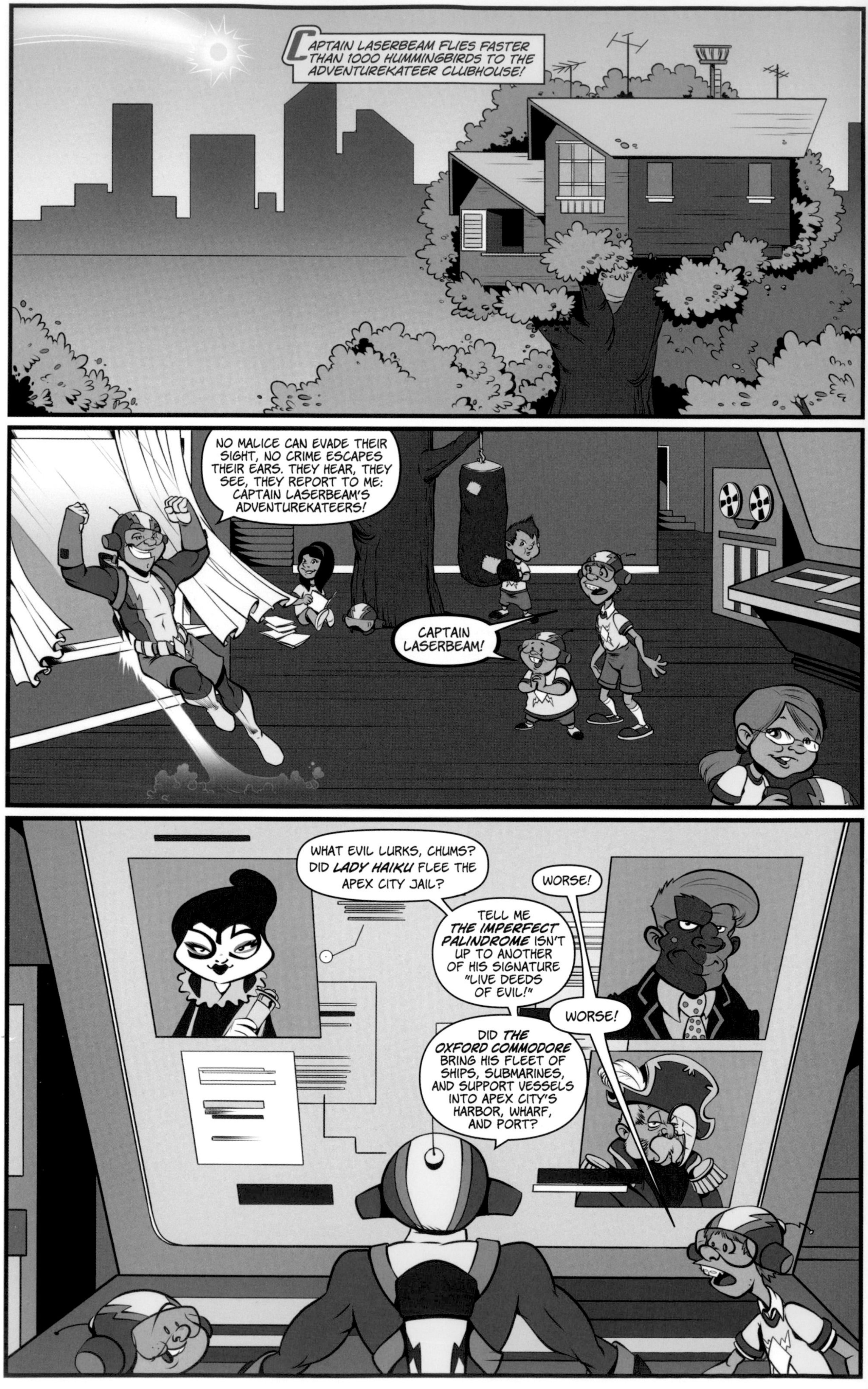
CAPTAIN LASERBEAM FLIES FASTER THAN 1000 HUMMINGBIRDS TO THE ADVENTUREKATEER CLUBHOUSE!
NO MALICE CAN EVADE THEIR SIGHT, NO CRIME ESCAPES THEIR EARS. THEY HEAR, THEY SEE, THEY REPORT TO ME: CAPTAIN LASERBEAM'S ADVENTUREKATEERS!
CAPTAIN LASERBEAM!
WHAT EVIL LURKS, CHUMS? DID LADY HAIKU FLEE THE APEX CITY JAIL?
WORSE!
TELL ME THE IMPERFECT PALINDROME ISN'T UP TO ANOTHER OF HIS SIGNATURE "LIVE DEEDS OF EVIL!"
WORSE!
DID THE OXFORD COMMODORE BRING HIS FLEET OF SHIPS, SUBMARINES, AND SUPPORT VESSELS INTO APEX CITY'S HARBOR, WHARF, AND PORT?

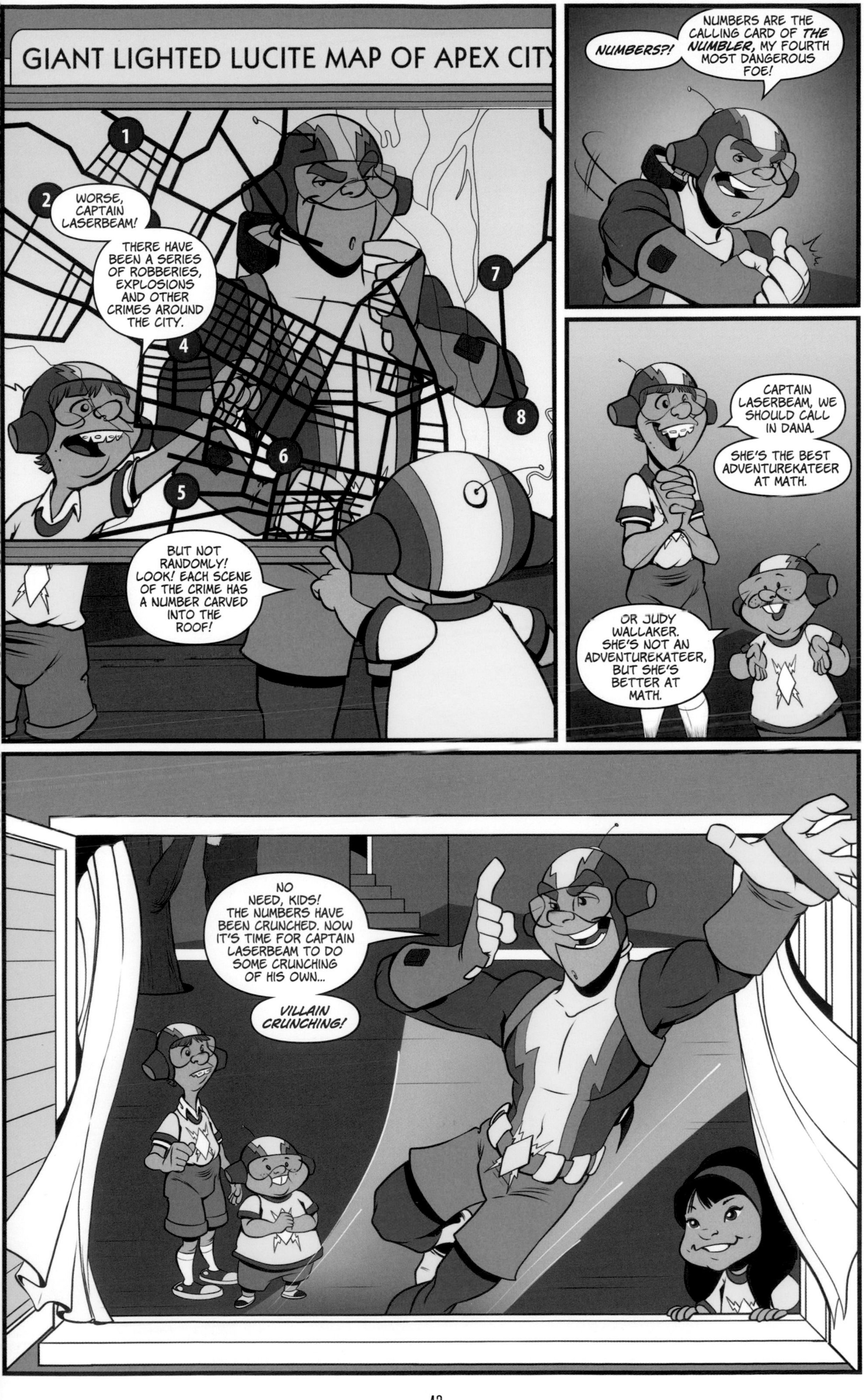
GIANT LIGHTED LUCITE MAP OF APEX CITY
1
2
4
5
6
7
8
WORSE, CAPTAIN LASERBEAM!
THERE HAVE BEEN A SERIES OF ROBBERIES, EXPLOSIONS AND OTHER CRIMES AROUND THE CITY.
BUT NOT RANDOMLY! LOOK! EACH SCENE OF THE CRIME HAS A NUMBER CARVED INTO THE ROOF!
NUMBERS?!
NUMBERS ARE THE CALLING CARD OF *THE NUMBLER*, MY FOURTH MOST DANGEROUS FOE!
CAPTAIN LASERBEAM, WE SHOULD CALL IN DANA.
SHE'S THE BEST ADVENTUREKATEER AT MATH.
OR JUDY WALLAKER. SHE'S NOT AN ADVENTUREKATEER, BUT SHE'S BETTER AT MATH.
NO NEED, KIDS! THE NUMBERS HAVE BEEN CRUNCHED. NOW IT'S TIME FOR CAPTAIN LASERBEAM TO DO SOME CRUNCHING OF HIS OWN...
*VILLAIN CRUNCHING!*

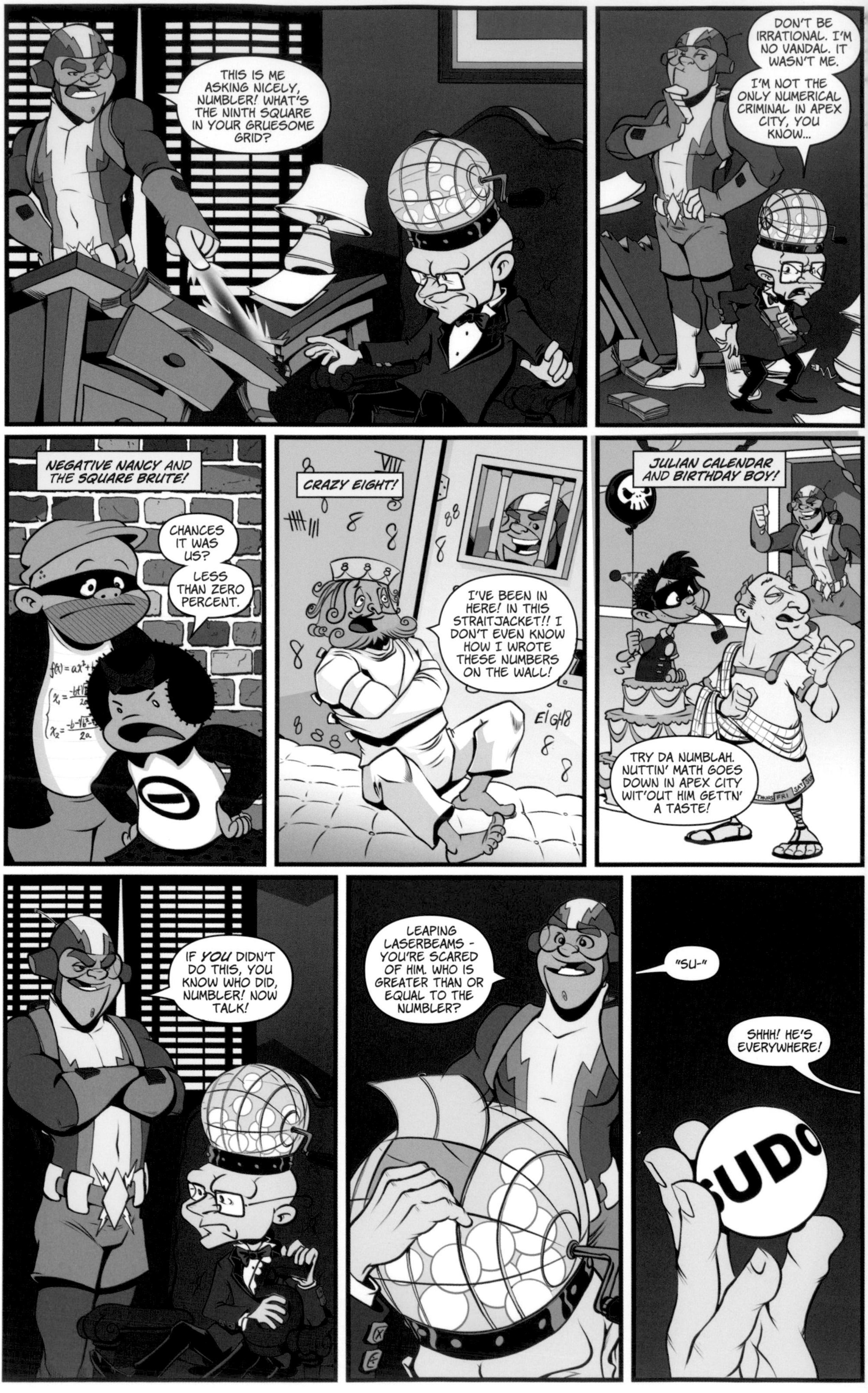
THIS IS ME ASKING NICELY, NUMBLER! WHAT'S THE NINTH SQUARE IN YOUR GRUESOME GRID?
DON'T BE IRRATIONAL. I'M NO VANDAL. IT WASN'T ME.
I'M NOT THE ONLY NUMERICAL CRIMINAL IN APEX CITY, YOU KNOW...
NEGATIVE NANCY AND THE SQUARE BRUTE!
CHANCES IT WAS US?
LESS THAN ZERO PERCENT.
CRAZY EIGHT!
I'VE BEEN IN HERE! IN THIS STRAITJACKET!! I DON'T EVEN KNOW HOW I WROTE THESE NUMBERS ON THE WALL!
JULIAN CALENDAR AND BIRTHDAY BOY!
TRY DA NUMBLAH. NUTTIN' MATH GOES DOWN IN APEX CITY WIT'OUT HIM GETTN' A TASTE!
IF YOU DIDN'T DO THIS, YOU KNOW WHO DID, NUMBLER! NOW TALK!
LEAPING LASERBEAMS - YOU'RE SCARED OF HIM. WHO IS GREATER THAN OR EQUAL TO THE NUMBLER?
"SU-"
SHHH! HE'S EVERYWHERE!
SUDO

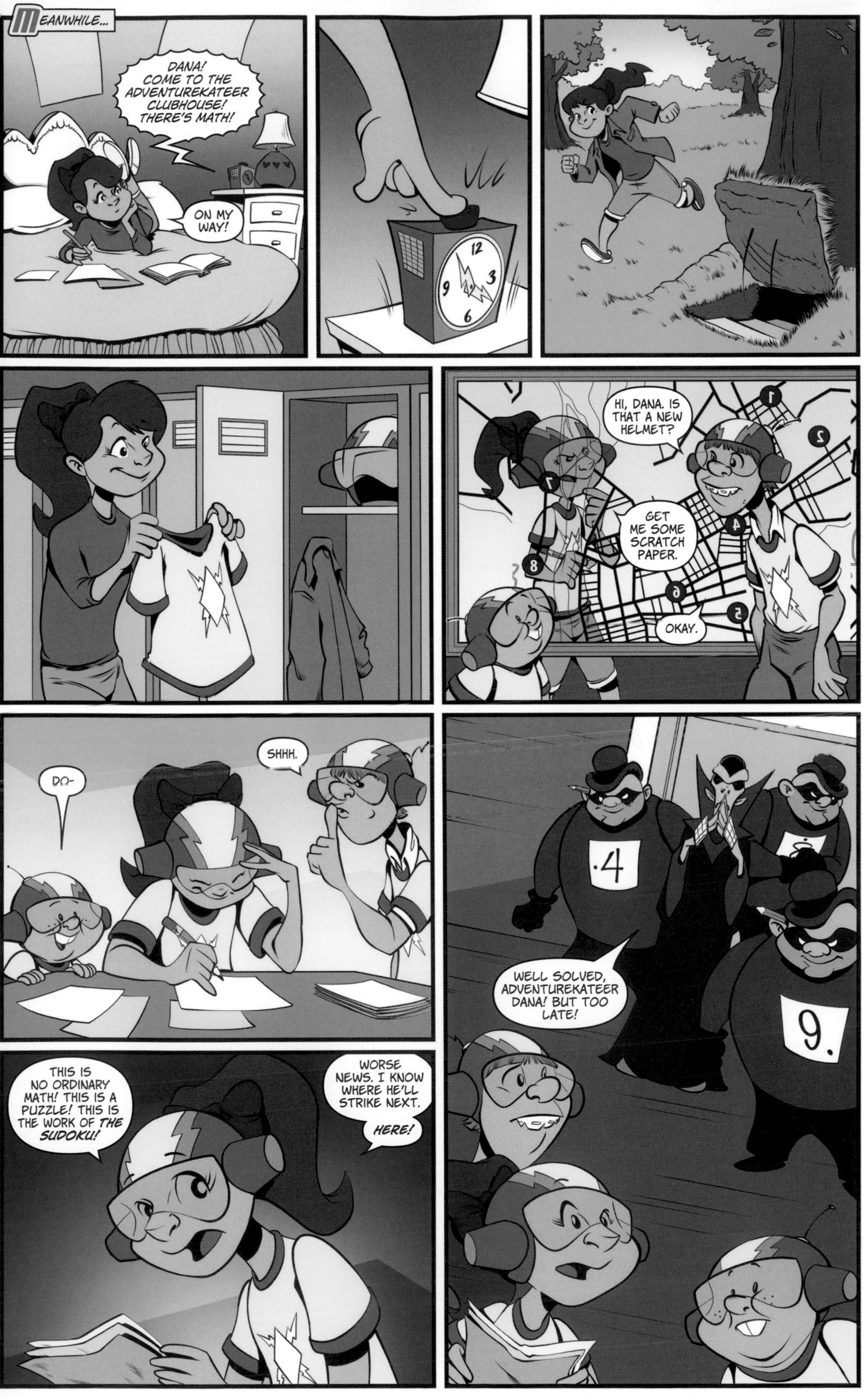
MEANWHILE...
DANA! COME TO THE ADVENTUREKATEER CLUBHOUSE! THERE'S MATH!
ON MY WAY!
12
3
6
9
HI, DANA. IS THAT A NEW HELMET?
GET ME SOME SCRATCH PAPER.
OKAY.
DO-
SHHH.
THIS IS NO ORDINARY MATH! THIS IS A PUZZLE! THIS IS THE WORK OF THE SUDOKU!
WORSE NEWS. I KNOW WHERE HE'LL STRIKE NEXT.
HERE!
WELL SOLVED, ADVENTUREKATEER DANA! BUT TOO LATE!
4
9

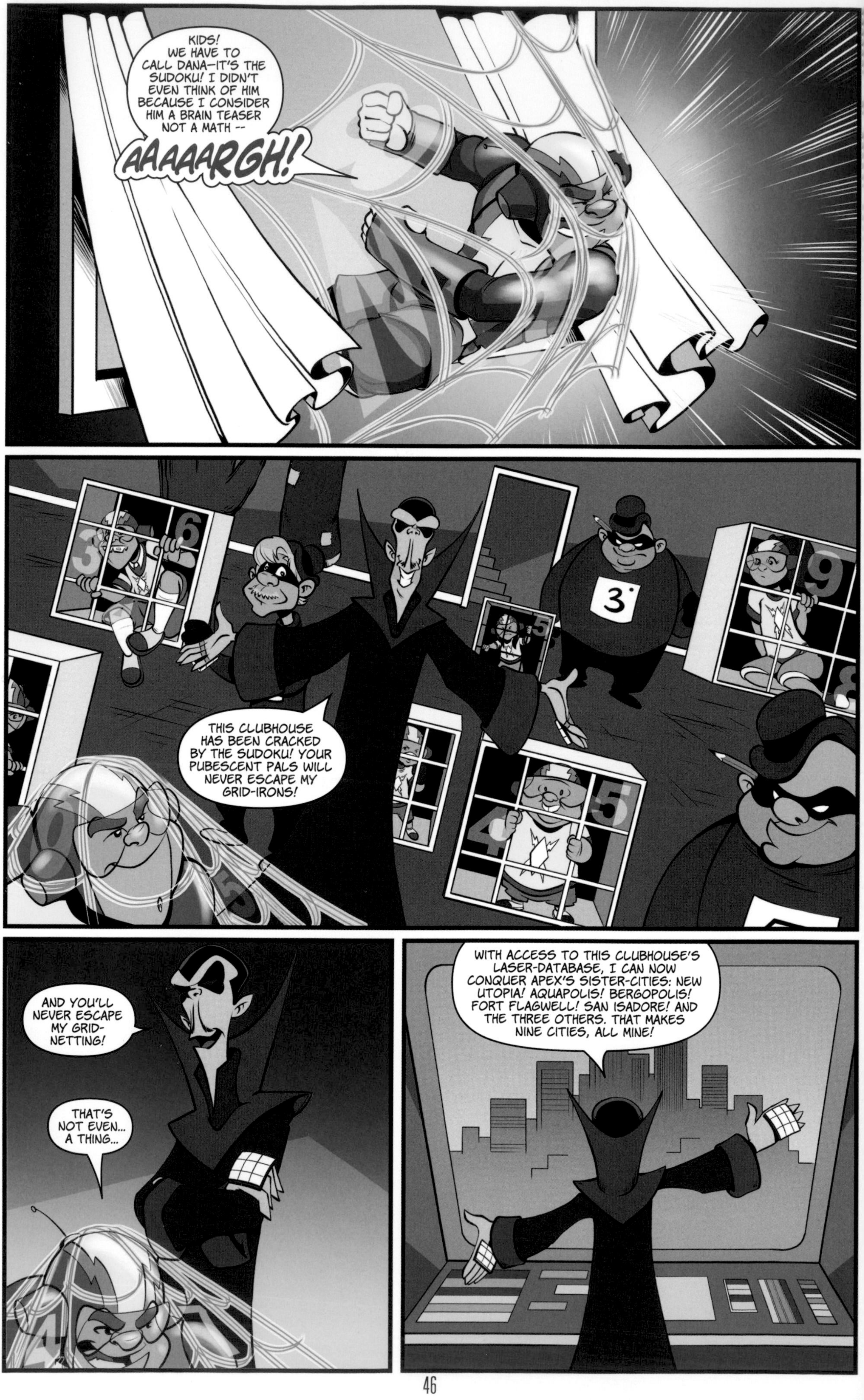
KIDS! WE HAVE TO CALL DANA—IT'S THE SUDOKU! I DIDN'T EVEN THINK OF HIM BECAUSE I CONSIDER HIM A BRAIN TEASER NOT A MATH --
AAAAARGH!
THIS CLUBHOUSE HAS BEEN CRACKED BY THE SUDOKU! YOUR PUBESCENT PALS WILL NEVER ESCAPE MY GRID-IRONS!
AND YOU'LL NEVER ESCAPE MY GRID-NETTING!
THAT'S NOT EVEN... A THING...
WITH ACCESS TO THIS CLUBHOUSE'S LASER-DATABASE, I CAN NOW CONQUER APEX'S SISTER-CITIES: NEW UTOPIA! AQUAPOLIS! BERGOPOLIS! FORT FLAGWELL! SAN ISADORE! AND THE THREE OTHERS. THAT MAKES NINE CITIES, ALL MINE!

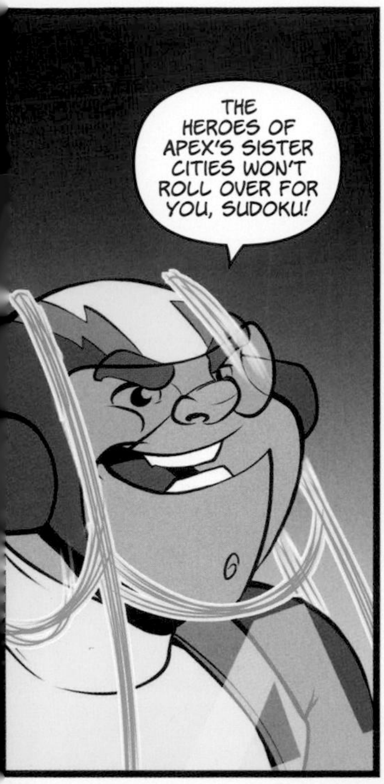
THE HEROES OF APEX'S SISTER CITIES WON'T ROLL OVER FOR YOU, SUDOKU!

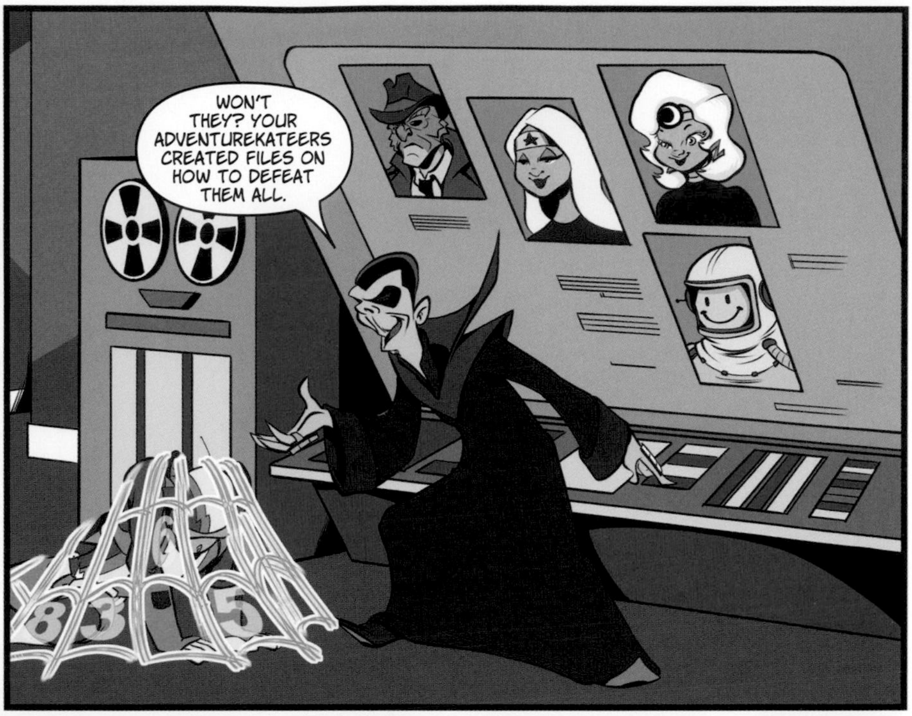
WON'T THEY? YOUR ADVENTUREKATEERS CREATED FILES ON HOW TO DEFEAT THEM ALL.

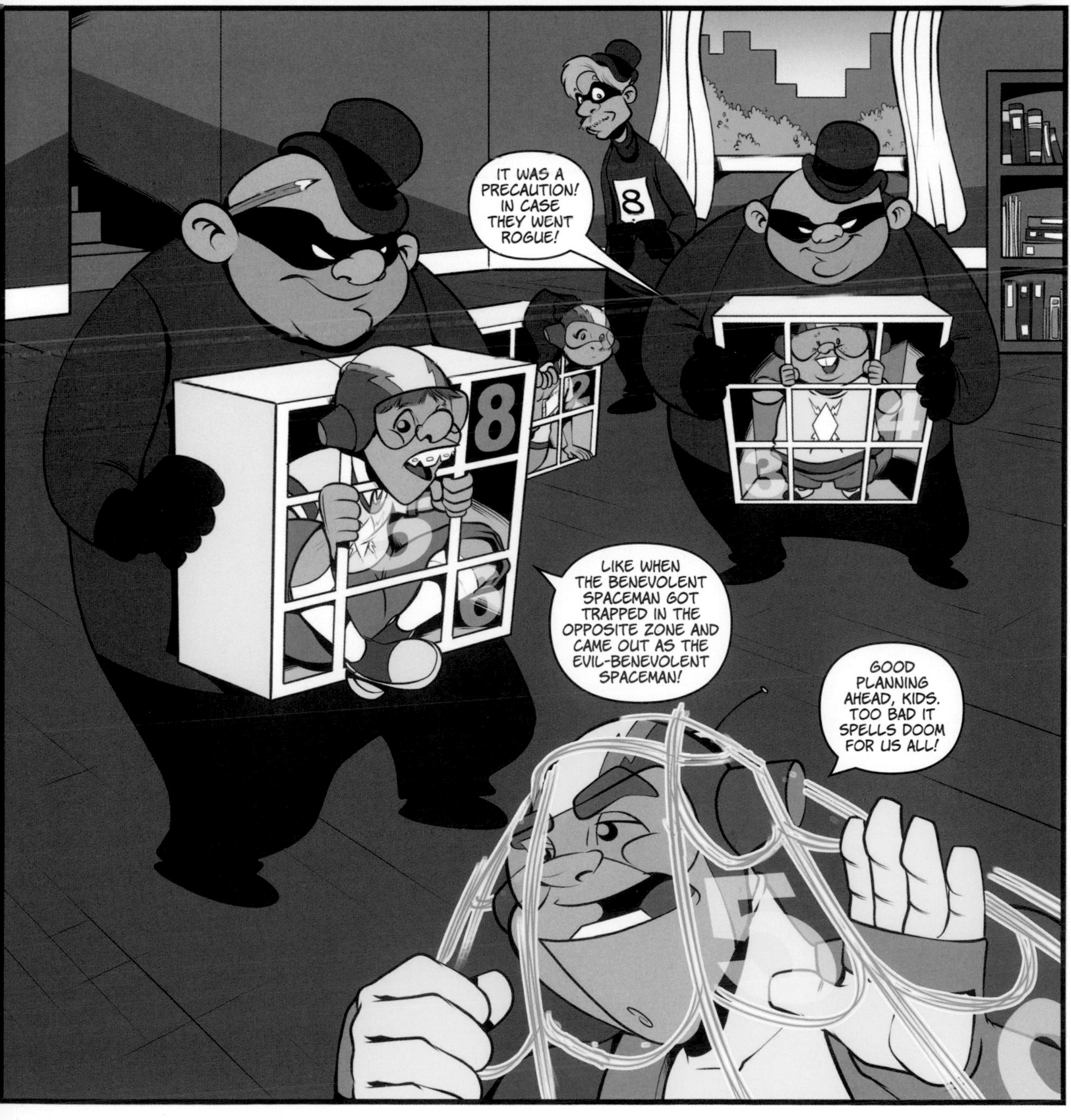
IT WAS A PRECAUTION! IN CASE THEY WENT ROGUE!
LIKE WHEN THE BENEVOLENT SPACEMAN GOT TRAPPED IN THE OPPOSITE ZONE AND CAME OUT AS THE EVIL-BENEVOLENT SPACEMAN!
GOOD PLANNING AHEAD, KIDS. TOO BAD IT SPELLS DOOM FOR US ALL!

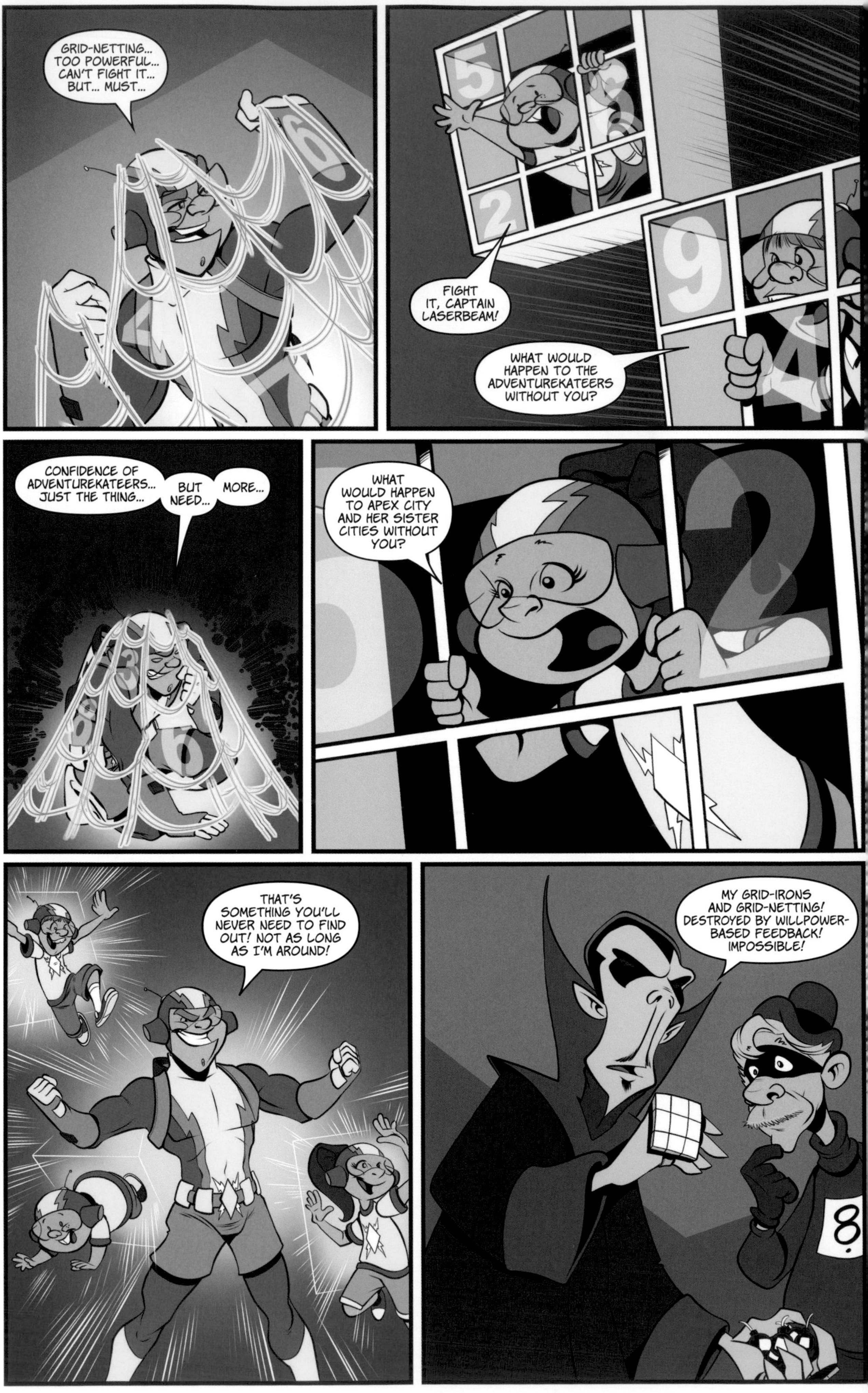
GRID-NETTING... TOO POWERFUL... CAN'T FIGHT IT... BUT... MUST...
FIGHT IT, CAPTAIN LASERBEAM!
WHAT WOULD HAPPEN TO THE ADVENTUREKATEERS WITHOUT YOU?
CONFIDENCE OF ADVENTUREKATEERS... JUST THE THING...
BUT NEED...
MORE...
WHAT WOULD HAPPEN TO APEX CITY AND HER SISTER CITIES WITHOUT YOU?
THAT'S SOMETHING YOU'LL NEVER NEED TO FIND OUT! NOT AS LONG AS I'M AROUND!
MY GRID-IRONS AND GRID-NETTING! DESTROYED BY WILLPOWER-BASED FEEDBACK! IMPOSSIBLE!

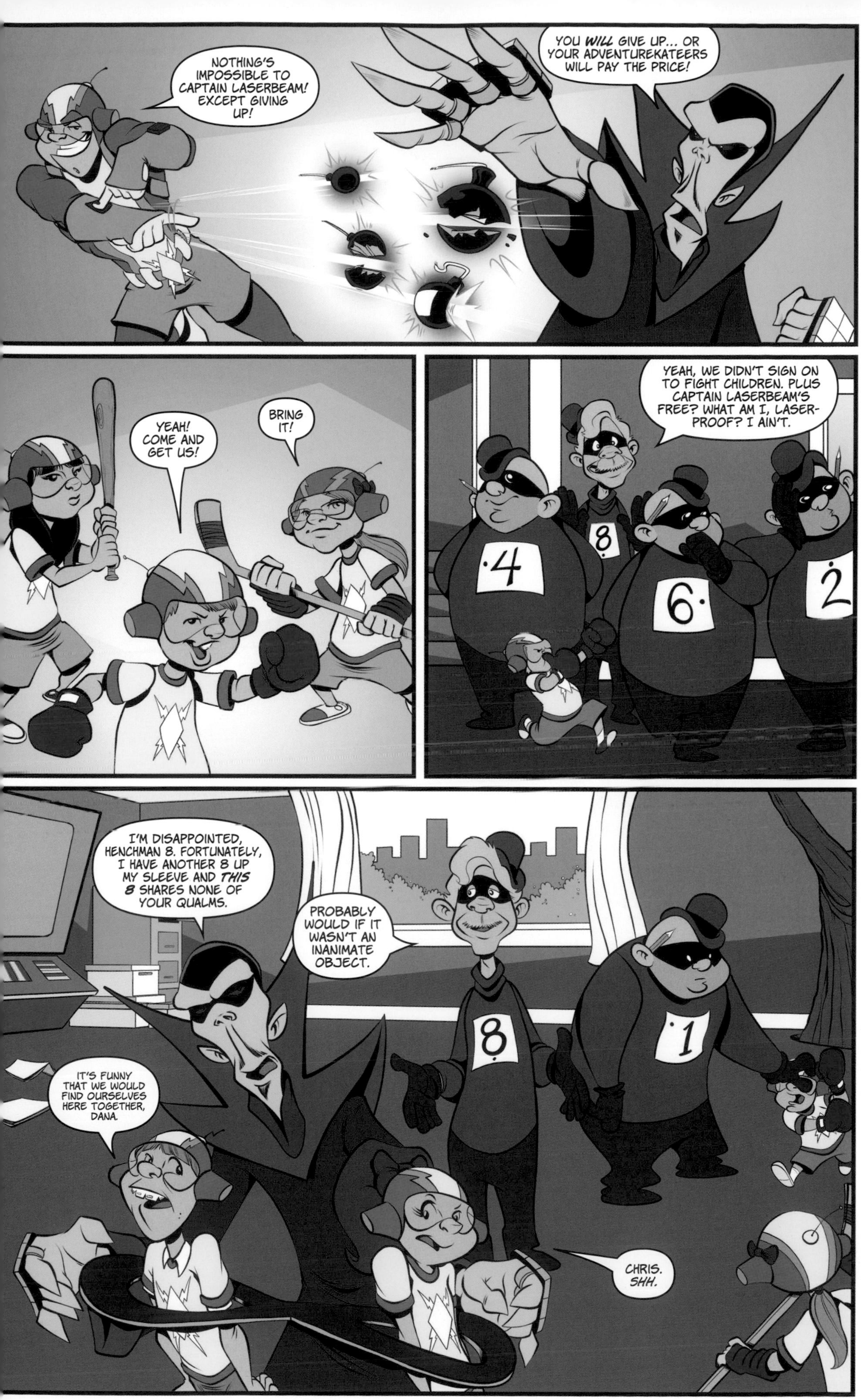
NOTHING'S IMPOSSIBLE TO CAPTAIN LASERBEAM! EXCEPT GIVING UP!
YOU *WILL* GIVE UP... OR YOUR ADVENTUREKATEERS WILL PAY THE PRICE!
YEAH! COME AND GET US!
BRING IT!
YEAH, WE DIDN'T SIGN ON TO FIGHT CHILDREN. PLUS CAPTAIN LASERBEAM'S FREE? WHAT AM I, LASER-PROOF? I AIN'T.
4
8
6
2
I'M DISAPPOINTED, HENCHMAN 8. FORTUNATELY, I HAVE ANOTHER 8 UP MY SLEEVE AND *THIS 8* SHARES NONE OF YOUR QUALMS.
PROBABLY WOULD IF IT WASN'T AN INANIMATE OBJECT.
8
1
IT'S FUNNY THAT WE WOULD FIND OURSELVES HERE TOGETHER, DANA.
CHRIS. SHH.

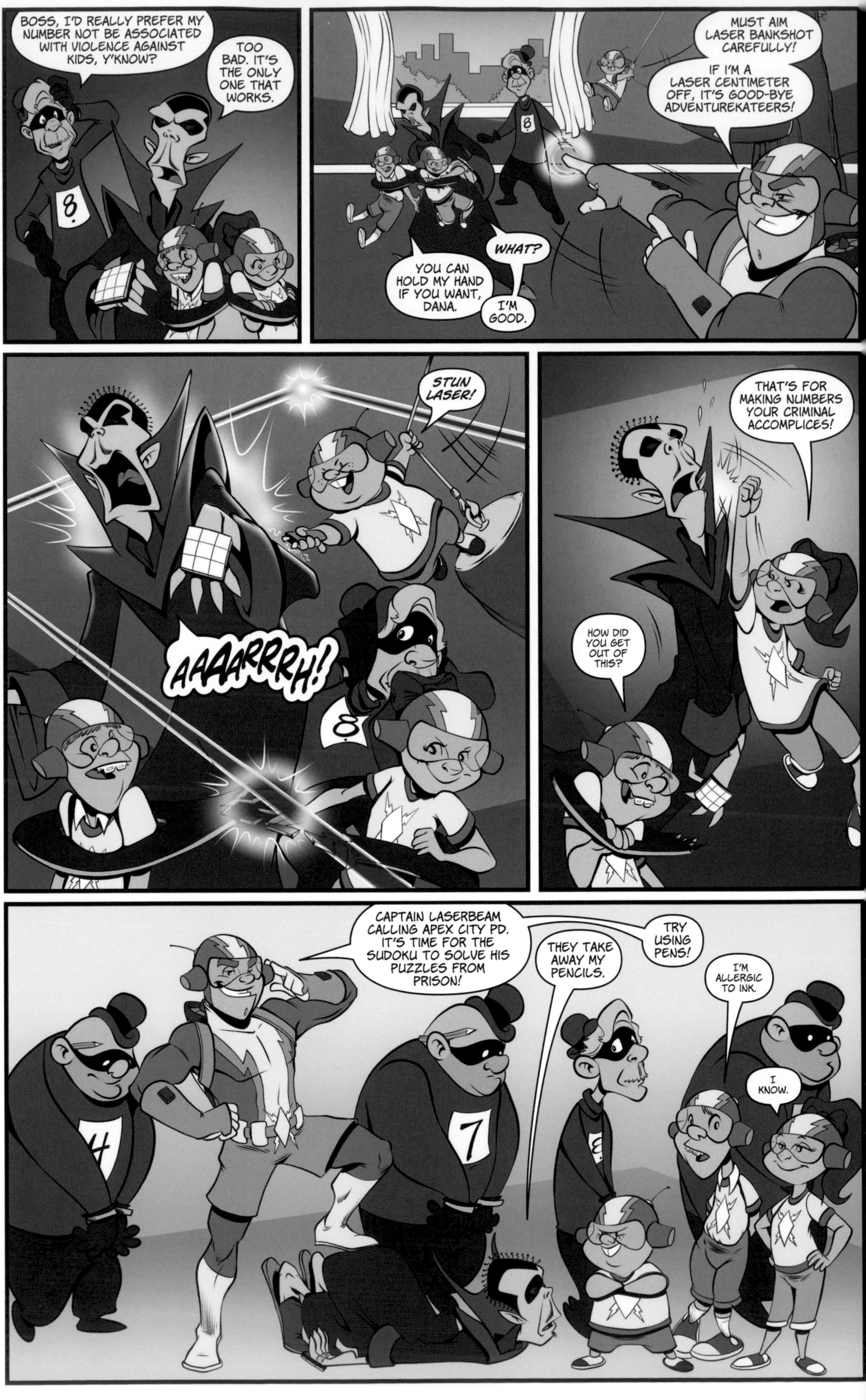
BOSS, I'D REALLY PREFER MY NUMBER NOT BE ASSOCIATED WITH VIOLENCE AGAINST KIDS, Y'KNOW?
TOO BAD. IT'S THE ONLY ONE THAT WORKS.
MUST AIM LASER BANKSHOT CAREFULLY!
IF I'M A LASER CENTIMETER OFF, IT'S GOOD-BYE ADVENTUREKATEERS!
YOU CAN HOLD MY HAND IF YOU WANT, DANA.
WHAT?
I'M GOOD.
STUN LASER!
AAAARRRH!
THAT'S FOR MAKING NUMBERS YOUR CRIMINAL ACCOMPLICES!
HOW DID YOU GET OUT OF THIS?
CAPTAIN LASERBEAM CALLING APEX CITY PD. IT'S TIME FOR THE SUDOKU TO SOLVE HIS PUZZLES FROM PRISON!
THEY TAKE AWAY MY PENCILS.
TRY USING PENS!
I'M ALLERGIC TO INK.
I KNOW.

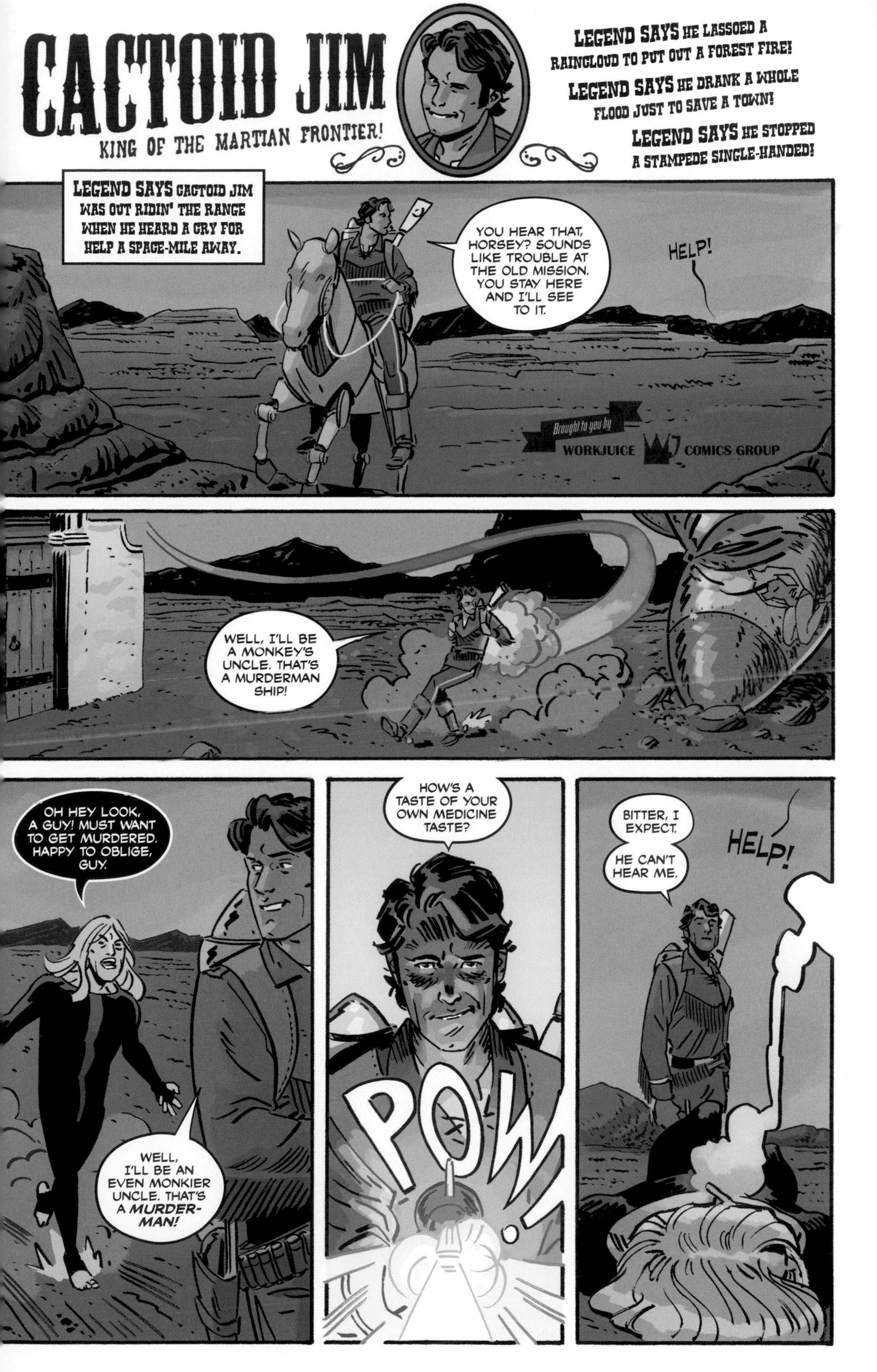
CACTOID JIM
KING OF THE MARTIAN FRONTIER!
LEGEND SAYS HE LASSOED A RAINCLOUD TO PUT OUT A FOREST FIRE!
LEGEND SAYS HE DRANK A WHOLE FLOOD JUST TO SAVE A TOWN!
LEGEND SAYS HE STOPPED A STAMPEDE SINGLE-HANDED!
LEGEND SAYS CACTOID JIM WAS OUT RIDIN' THE RANGE WHEN HE HEARD A CRY FOR HELP A SPACE-MILE AWAY.
YOU HEAR THAT, HORSEY? SOUNDS LIKE TROUBLE AT THE OLD MISSION. YOU STAY HERE AND I'LL SEE TO IT.
HELP!
Brought to you by WORKJUICE COMICS GROUP
WELL, I'LL BE A MONKEY'S UNCLE. THAT'S A MURDERMAN SHIP!
OH HEY LOOK, A GUY! MUST WANT TO GET MURDERED. HAPPY TO OBLIGE, GUY.
WELL, I'LL BE AN EVEN MONKIER UNCLE. THAT'S A MURDER-MAN!
HOW'S A TASTE OF YOUR OWN MEDICINE TASTE?
POW!
BITTER, I EXPECT.
HE CAN'T HEAR ME.
HELP!

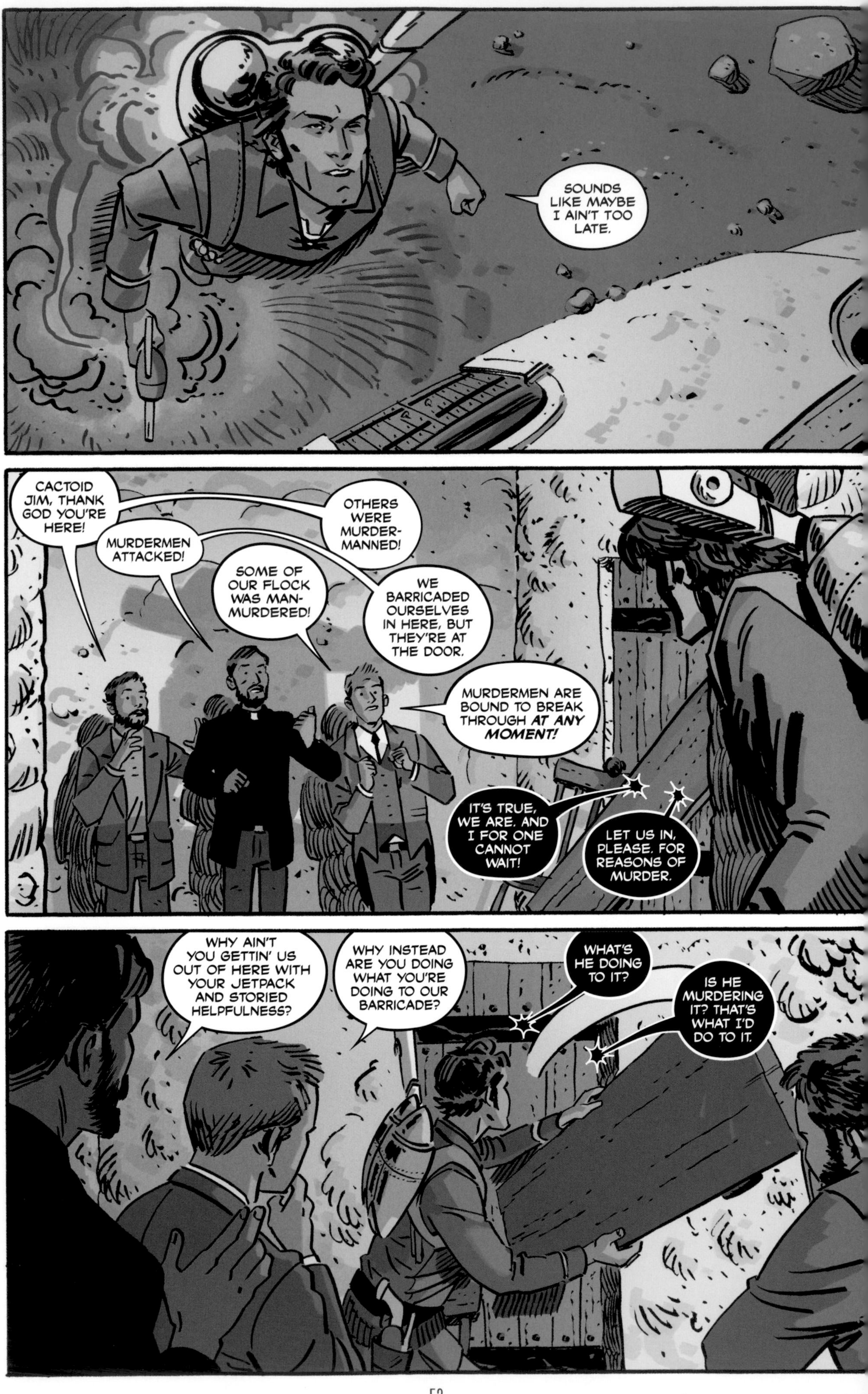
SOUNDS LIKE MAYBE I AIN'T TOO LATE.
CACTOID JIM, THANK GOD YOU'RE HERE!
OTHERS WERE MURDER-MANNED!
MURDERMEN ATTACKED!
SOME OF OUR FLOCK WAS MAN-MURDERED!
WE BARRICADED OURSELVES IN HERE, BUT THEY'RE AT THE DOOR.
MURDERMEN ARE BOUND TO BREAK THROUGH *AT ANY MOMENT!*
IT'S TRUE, WE ARE. AND I FOR ONE CANNOT WAIT!
LET US IN, PLEASE. FOR REASONS OF MURDER.
WHY AIN'T YOU GETTIN' US OUT OF HERE WITH YOUR JETPACK AND STORIED HELPFULNESS?
WHY INSTEAD ARE YOU DOING WHAT YOU'RE DOING TO OUR BARRICADE?
WHAT'S HE DOING TO IT?
IS HE MURDERING IT? THAT'S WHAT I'D DO TO IT.

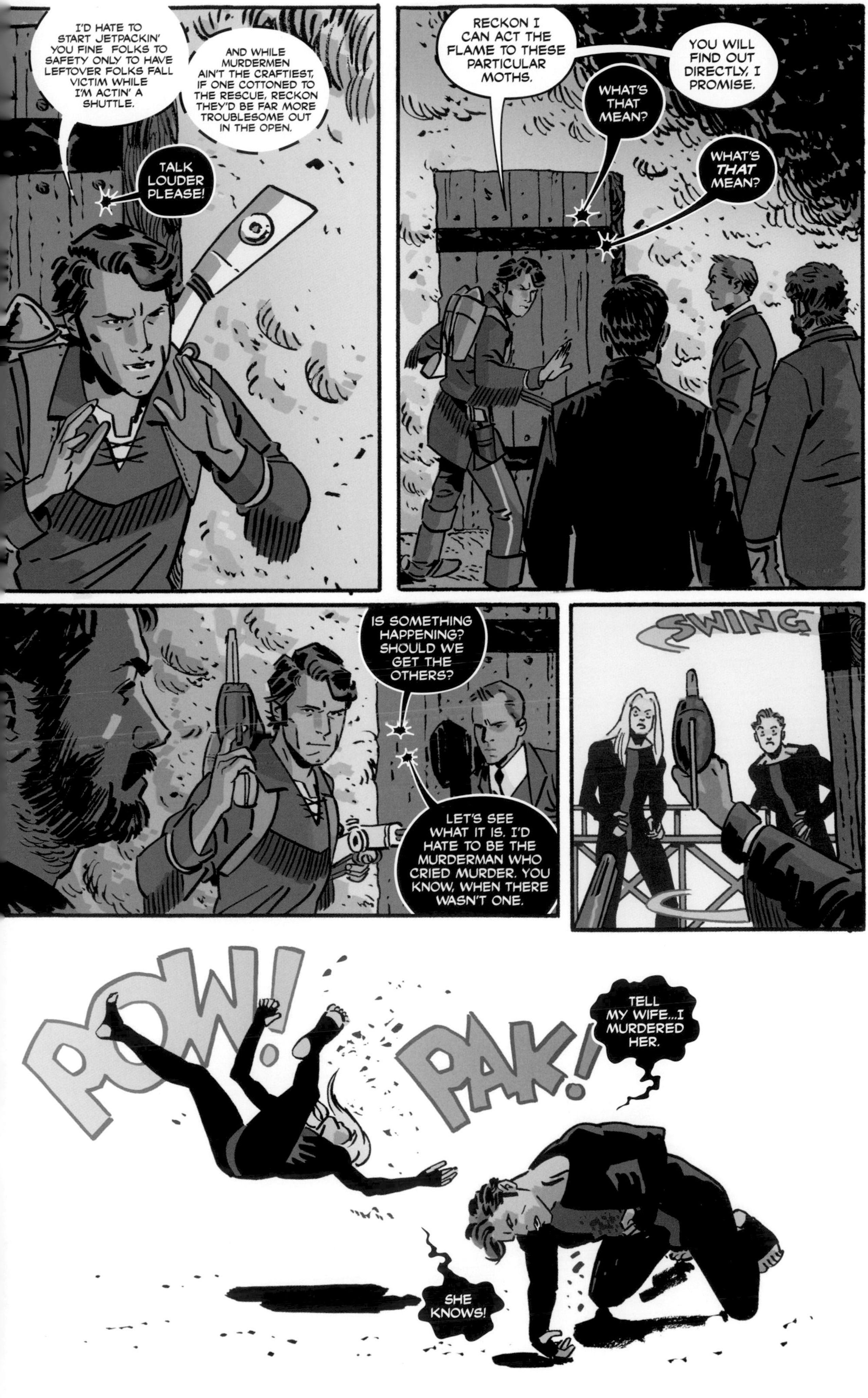

I'D HATE TO START JETPACKIN' YOU FINE FOLKS TO SAFETY ONLY TO HAVE LEFTOVER FOLKS FALL VICTIM WHILE I'M ACTIN' A SHUTTLE.
AND WHILE MURDERMEN AIN'T THE CRAFTIEST, IF ONE COTTONED TO THE RESCUE, RECKON THEY'D BE FAR MORE TROUBLESOME OUT IN THE OPEN.
TALK LOUDER PLEASE!
RECKON I CAN ACT THE FLAME TO THESE PARTICULAR MOTHS.
YOU WILL FIND OUT DIRECTLY, I PROMISE.
WHAT'S THAT MEAN?
WHAT'S *THAT* MEAN?
IS SOMETHING HAPPENING? SHOULD WE GET THE OTHERS?
LET'S SEE WHAT IT IS. I'D HATE TO BE THE MURDERMAN WHO CRIED MURDER. YOU KNOW, WHEN THERE WASN'T ONE.
SWING
POW!
PAK!
TELL MY WIFE...I MURDERED HER.
SHE KNOWS!

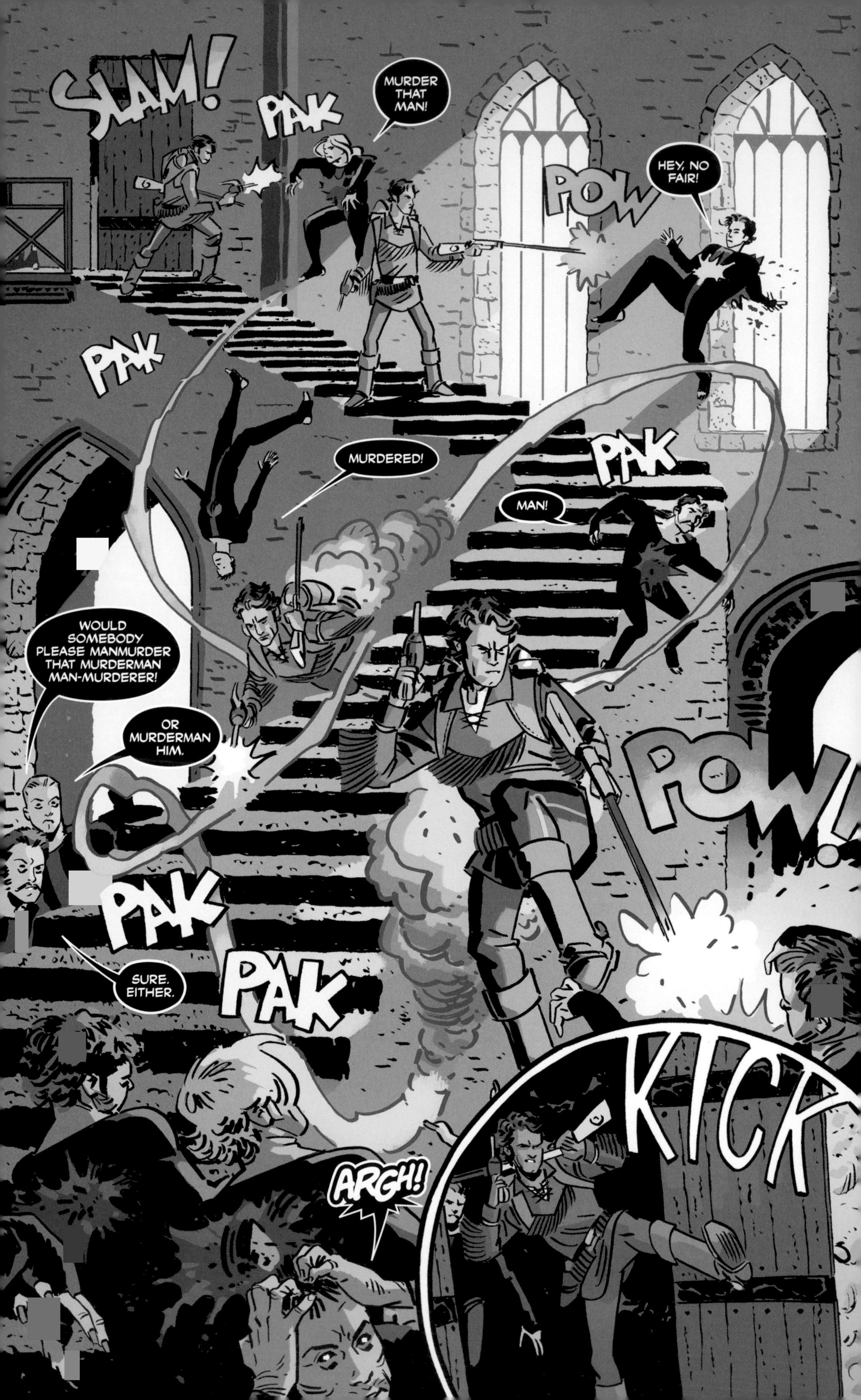
SLAM!
PAK
MURDER THAT MAN!
POW
HEY, NO FAIR!
PAK
MURDERED!
PAK
MAN!
WOULD SOMEBODY PLEASE MANMURDER THAT MURDERMAN MAN-MURDERER!
OR MURDERMAN HIM.
POW!
PAK
SURE. EITHER.
PAK
KICK
ARGH!

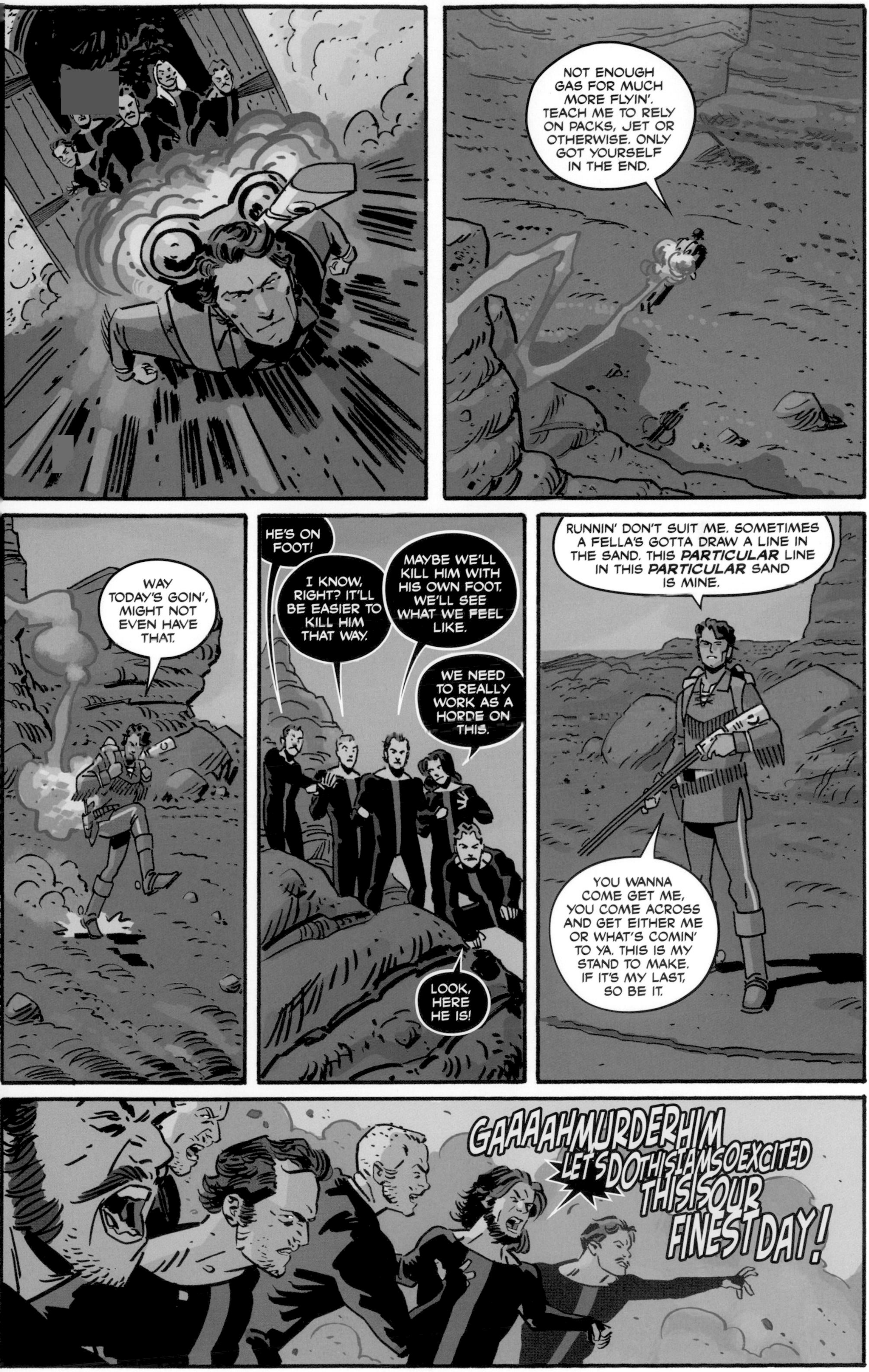
NOT ENOUGH GAS FOR MUCH MORE FLYIN'. TEACH ME TO RELY ON PACKS, JET OR OTHERWISE. ONLY GOT YOURSELF IN THE END.
WAY TODAY'S GOIN', MIGHT NOT EVEN HAVE THAT.
HE'S ON FOOT!
I KNOW, RIGHT? IT'LL BE EASIER TO KILL HIM THAT WAY.
MAYBE WE'LL KILL HIM WITH HIS OWN FOOT. WE'LL SEE WHAT WE FEEL LIKE.
WE NEED TO REALLY WORK AS A HORDE ON THIS.
LOOK, HERE HE IS!
RUNNIN' DON'T SUIT ME. SOMETIMES A FELLA'S GOTTA DRAW A LINE IN THE SAND. THIS PARTICULAR LINE IN THIS PARTICULAR SAND IS MINE.
YOU WANNA COME GET ME, YOU COME ACROSS AND GET EITHER ME OR WHAT'S COMIN' TO YA. THIS IS MY STAND TO MAKE. IF IT'S MY LAST, SO BE IT.
GAAAAHMURDERHIM
LETSDOTHISIAMSOEXCITED
THISISOUR
FINESTDAY!

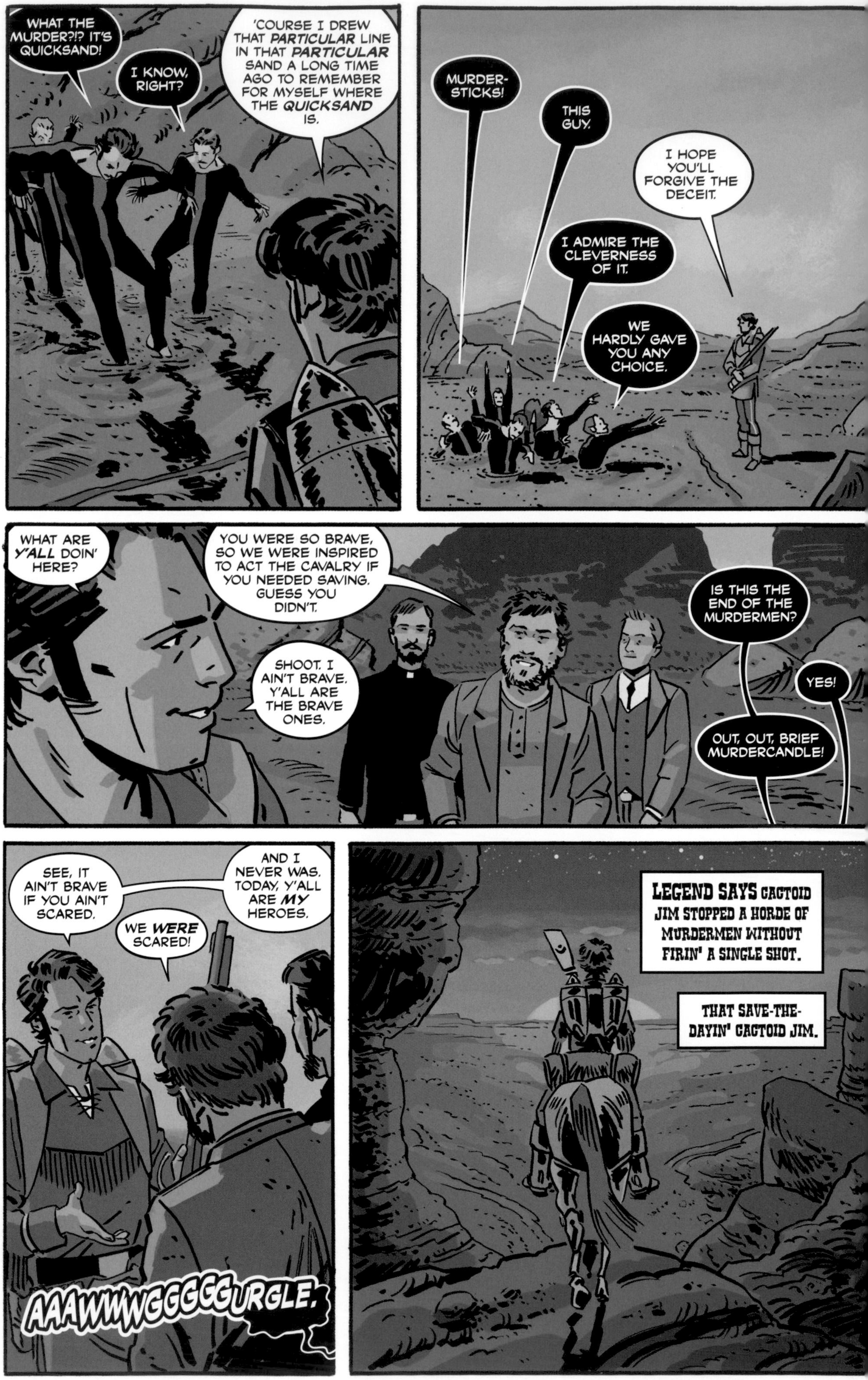
WHAT THE MURDER?!? IT'S QUICKSAND!
I KNOW, RIGHT?
'COURSE I DREW THAT PARTICULAR LINE IN THAT PARTICULAR SAND A LONG TIME AGO TO REMEMBER FOR MYSELF WHERE THE QUICKSAND IS.
MURDER-STICKS!
THIS GUY.
I HOPE YOU'LL FORGIVE THE DECEIT.
I ADMIRE THE CLEVERNESS OF IT.
WE HARDLY GAVE YOU ANY CHOICE.
WHAT ARE Y'ALL DOIN' HERE?
YOU WERE SO BRAVE, SO WE WERE INSPIRED TO ACT THE CAVALRY IF YOU NEEDED SAVING. GUESS YOU DIDN'T.
SHOOT. I AIN'T BRAVE. Y'ALL ARE THE BRAVE ONES.
IS THIS THE END OF THE MURDERMEN?
YES!
OUT, OUT, BRIEF MURDERCANDLE!
SEE, IT AIN'T BRAVE IF YOU AIN'T SCARED.
WE WERE SCARED!
AND I NEVER WAS. TODAY, Y'ALL ARE MY HEROES.
AAAWWWGGGGGURGLE.
LEGEND SAYS CACTOID JIM STOPPED A HORDE OF MURDERMEN WITHOUT FIRIN' A SINGLE SHOT.
THAT SAVE-THE-DAYIN' CACTOID JIM.

# JEFFERSON REID ☆ ACE AMERICAN

Sponsored by WORKJUICE COMICS GROUP

★★★★★ PATRIOT BRAND CIGARETTES ★★★★★

BROUGHT TO YOU BY PATRIOT BRAND CIGARETTES
*they're good for your Constitution!*

**NEWS ON PARADE!**

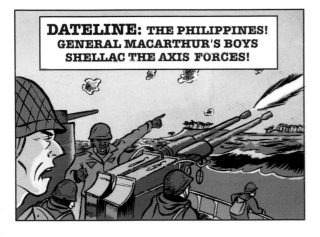

**DATELINE:** THE PHILIPPINES! GENERAL MACARTHUR'S BOYS SHELLAC THE AXIS FORCES!

AND THEY'RE NOT ALONE IN THE FIGHT FOR FREEDOM!

AMERICAN FORCES ARE BOLSTERED UNSEEN BY THE CLANDESTINE SOLDIERS OF THE CLOAK-AND-DAGGER OUTFIT KNOWN AS THE A.V.C - THE AMERICAN VICTORY COMMISSION!

THE COMMANDER OF THE TOP SECRET A.V.C., GENERAL REX FLAGWELL, HAD THIS TO SAY:

GET YOUR FLOAT PARADE READY, AMERICA! WE'RE WINNING THIS WAR!

THAT'S GOOD NEWS, AMERICA!

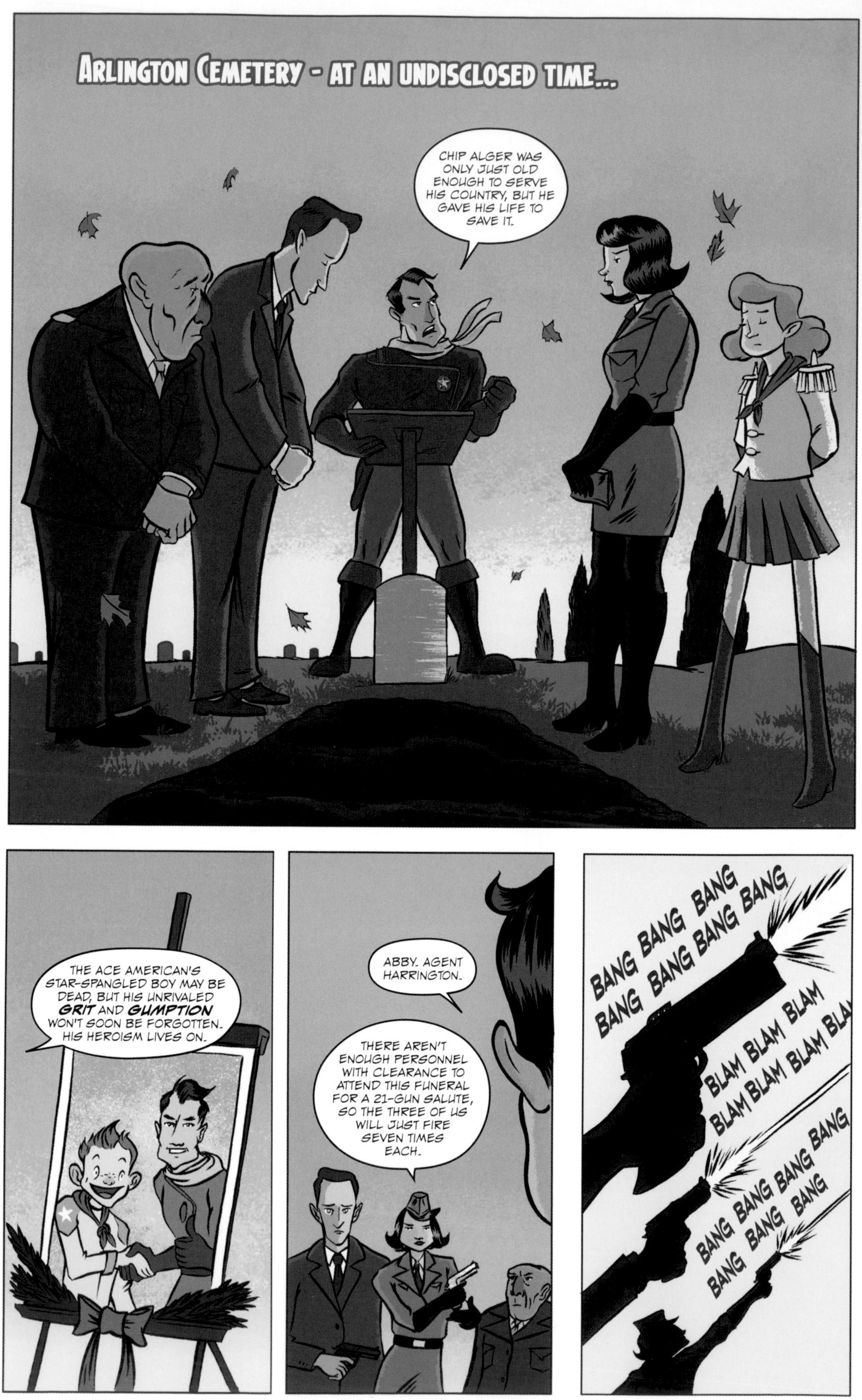
ARLINGTON CEMETERY - AT AN UNDISCLOSED TIME...
CHIP ALGER WAS ONLY JUST OLD ENOUGH TO SERVE HIS COUNTRY, BUT HE GAVE HIS LIFE TO SAVE IT.
THE ACE AMERICAN'S STAR-SPANGLED BOY MAY BE DEAD, BUT HIS UNRIVALED GRIT AND GUMPTION WON'T SOON BE FORGOTTEN. HIS HEROISM LIVES ON.
ABBY. AGENT HARRINGTON.
THERE AREN'T ENOUGH PERSONNEL WITH CLEARANCE TO ATTEND THIS FUNERAL FOR A 21-GUN SALUTE, SO THE THREE OF US WILL JUST FIRE SEVEN TIMES EACH.
BANG BANG BANG
BANG BANG BANG BANG
BLAM BLAM BLAM
BLAM BLAM BLAM BLAM
BANG BANG BANG BANG
BANG BANG BANG

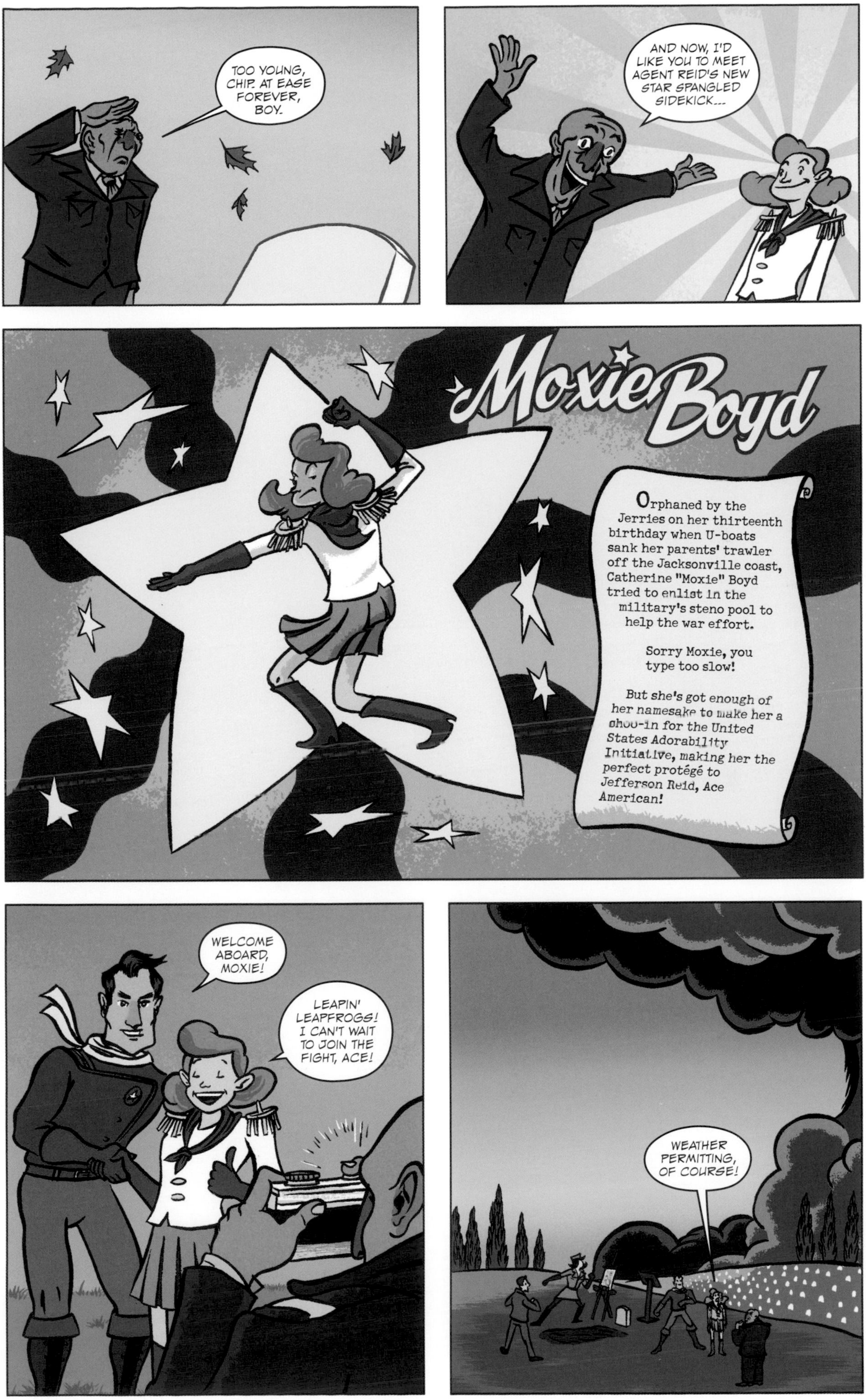
TOO YOUNG, CHIP. AT EASE FOREVER, BOY.
AND NOW, I'D LIKE YOU TO MEET AGENT REID'S NEW STAR SPANGLED SIDEKICK...
Moxie Boyd
Orphaned by the Jerries on her thirteenth birthday when U-boats sank her parents' trawler off the Jacksonville coast, Catherine "Moxie" Boyd tried to enlist in the military's steno pool to help the war effort.
Sorry Moxie, you type too slow!
But she's got enough of her namesake to make her a shoo-in for the United States Adorability Initiative, making her the perfect protégé to Jefferson Reid, Ace American!
WELCOME ABOARD, MOXIE!
LEAPIN' LEAPFROGS! I CAN'T WAIT TO JOIN THE FIGHT, ACE!
WEATHER PERMITTING, OF COURSE!

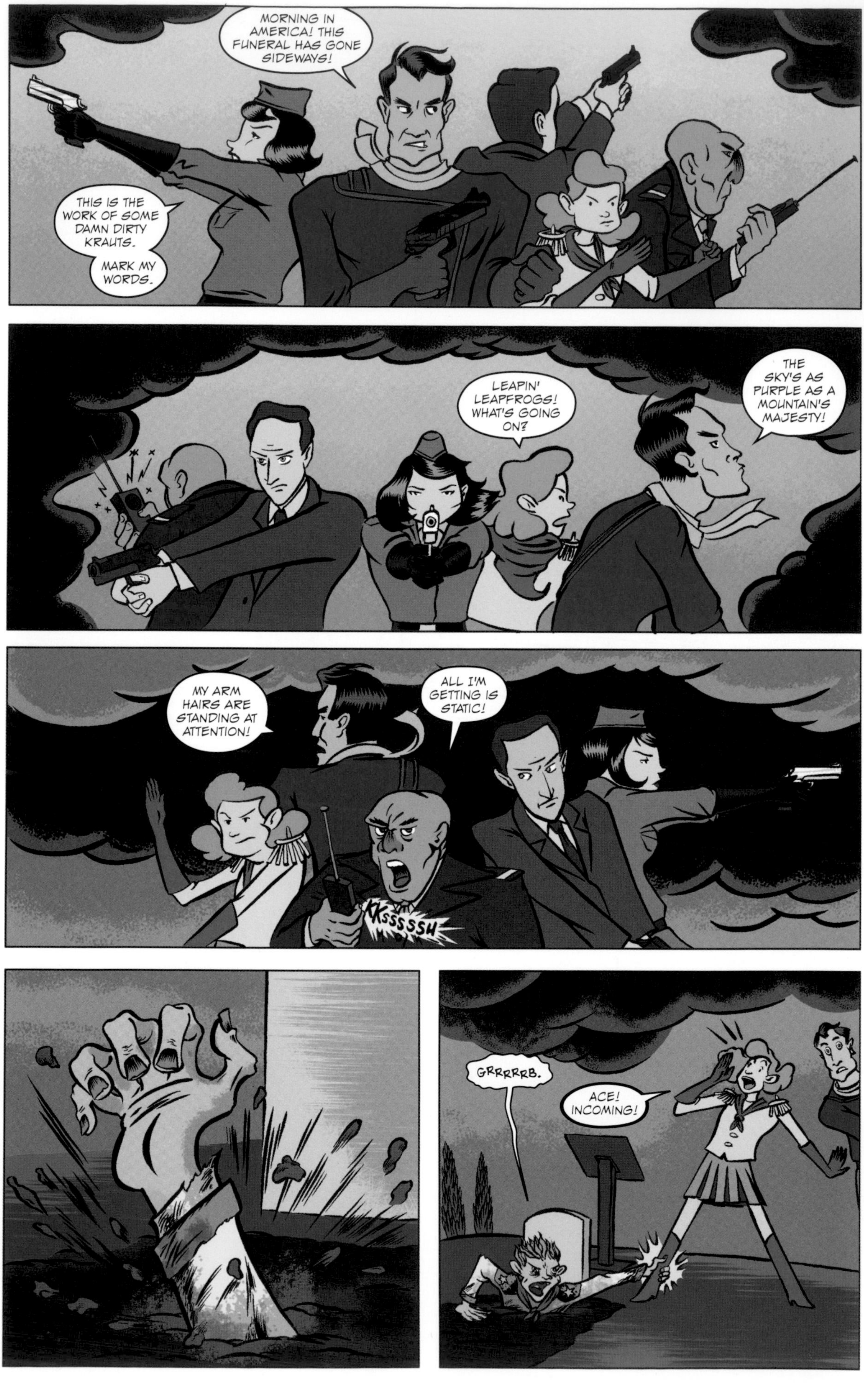
MORNING IN AMERICA! THIS FUNERAL HAS GONE SIDEWAYS!
THIS IS THE WORK OF SOME DAMN DIRTY KRAUTS.
MARK MY WORDS.
LEAPIN' LEAPFROGS! WHAT'S GOING ON?
THE SKY'S AS PURPLE AS A MOUNTAIN'S MAJESTY!
MY ARM HAIRS ARE STANDING AT ATTENTION!
ALL I'M GETTING IS STATIC!
KKSSSSSSH
GRRRRRB.
ACE! INCOMING!

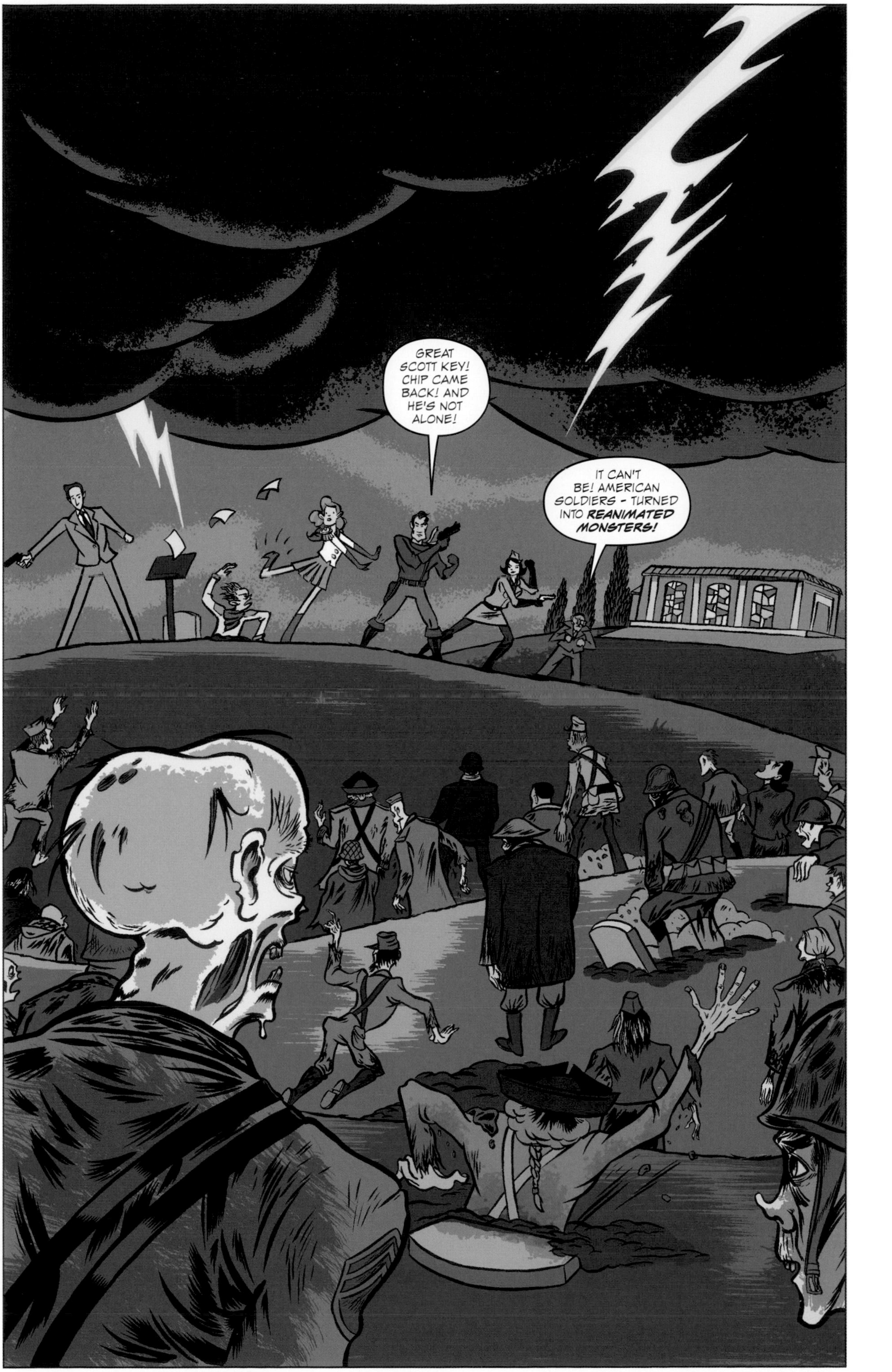
GREAT SCOTT KEY! CHIP CAME BACK! AND HE'S NOT ALONE!
IT CAN'T BE! AMERICAN SOLDIERS - TURNED INTO **REANIMATED MONSTERS!**

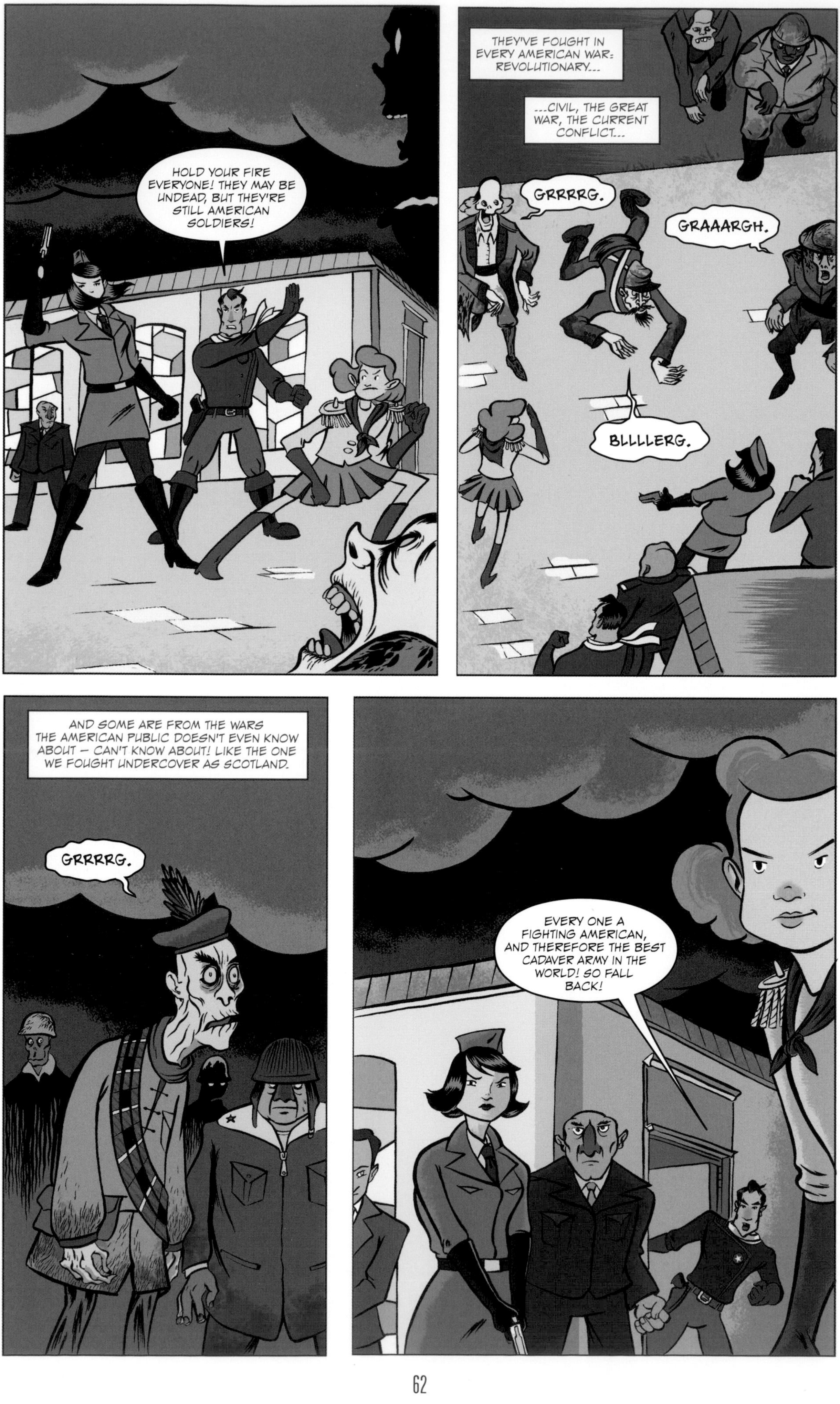
HOLD YOUR FIRE EVERYONE! THEY MAY BE UNDEAD, BUT THEY'RE STILL AMERICAN SOLDIERS!
THEY'VE FOUGHT IN EVERY AMERICAN WAR: REVOLUTIONARY...
...CIVIL, THE GREAT WAR, THE CURRENT CONFLICT...
GRRRRG.
GRAAARGH.
BLLLLERG.
AND SOME ARE FROM THE WARS THE AMERICAN PUBLIC DOESN'T EVEN KNOW ABOUT – CAN'T KNOW ABOUT! LIKE THE ONE WE FOUGHT UNDERCOVER AS SCOTLAND.
GRRRRG.
EVERY ONE A FIGHTING AMERICAN, AND THEREFORE THE BEST CADAVER ARMY IN THE WORLD! SO FALL BACK!

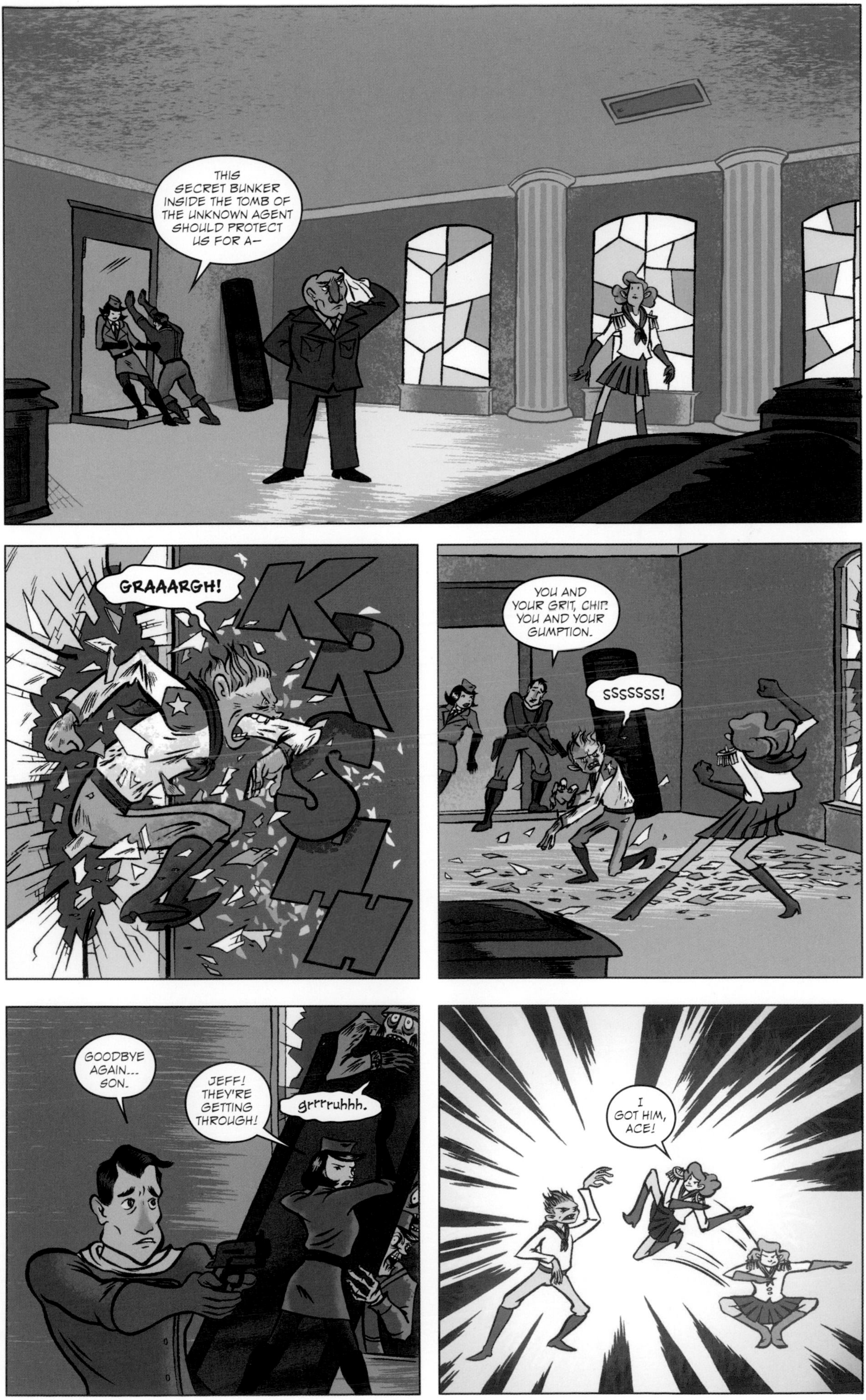
THIS SECRET BUNKER INSIDE THE TOMB OF THE UNKNOWN AGENT SHOULD PROTECT US FOR A—
GRAAARGH!
KRSHH
YOU AND YOUR GRIT, CHIP. YOU AND YOUR GUMPTION.
SSSSSSS!
GOODBYE AGAIN... SON.
JEFF! THEY'RE GETTING THROUGH!
grrrruhhh.
I GOT HIM, ACE!

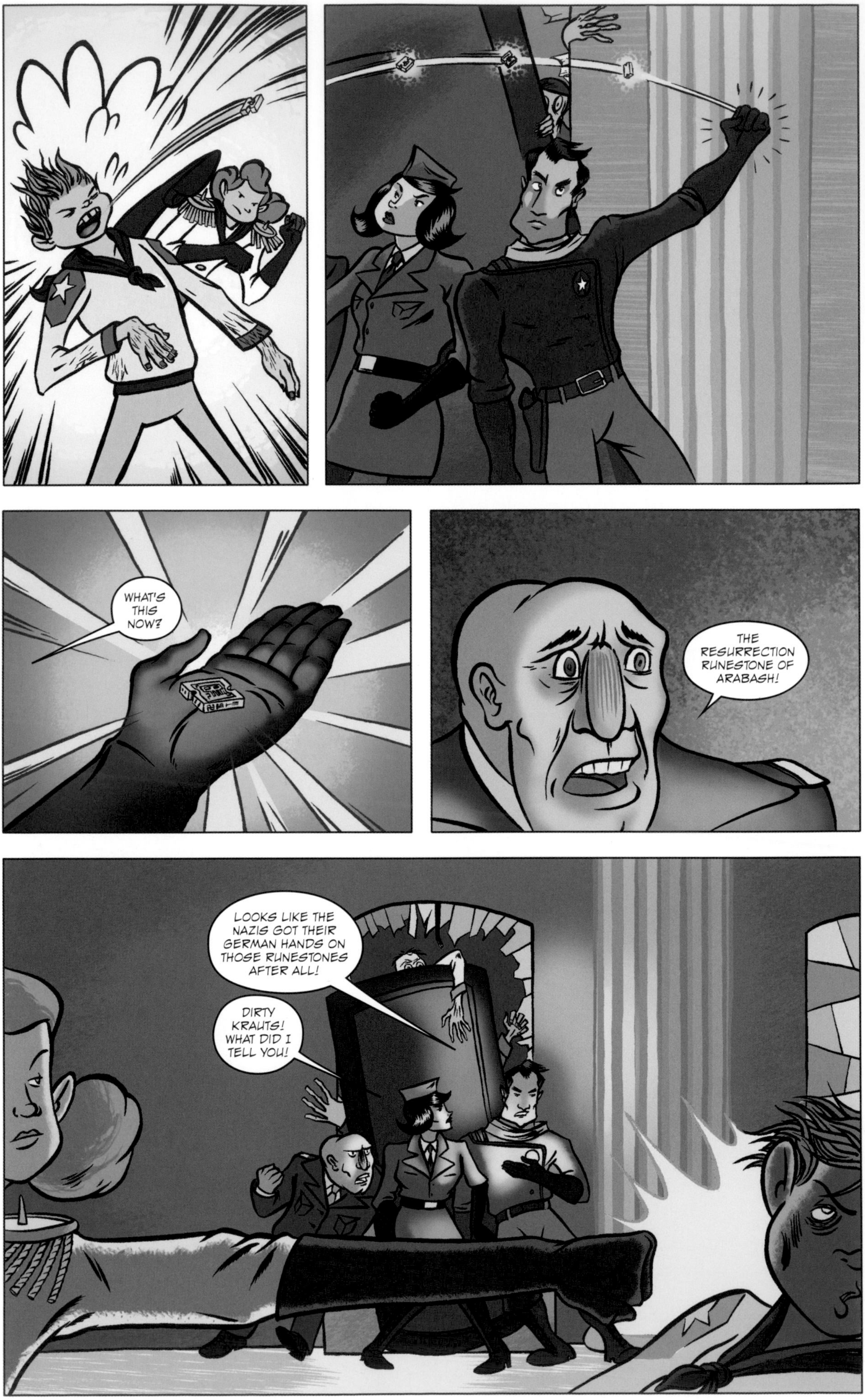
WHAT'S THIS NOW?
THE RESURRECTION RUNESTONE OF ARABASH!
LOOKS LIKE THE NAZIS GOT THEIR GERMAN HANDS ON THOSE RUNESTONES AFTER ALL!
DIRTY KRAUTS! WHAT DID I TELL YOU!

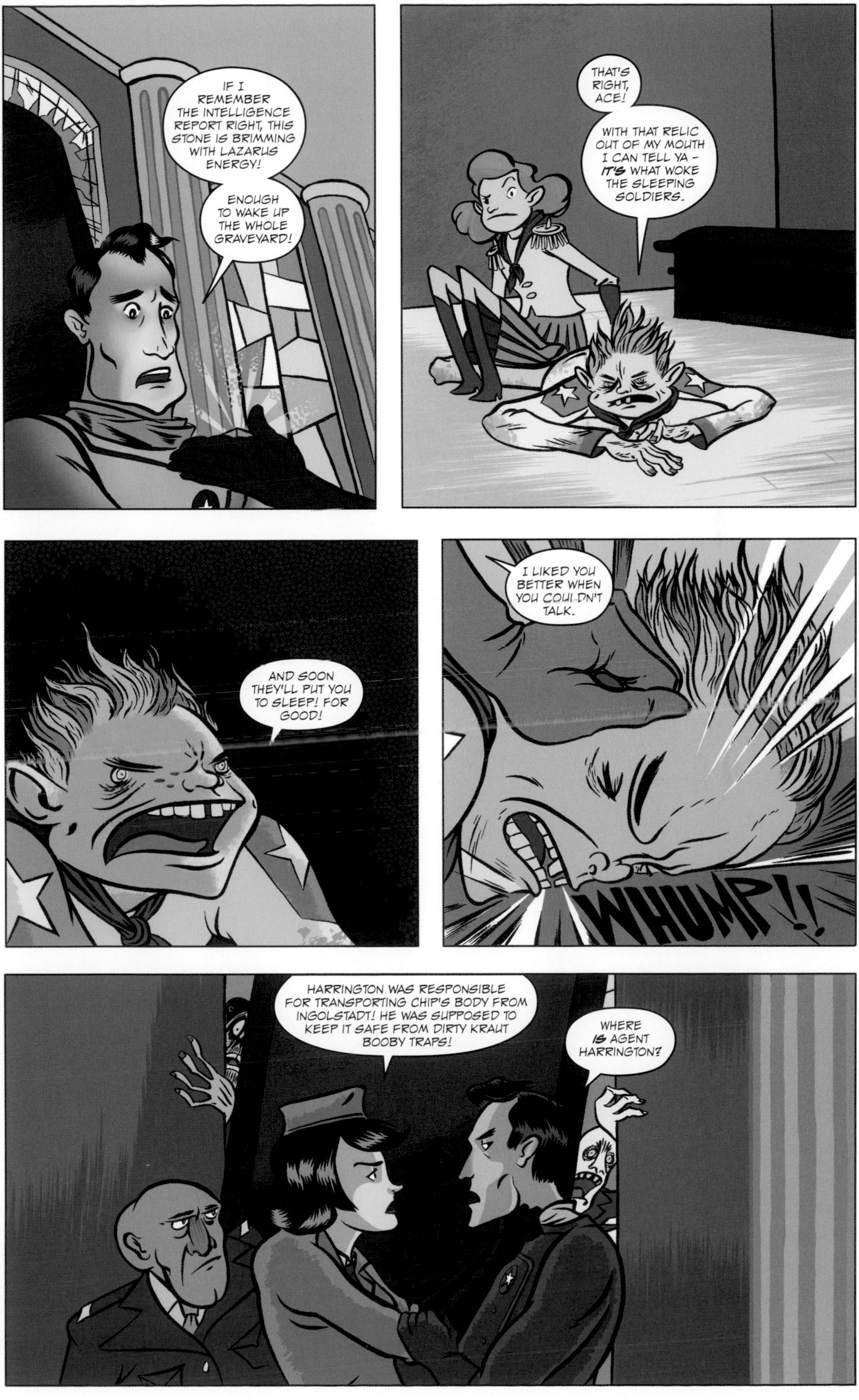
IF I REMEMBER THE INTELLIGENCE REPORT RIGHT, THIS STONE IS BRIMMING WITH LAZARUS ENERGY!
ENOUGH TO WAKE UP THE WHOLE GRAVEYARD!
THAT'S RIGHT, ACE!
WITH THAT RELIC OUT OF MY MOUTH I CAN TELL YA - IT'S WHAT WOKE THE SLEEPING SOLDIERS.
AND SOON THEY'LL PUT YOU TO SLEEP! FOR GOOD!
I LIKED YOU BETTER WHEN YOU COULDN'T TALK.
WHUMP!!
HARRINGTON WAS RESPONSIBLE FOR TRANSPORTING CHIP'S BODY FROM INGOLSTADT! HE WAS SUPPOSED TO KEEP IT SAFE FROM DIRTY KRAUT BOOBY TRAPS!
WHERE IS AGENT HARRINGTON?

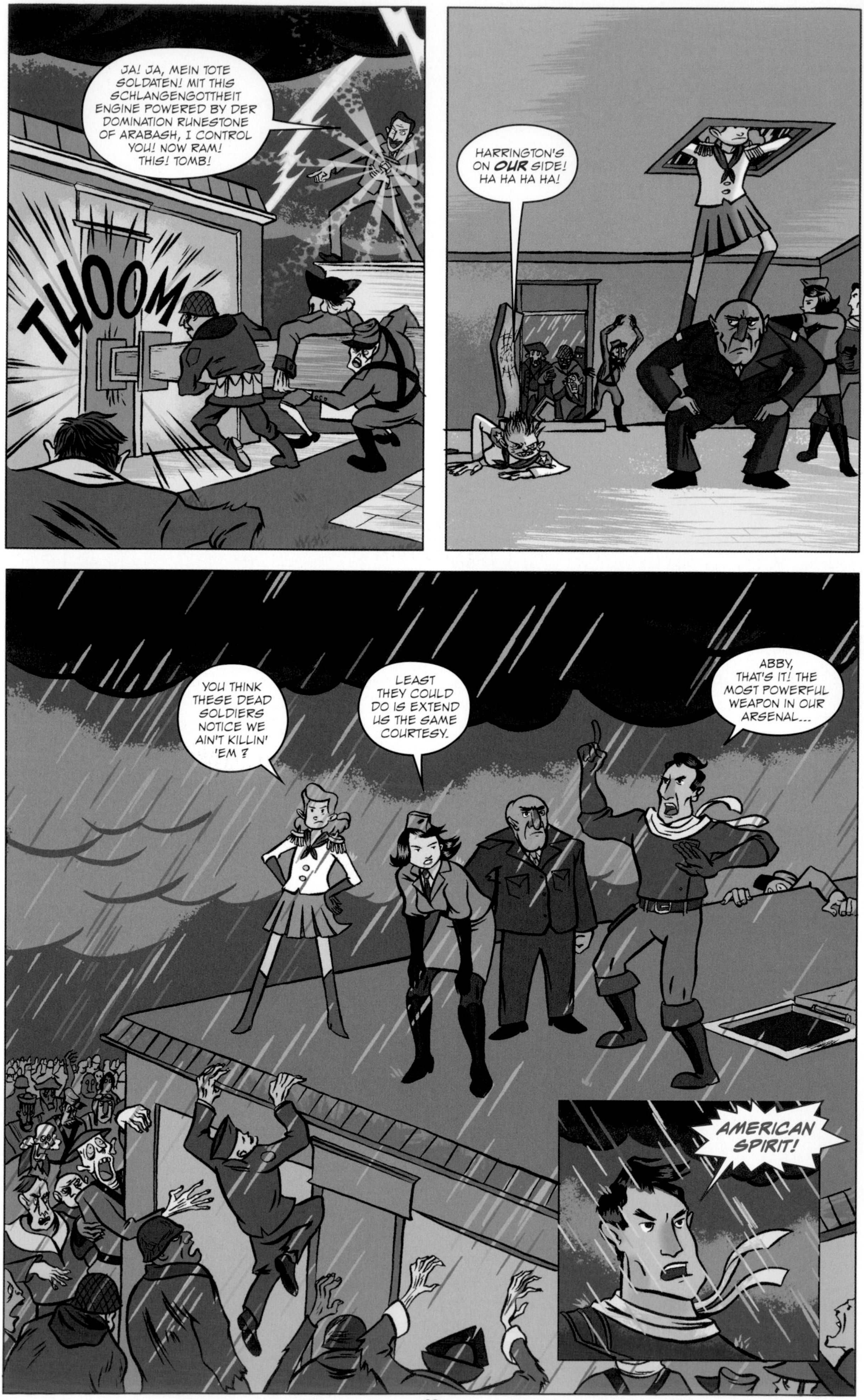
JA! JA, MEIN TOTE SOLDATEN! MIT THIS SCHLANGENGOTTHEIT ENGINE POWERED BY DER DOMINATION RUNESTONE OF ARABASH, I CONTROL YOU! NOW RAM! THIS! TOMB!
THOOM
HARRINGTON'S ON **OUR** SIDE! HA HA HA HA!
YOU THINK THESE DEAD SOLDIERS NOTICE WE AIN'T KILLIN' 'EM ?
LEAST THEY COULD DO IS EXTEND US THE SAME COURTESY.
ABBY, THAT'S IT! THE MOST POWERFUL WEAPON IN OUR ARSENAL...
AMERICAN SPIRIT!

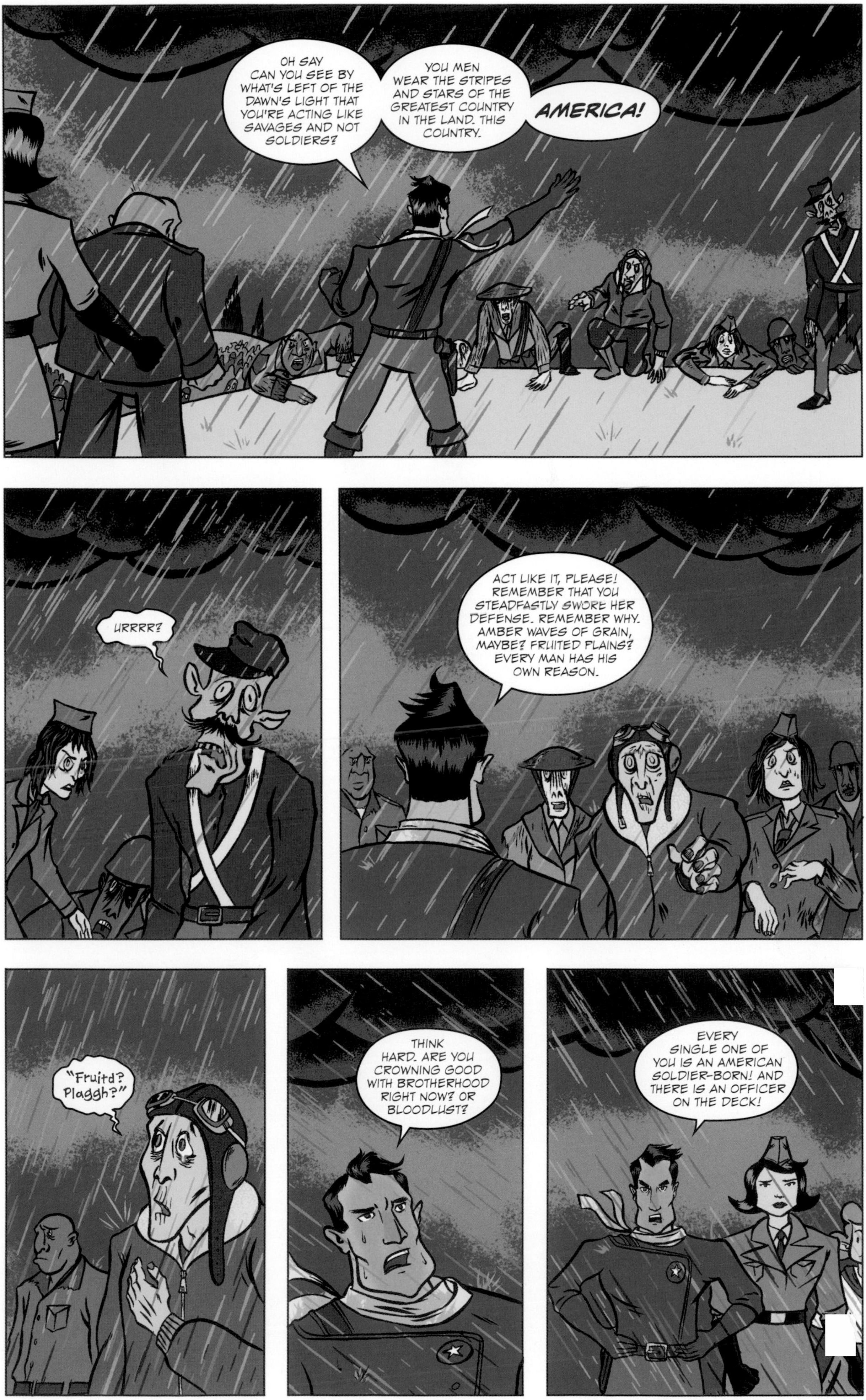
OH SAY CAN YOU SEE BY WHAT'S LEFT OF THE DAWN'S LIGHT THAT YOU'RE ACTING LIKE SAVAGES AND NOT SOLDIERS?
YOU MEN WEAR THE STRIPES AND STARS OF THE GREATEST COUNTRY IN THE LAND. THIS COUNTRY.
AMERICA!
URRRR?
ACT LIKE IT, PLEASE! REMEMBER THAT YOU STEADFASTLY SWORE HER DEFENSE. REMEMBER WHY. AMBER WAVES OF GRAIN, MAYBE? FRUITED PLAINS? EVERY MAN HAS HIS OWN REASON.
"Fruitd? Plaggh?"
THINK HARD. ARE YOU CROWNING GOOD WITH BROTHERHOOD RIGHT NOW? OR BLOODLUST?
EVERY SINGLE ONE OF YOU IS AN AMERICAN SOLDIER-BORN! AND THERE IS AN OFFICER ON THE DECK!

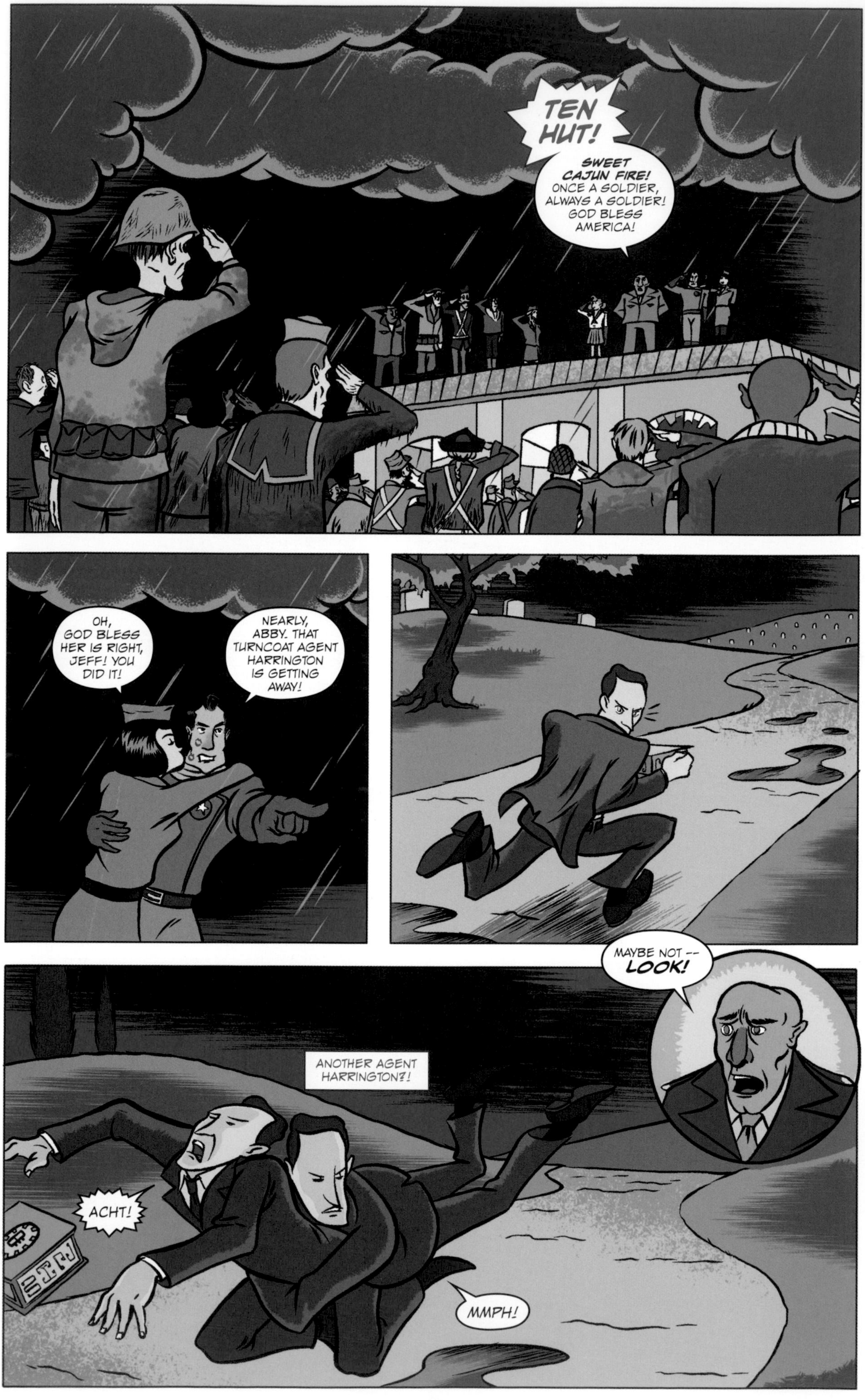
TEN HUT!
SWEET CAJUN FIRE! ONCE A SOLDIER, ALWAYS A SOLDIER! GOD BLESS AMERICA!
OH, GOD BLESS HER IS RIGHT, JEFF! YOU DID IT!
NEARLY, ABBY. THAT TURNCOAT AGENT HARRINGTON IS GETTING AWAY!
MAYBE NOT -- LOOK!
ANOTHER AGENT HARRINGTON?!
ACHT!
MMPH!

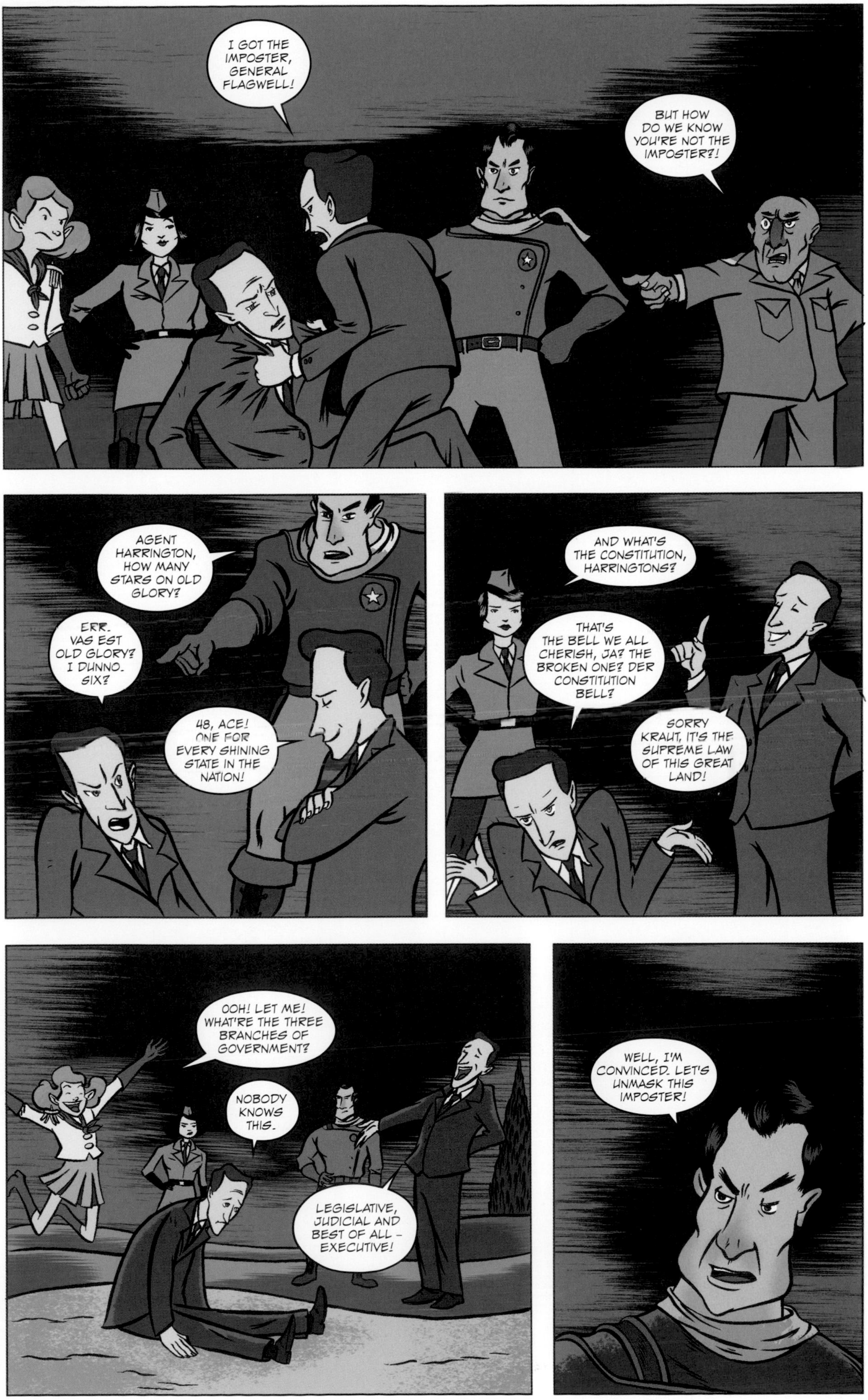

I GOT THE IMPOSTER, GENERAL FLAGWELL!
BUT HOW DO WE KNOW YOU'RE NOT THE IMPOSTER?!
AGENT HARRINGTON, HOW MANY STARS ON OLD GLORY?
ERR. VAS EST OLD GLORY? I DUNNO. SIX?
48, ACE! ONE FOR EVERY SHINING STATE IN THE NATION!
AND WHAT'S THE CONSTITUTION, HARRINGTONS?
THAT'S THE BELL WE ALL CHERISH, JA? THE BROKEN ONE? DER CONSTITUTION BELL?
SORRY KRAUT, IT'S THE SUPREME LAW OF THIS GREAT LAND!
OOH! LET ME! WHAT'RE THE THREE BRANCHES OF GOVERNMENT?
NOBODY KNOWS THIS.
LEGISLATIVE, JUDICIAL AND BEST OF ALL - EXECUTIVE!
WELL, I'M CONVINCED. LET'S UNMASK THIS IMPOSTER!

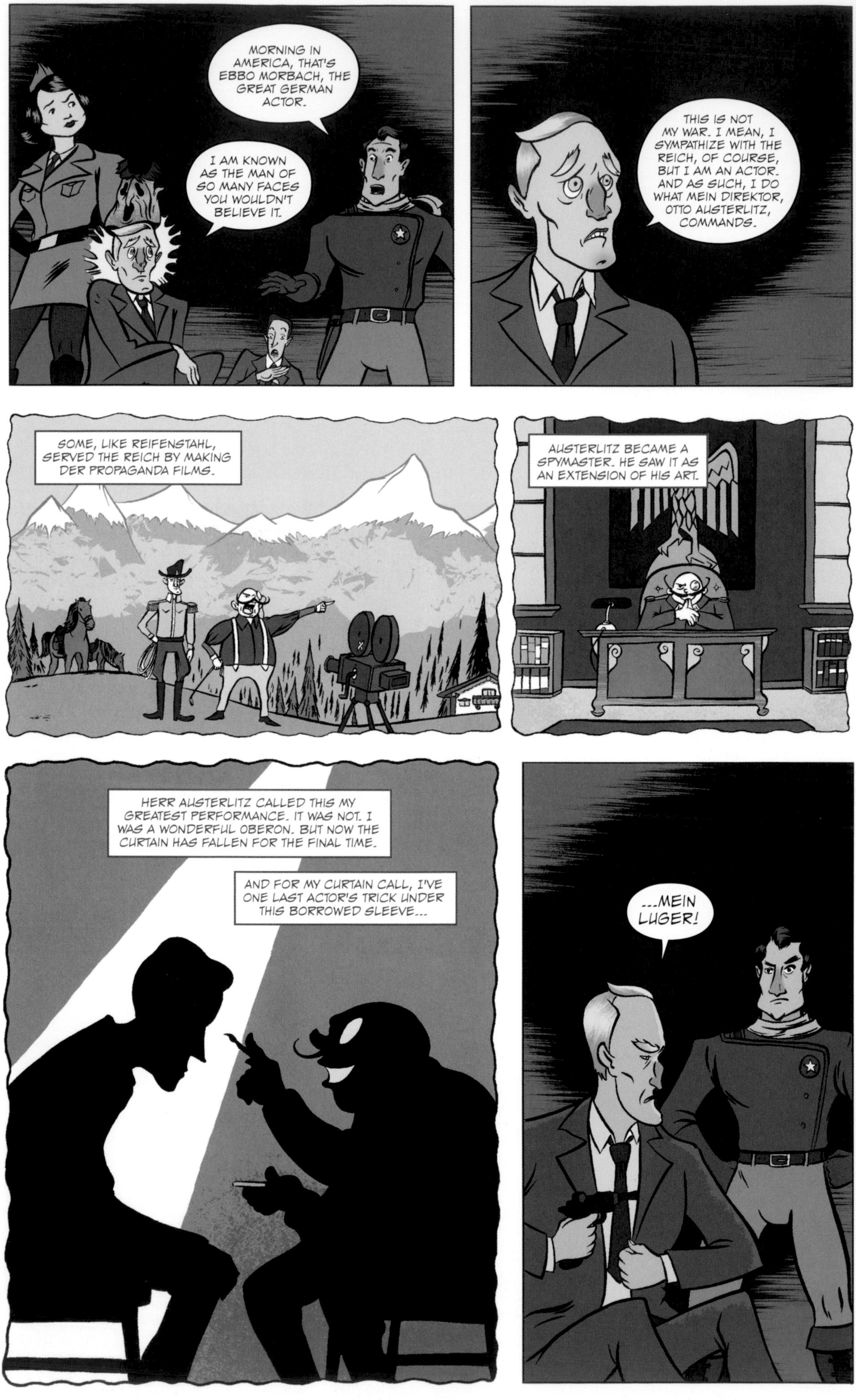
MORNING IN AMERICA, THAT'S EBBO MORBACH, THE GREAT GERMAN ACTOR.
I AM KNOWN AS THE MAN OF SO MANY FACES YOU WOULDN'T BELIEVE IT.
THIS IS NOT MY WAR. I MEAN, I SYMPATHIZE WITH THE REICH, OF COURSE, BUT I AM AN ACTOR. AND AS SUCH, I DO WHAT MEIN DIREKTOR, OTTO AUSTERLITZ, COMMANDS.
SOME, LIKE REIFENSTAHL, SERVED THE REICH BY MAKING DER PROPAGANDA FILMS.
AUSTERLITZ BECAME A SPYMASTER. HE SAW IT AS AN EXTENSION OF HIS ART.
HERR AUSTERLITZ CALLED THIS MY GREATEST PERFORMANCE. IT WAS NOT. I WAS A WONDERFUL OBERON. BUT NOW THE CURTAIN HAS FALLEN FOR THE FINAL TIME.
AND FOR MY CURTAIN CALL, I'VE ONE LAST ACTOR'S TRICK UNDER THIS BORROWED SLEEVE...
...MEIN LUGER!

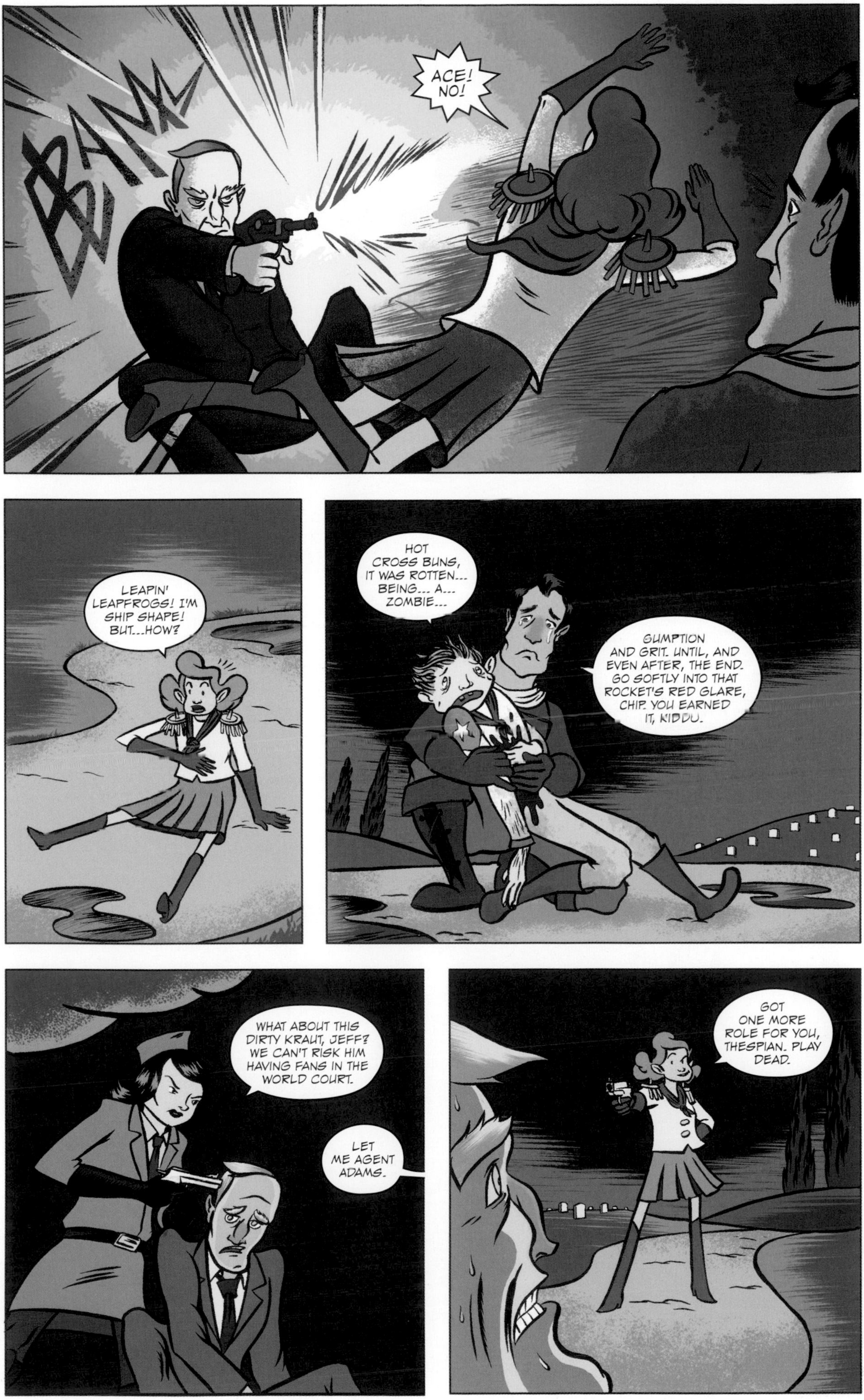
ACE! NO!
LEAPIN' LEAPFROGS! I'M SHIP SHAPE! BUT...HOW?
HOT CROSS BUNS, IT WAS ROTTEN... BEING... A... ZOMBIE...
GUMPTION AND GRIT. UNTIL, AND EVEN AFTER, THE END. GO SOFTLY INTO THAT ROCKET'S RED GLARE, CHIP. YOU EARNED IT, KIDDO.
WHAT ABOUT THIS DIRTY KRAUT, JEFF? WE CAN'T RISK HIM HAVING FANS IN THE WORLD COURT.
LET ME AGENT ADAMS.
GOT ONE MORE ROLE FOR YOU, THESPIAN. PLAY DEAD.

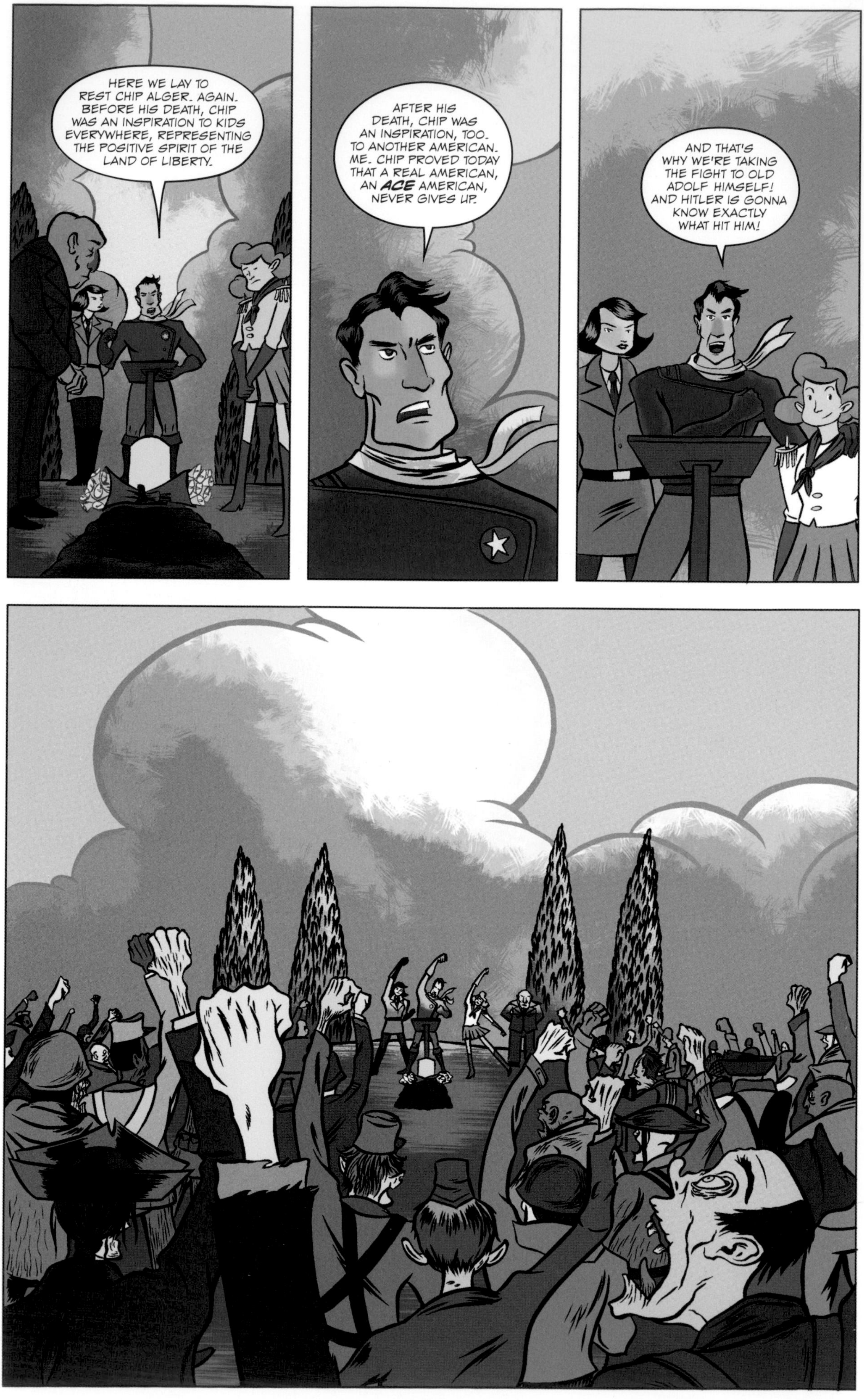
HERE WE LAY TO REST CHIP ALGER. AGAIN. BEFORE HIS DEATH, CHIP WAS AN INSPIRATION TO KIDS EVERYWHERE, REPRESENTING THE POSITIVE SPIRIT OF THE LAND OF LIBERTY.
AFTER HIS DEATH, CHIP WAS AN INSPIRATION, TOO. TO ANOTHER AMERICAN. ME. CHIP PROVED TODAY THAT A REAL AMERICAN, AN ACE AMERICAN, NEVER GIVES UP.
AND THAT'S WHY WE'RE TAKING THE FIGHT TO OLD ADOLF HIMSELF! AND HITLER IS GONNA KNOW EXACTLY WHAT HIT HIM!

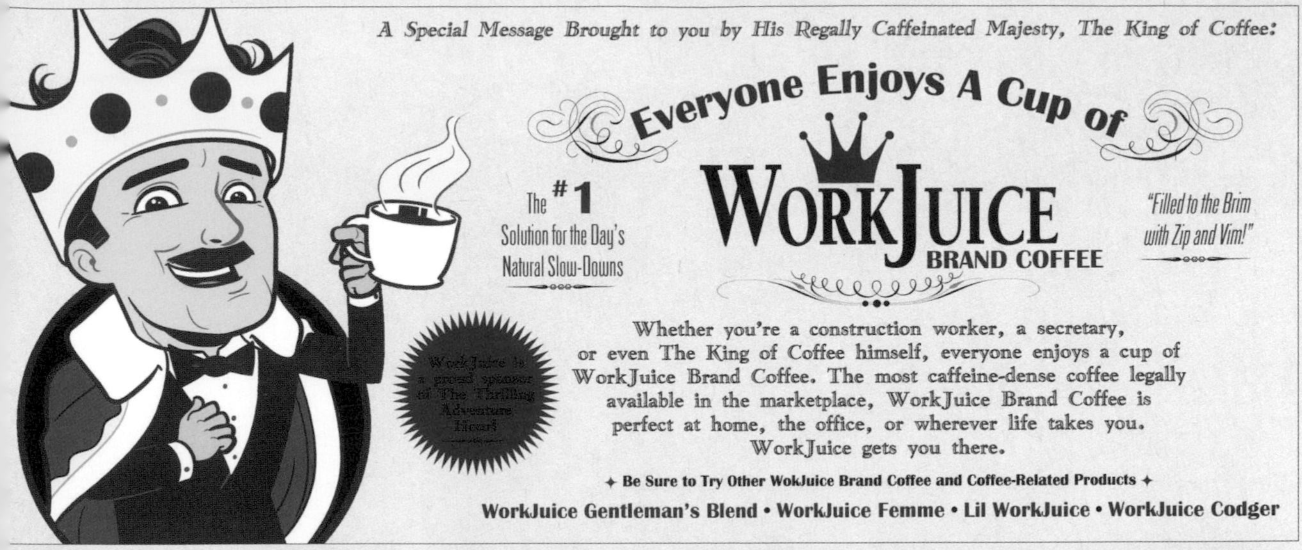
A Special Message Brought to you by His Regally Caffeinated Majesty, The King of Coffee:
Everyone Enjoys A Cup of
WorkJuice
Brand Coffee
The #1 Solution for the Day's Natural Slow-Downs
"Filled to the Brim with Zip and Vim!"
WorkJuice is a proud sponsor of The Thrilling Adventure Hour!
Whether you're a construction worker, a secretary, or even The King of Coffee himself, everyone enjoys a cup of WorkJuice Brand Coffee. The most caffeine-dense coffee legally available in the marketplace, WorkJuice Brand Coffee is perfect at home, the office, or wherever life takes you. WorkJuice gets you there.
✦ Be Sure to Try Other WokJuice Brand Coffee and Coffee-Related Products ✦
WorkJuice Gentleman's Blend • WorkJuice Femme • Lil WorkJuice • WorkJuice Codger

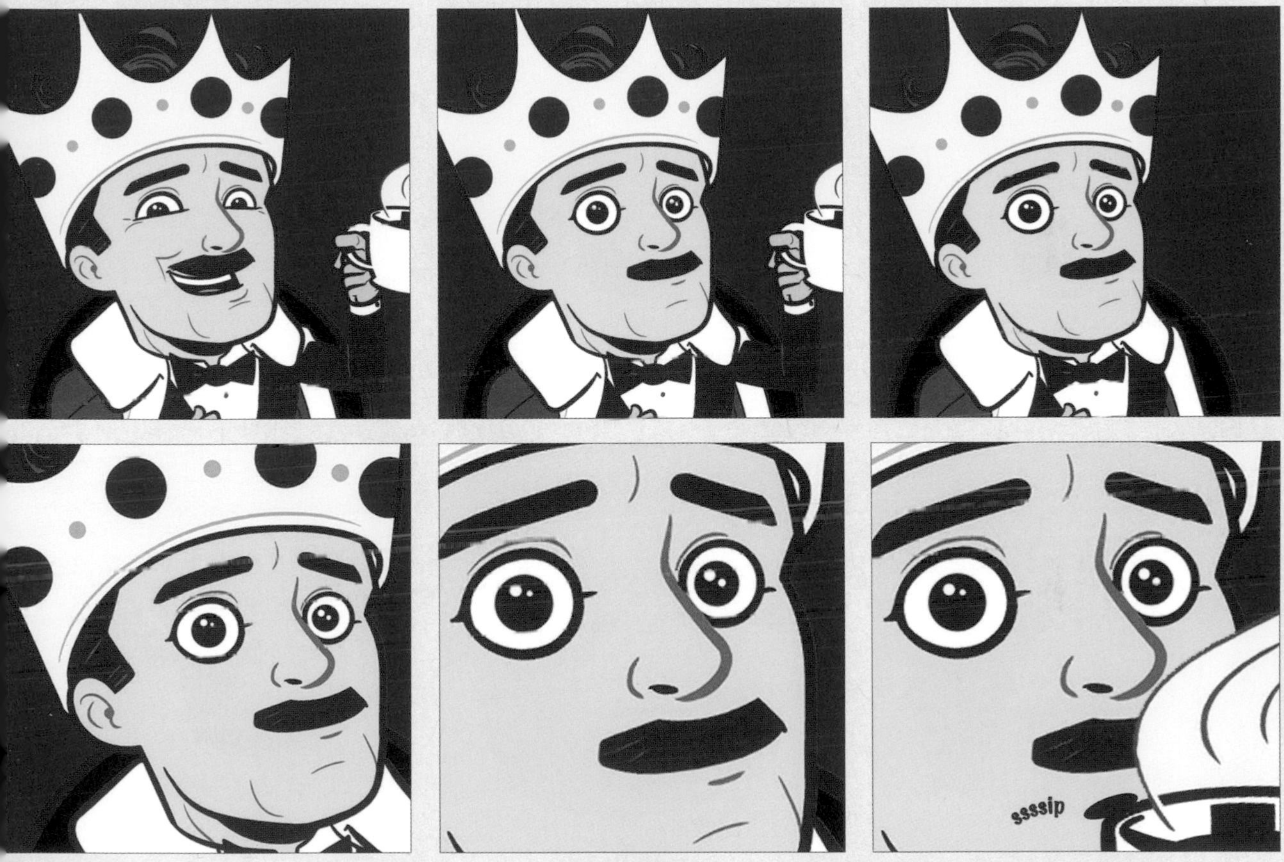
ssssip

"Ladies and Gentlemen, it is me, **JOHN HODGMAN**, who offers this testimonial. It has been only 21 months since I first encountered ***THE THRILLING ADVENTURE HOUR***, and my life has not been the same since. Beyond being the best staged episodic radio comedy of the 21st century, ***THRILLING*** is also and more plainly just wonderful: one of the most joyously and smartly written entertainments that I have encountered. Acker, Blacker, and the WorkJuice Players just make me happy. And also I am generally more alert and my eczema has cleared up. So it is extra exciting to welcome THRILLING to the funny pages, thus merging two great marginal American art forms into one, and eliminating the need for all those human actors and singers, who are generally longwinded jerks. Myself most of all."

John Hodgman

Author of the trilogy of *Complete World Knowledge*, humorist, frequent contributor to *The Daily Show*

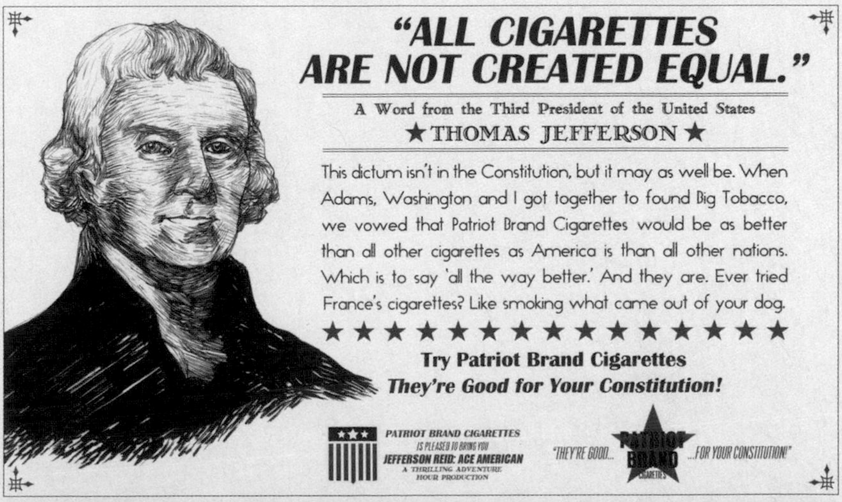
"ALL CIGARETTES ARE NOT CREATED EQUAL."
A Word from the Third President of the United States
★ THOMAS JEFFERSON ★
This dictum isn't in the Constitution, but it may as well be. When Adams, Washington and I got together to found Big Tobacco, we vowed that Patriot Brand Cigarettes would be as better than all other cigarettes as America is than all other nations. Which is to say 'all the way better.' And they are. Ever tried France's cigarettes? Like smoking what came out of your dog.
Try Patriot Brand Cigarettes
They're Good for Your Constitution!
PATRIOT BRAND CIGARETTES IS PLEASED TO BRING YOU JEFFERSON REID: ACE AMERICAN A THRILLING ADVENTURE HOUR PRODUCTION
"THEY'RE GOOD... ...FOR YOUR CONSTITUTION!"

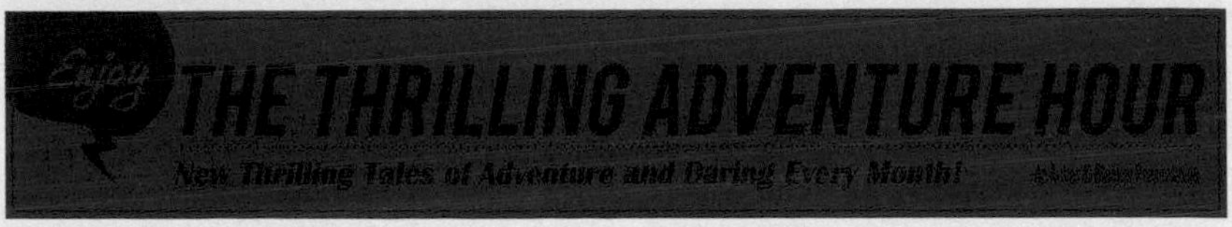
Enjoy
THE THRILLING ADVENTURE HOUR
New Thrilling Tales of Adventure and Daring Every Month!

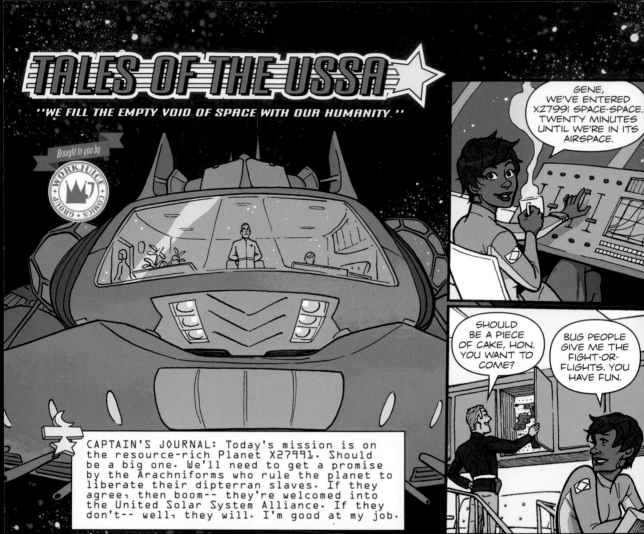

# TALES OF THE USSA ★

"WE FILL THE EMPTY VOID OF SPACE WITH OUR HUMANITY."

Brought to you by
WORKJUICE
COMICS • GROUP • POP

GENE, WE'VE ENTERED X27991 SPACE-SPACE. TWENTY MINUTES UNTIL WE'RE IN ITS AIRSPACE.

CAPTAIN'S JOURNAL: Today's mission is on the resource-rich Planet X27991. Should be a big one. We'll need to get a promise by the Arachniforms who rule the planet to liberate their dipterran slaves. If they agree, then boom-- they're welcomed into the United Solar System Alliance. If they don't-- well, they will. I'm good at my job.

SHOULD BE A PIECE OF CAKE, HON. YOU WANT TO COME?

BUG PEOPLE GIVE ME THE FIGHT-OR-FLIGHTS. YOU HAVE FUN.

I JUST SENT YOU THE GROUND CREW MANIFEST.

OH! YOU'RE BRINGING LEWIS PLANETSIDE? I'M SURPRISED. BUT ERICA WILL BE HAPPY.

YOU'LL - GENE, YOU'LL BE NICE TO HIM DOWN THERE, WON'T YOU?

I'M HIS CAPTAIN. I'LL BE CAPTAIN TO HIM DOWN THERE.

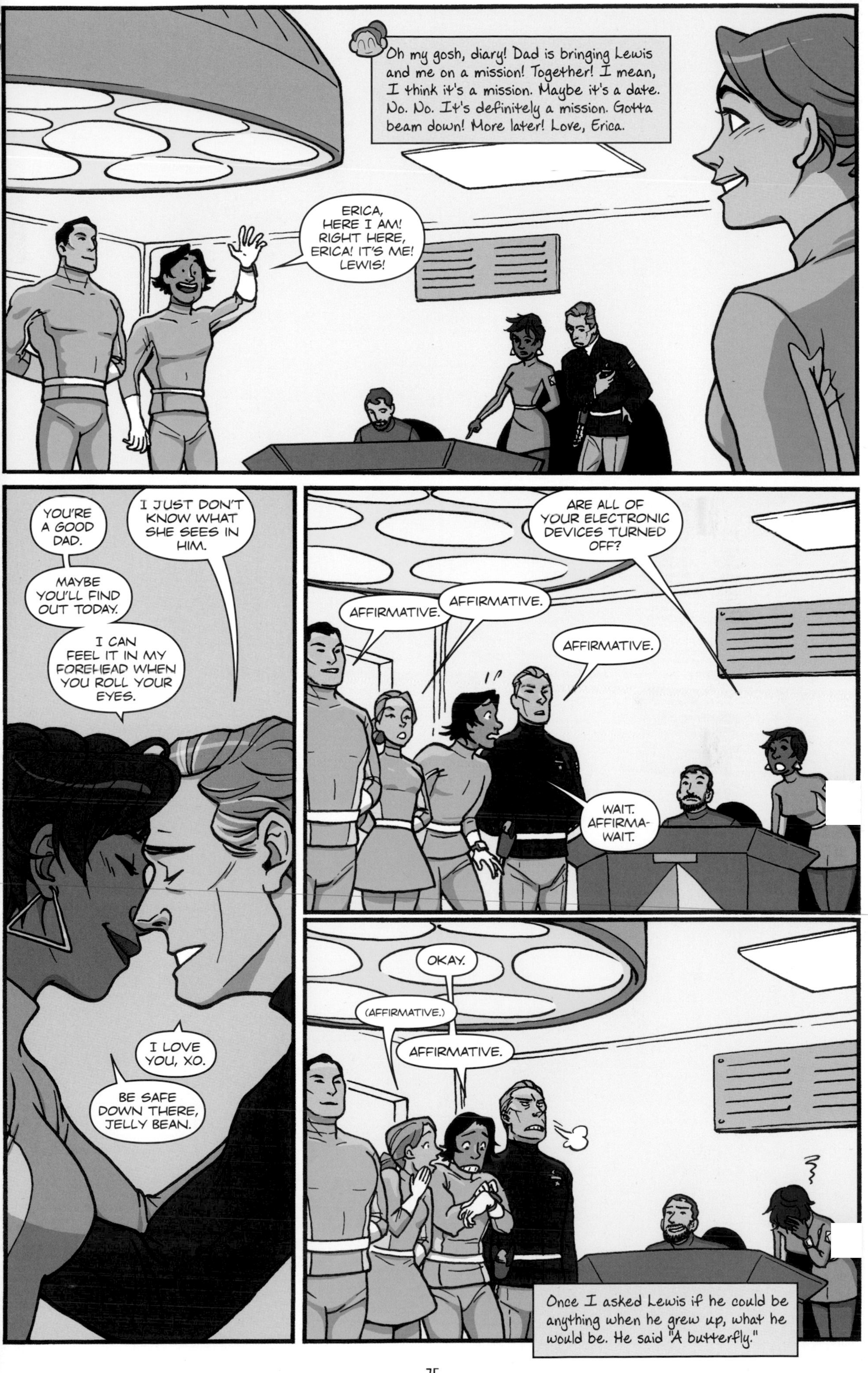

Oh my gosh, diary! Dad is bringing Lewis and me on a mission! Together! I mean, I think it's a mission. Maybe it's a date. No. No. It's definitely a mission. Gotta beam down! More later! Love, Erica.
ERICA, HERE I AM! RIGHT HERE, ERICA! IT'S ME! LEWIS!
YOU'RE A GOOD DAD.
I JUST DON'T KNOW WHAT SHE SEES IN HIM.
MAYBE YOU'LL FIND OUT TODAY.
I CAN FEEL IT IN MY FOREHEAD WHEN YOU ROLL YOUR EYES.
I LOVE YOU, XO.
BE SAFE DOWN THERE, JELLY BEAN.
ARE ALL OF YOUR ELECTRONIC DEVICES TURNED OFF?
AFFIRMATIVE.
AFFIRMATIVE.
AFFIRMATIVE.
WAIT. AFFIRMA- WAIT.
OKAY.
(AFFIRMATIVE.)
AFFIRMATIVE.
Once I asked Lewis if he could be anything when he grew up, what he would be. He said "A butterfly."

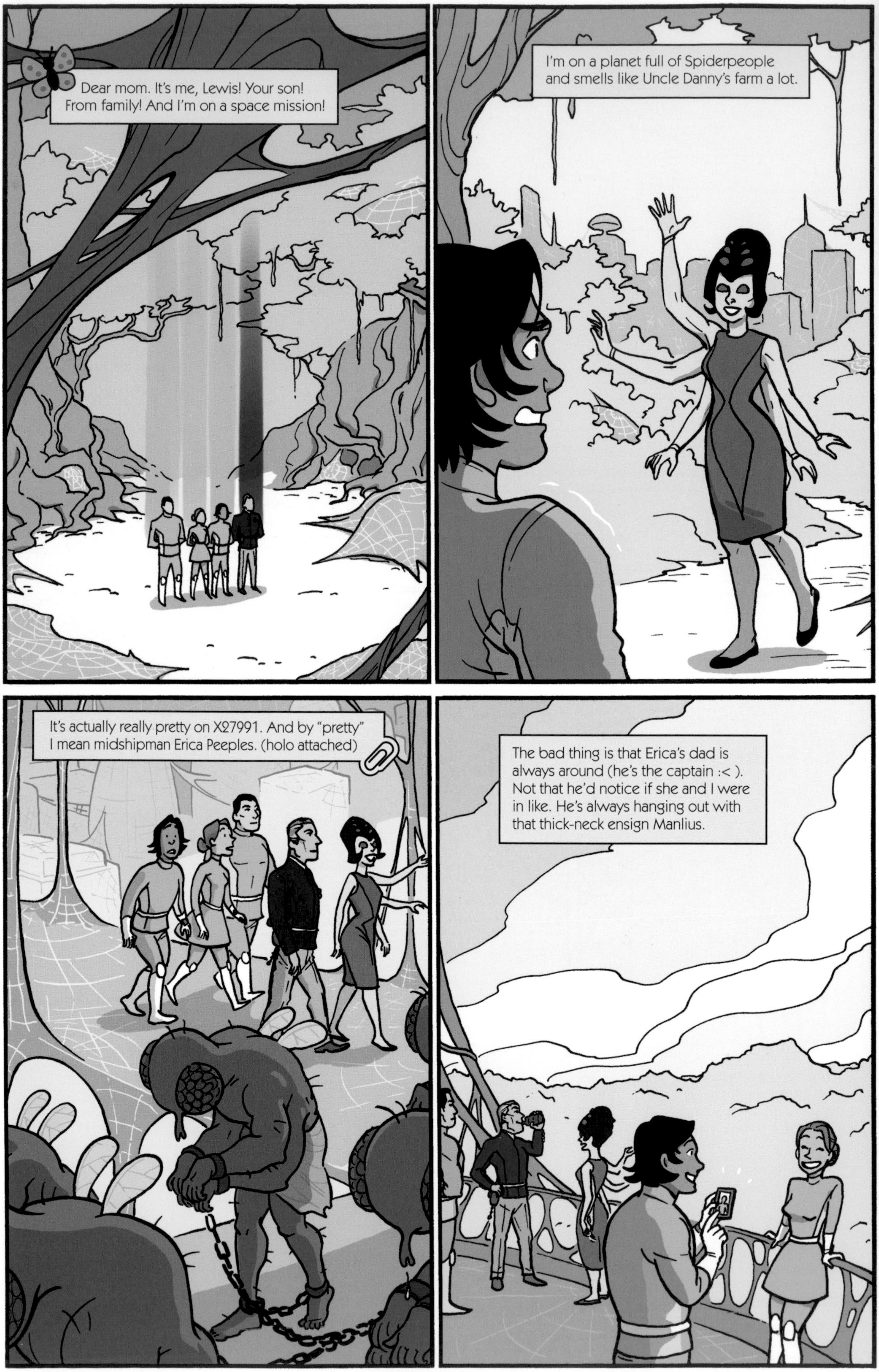
Dear mom. It's me, Lewis! Your son! From family! And I'm on a space mission!
I'm on a planet full of Spiderpeople and smells like Uncle Danny's farm a lot.
It's actually really pretty on X27991. And by "pretty" I mean midshipman Erica Peeples. (holo attached)
The bad thing is that Erica's dad is always around (he's the captain :< ). Not that he'd notice if she and I were in like. He's always hanging out with that thick-neck ensign Manlius.

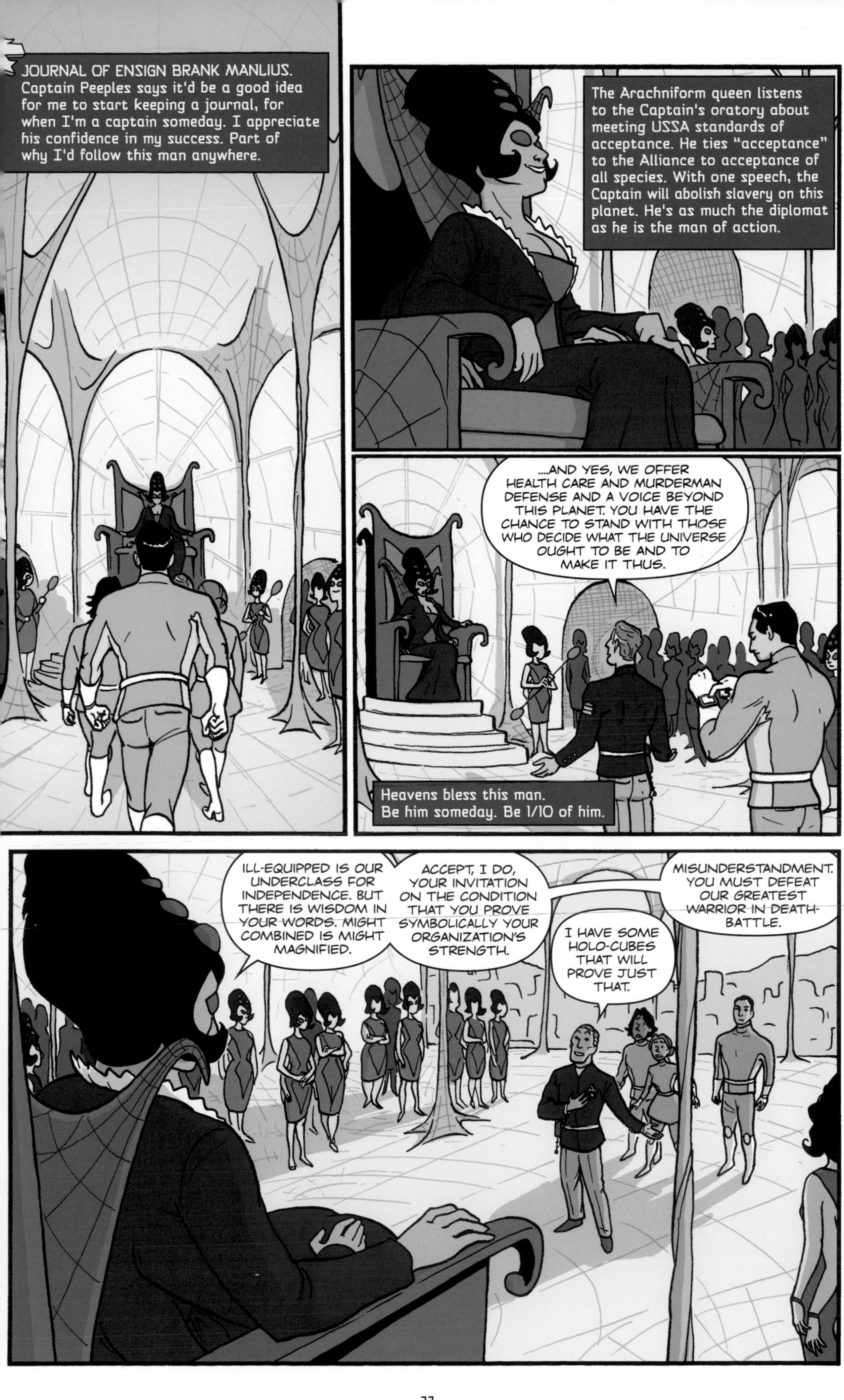
JOURNAL OF ENSIGN BRANK MANLIUS. Captain Peeples says it'd be a good idea for me to start keeping a journal, for when I'm a captain someday. I appreciate his confidence in my success. Part of why I'd follow this man anywhere.
The Arachniform queen listens to the Captain's oratory about meeting USSA standards of acceptance. He ties "acceptance" to the Alliance to acceptance of all species. With one speech, the Captain will abolish slavery on this planet. He's as much the diplomat as he is the man of action.
....AND YES, WE OFFER HEALTH CARE AND MURDERMAN DEFENSE AND A VOICE BEYOND THIS PLANET. YOU HAVE THE CHANCE TO STAND WITH THOSE WHO DECIDE WHAT THE UNIVERSE OUGHT TO BE AND TO MAKE IT THUS.
Heavens bless this man. Be him someday. Be 1/10 of him.
ILL-EQUIPPED IS OUR UNDERCLASS FOR INDEPENDENCE. BUT THERE IS WISDOM IN YOUR WORDS. MIGHT COMBINED IS MIGHT MAGNIFIED.
ACCEPT, I DO, YOUR INVITATION ON THE CONDITION THAT YOU PROVE SYMBOLICALLY YOUR ORGANIZATION'S STRENGTH.
I HAVE SOME HOLO-CUBES THAT WILL PROVE JUST THAT.
MISUNDERSTANDMENT. YOU MUST DEFEAT OUR GREATEST WARRIOR IN DEATH-BATTLE.

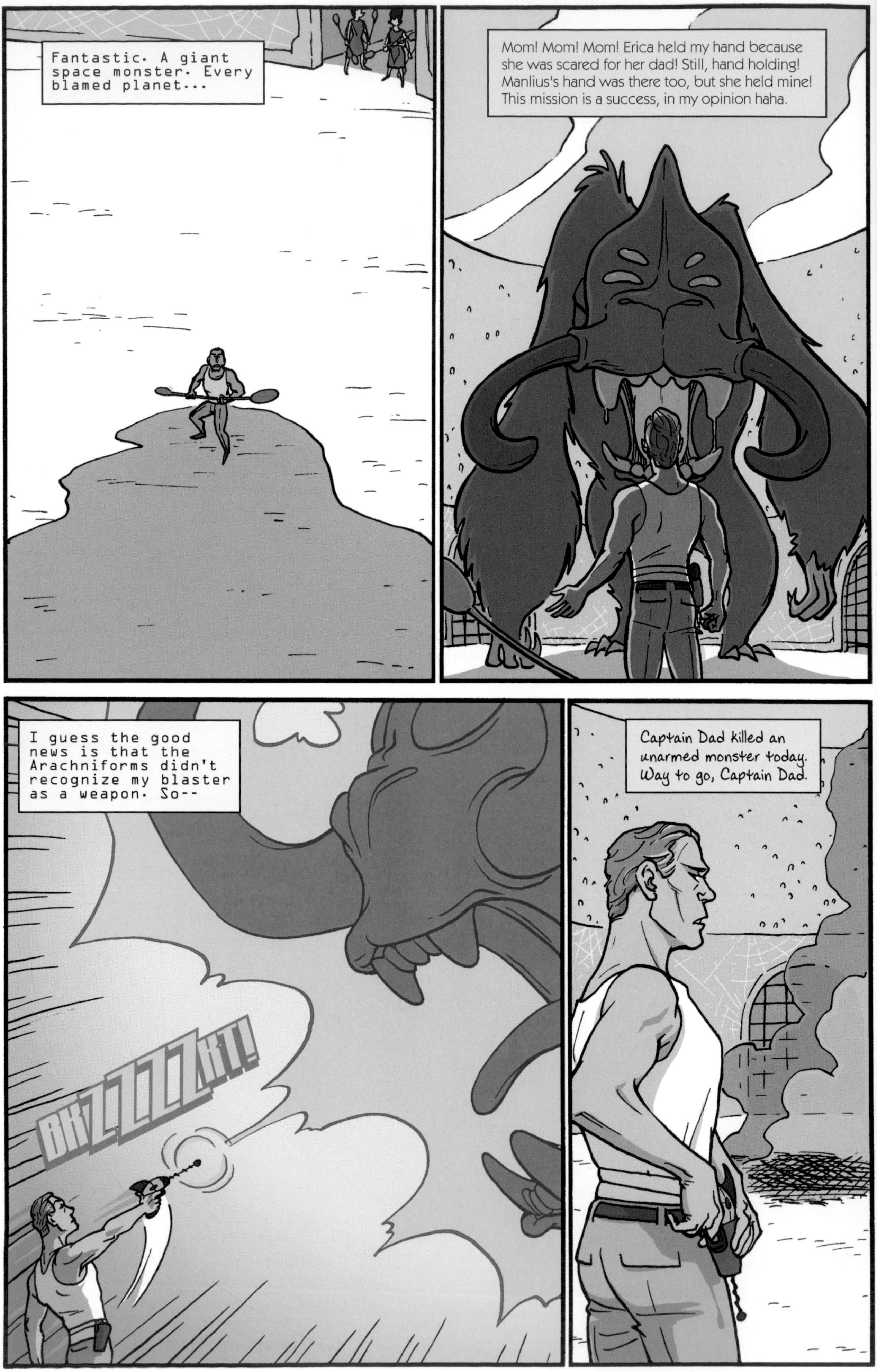
Fantastic. A giant space monster. Every blamed planet...
Mom! Mom! Mom! Erica held my hand because she was scared for her dad! Still, hand holding! Manlius's hand was there too, but she held mine! This mission is a success, in my opinion haha.
I guess the good news is that the Arachniforms didn't recognize my blaster as a weapon. So--
BKZZZZKT!
Captain Dad killed an unarmed monster today. Way to go, Captain Dad.

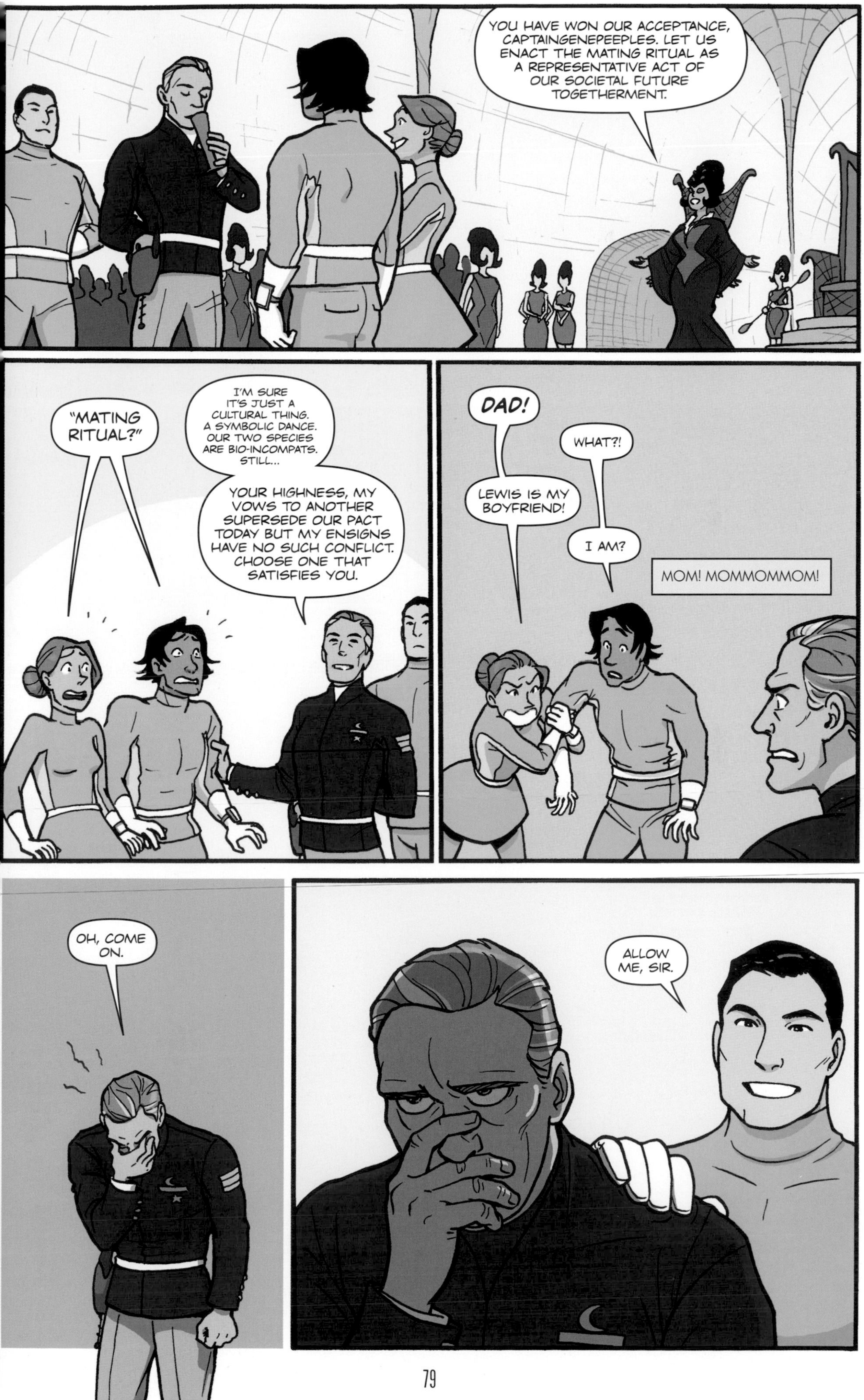
YOU HAVE WON OUR ACCEPTANCE, CAPTAINGENEPEEPLES. LET US ENACT THE MATING RITUAL AS A REPRESENTATIVE ACT OF OUR SOCIETAL FUTURE TOGETHERMENT.
"MATING RITUAL?"
I'M SURE IT'S JUST A CULTURAL THING. A SYMBOLIC DANCE. OUR TWO SPECIES ARE BIO-INCOMPATS. STILL...
YOUR HIGHNESS, MY VOWS TO ANOTHER SUPERSEDE OUR PACT TODAY BUT MY ENSIGNS HAVE NO SUCH CONFLICT. CHOOSE ONE THAT SATISFIES YOU.
DAD!
WHAT?!
LEWIS IS MY BOYFRIEND!
I AM?
MOM! MOMMOMMOM!
OH, COME ON.
ALLOW ME, SIR.

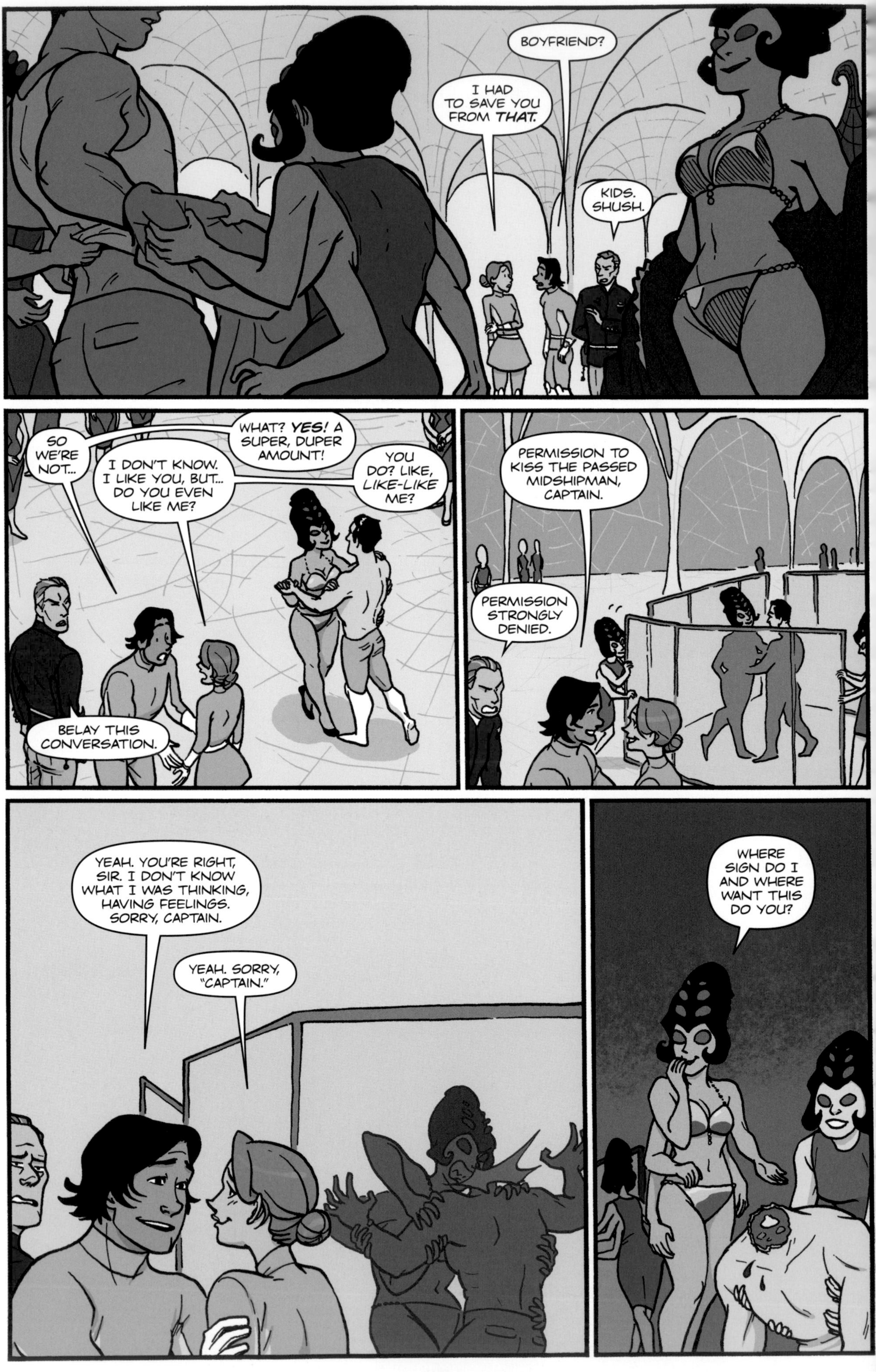
BOYFRIEND?
I HAD TO SAVE YOU FROM THAT.
KIDS. SHUSH.
SO WE'RE NOT...
WHAT? YES! A SUPER, DUPER AMOUNT!
I DON'T KNOW. I LIKE YOU, BUT... DO YOU EVEN LIKE ME?
YOU DO? LIKE, LIKE-LIKE ME?
BELAY THIS CONVERSATION.
PERMISSION TO KISS THE PASSED MIDSHIPMAN, CAPTAIN.
PERMISSION STRONGLY DENIED.
YEAH. YOU'RE RIGHT, SIR. I DON'T KNOW WHAT I WAS THINKING, HAVING FEELINGS. SORRY, CAPTAIN.
YEAH. SORRY, "CAPTAIN."
WHERE SIGN DO I AND WHERE WANT THIS DO YOU?

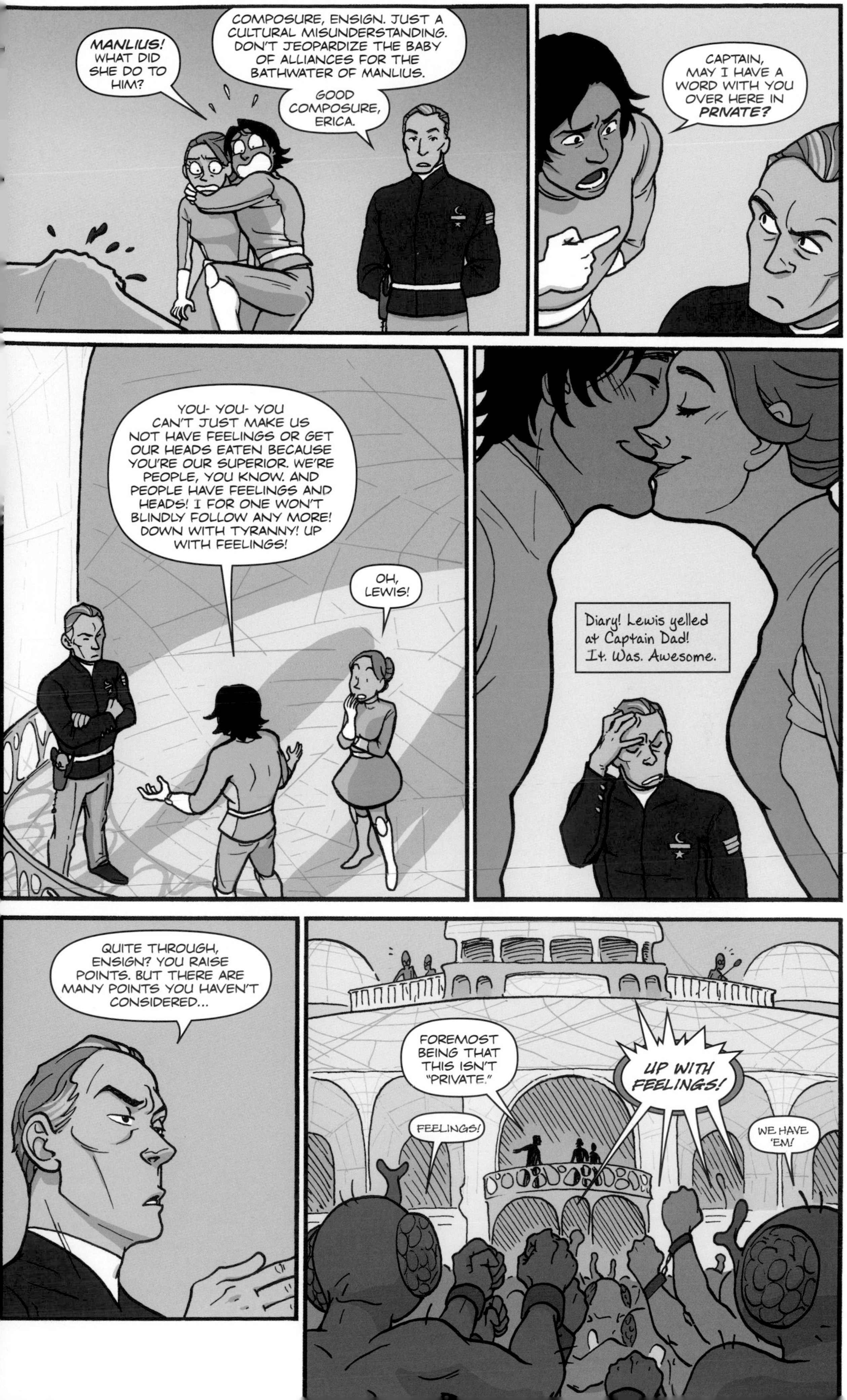
MANLIUS! WHAT DID SHE DO TO HIM?
COMPOSURE, ENSIGN. JUST A CULTURAL MISUNDERSTANDING. DON'T JEOPARDIZE THE BABY OF ALLIANCES FOR THE BATHWATER OF MANLIUS.
GOOD COMPOSURE, ERICA.
CAPTAIN, MAY I HAVE A WORD WITH YOU OVER HERE IN PRIVATE?
YOU- YOU- YOU CAN'T JUST MAKE US NOT HAVE FEELINGS OR GET OUR HEADS EATEN BECAUSE YOU'RE OUR SUPERIOR. WE'RE PEOPLE, YOU KNOW. AND PEOPLE HAVE FEELINGS AND HEADS! I FOR ONE WON'T BLINDLY FOLLOW ANY MORE! DOWN WITH TYRANNY! UP WITH FEELINGS!
OH, LEWIS!
Diary! Lewis yelled at Captain Dad! It. Was. Awesome.
QUITE THROUGH, ENSIGN? YOU RAISE POINTS. BUT THERE ARE MANY POINTS YOU HAVEN'T CONSIDERED...
FOREMOST BEING THAT THIS ISN'T "PRIVATE."
UP WITH FEELINGS!
FEELINGS!
WE HAVE 'EM!

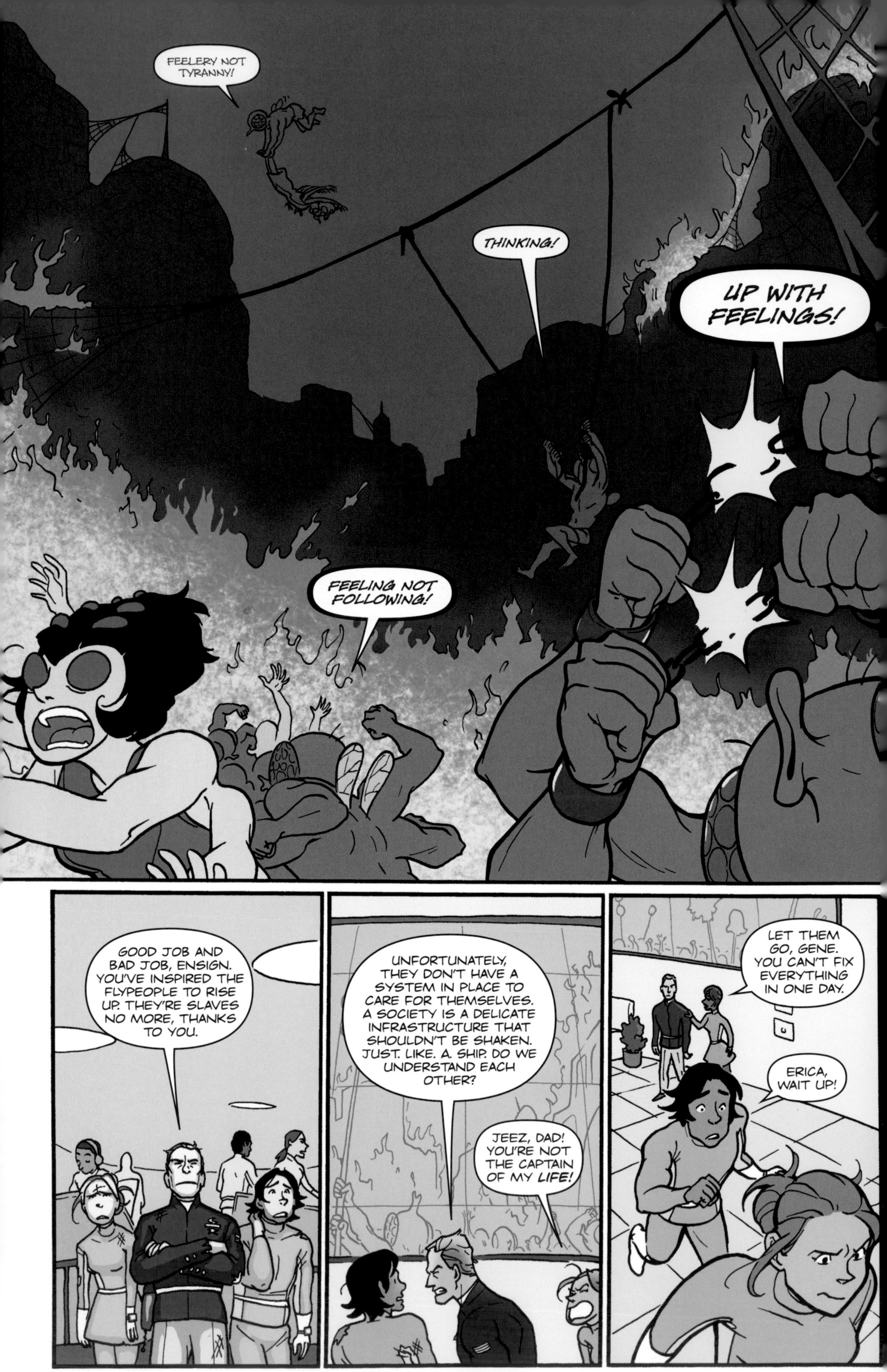
FEELERY NOT TYRANNY!
THINKING!
UP WITH FEELINGS!
FEELING NOT FOLLOWING!
GOOD JOB AND BAD JOB, ENSIGN. YOU'VE INSPIRED THE FLYPEOPLE TO RISE UP. THEY'RE SLAVES NO MORE, THANKS TO YOU.
UNFORTUNATELY, THEY DON'T HAVE A SYSTEM IN PLACE TO CARE FOR THEMSELVES. A SOCIETY IS A DELICATE INFRASTRUCTURE THAT SHOULDN'T BE SHAKEN. JUST. LIKE. A. SHIP. DO WE UNDERSTAND EACH OTHER?
JEEZ, DAD! YOU'RE NOT THE CAPTAIN OF MY *LIFE*!
LET THEM GO, GENE. YOU CAN'T FIX EVERYTHING IN ONE DAY.
ERICA, WAIT UP!

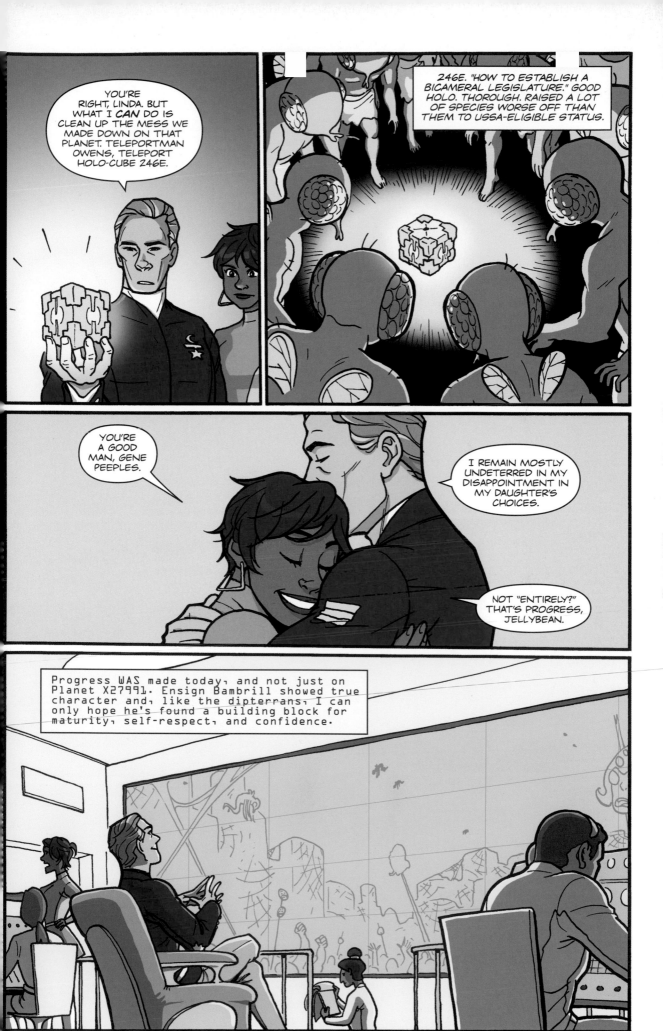

YOU'RE RIGHT, LINDA. BUT WHAT I *CAN* DO IS CLEAN UP THE MESS WE MADE DOWN ON THAT PLANET. TELEPORTMAN OWENS, TELEPORT HOLO-CUBE 246E.

246E. "HOW TO ESTABLISH A BICAMERAL LEGISLATURE." GOOD HOLO. THOROUGH. RAISED A LOT OF SPECIES WORSE OFF THAN THEM TO USSA-ELIGIBLE STATUS.

YOU'RE A GOOD MAN, GENE PEEPLES.

I REMAIN MOSTLY UNDETERRED IN MY DISAPPOINTMENT IN MY DAUGHTER'S CHOICES.

NOT "ENTIRELY?" THAT'S PROGRESS, JELLYBEAN.

Progress WAS made today, and not just on Planet X27991. Ensign Bambrill showed true character and, like the dipterrans, I can only hope he's found a building block for maturity, self-respect, and confidence.

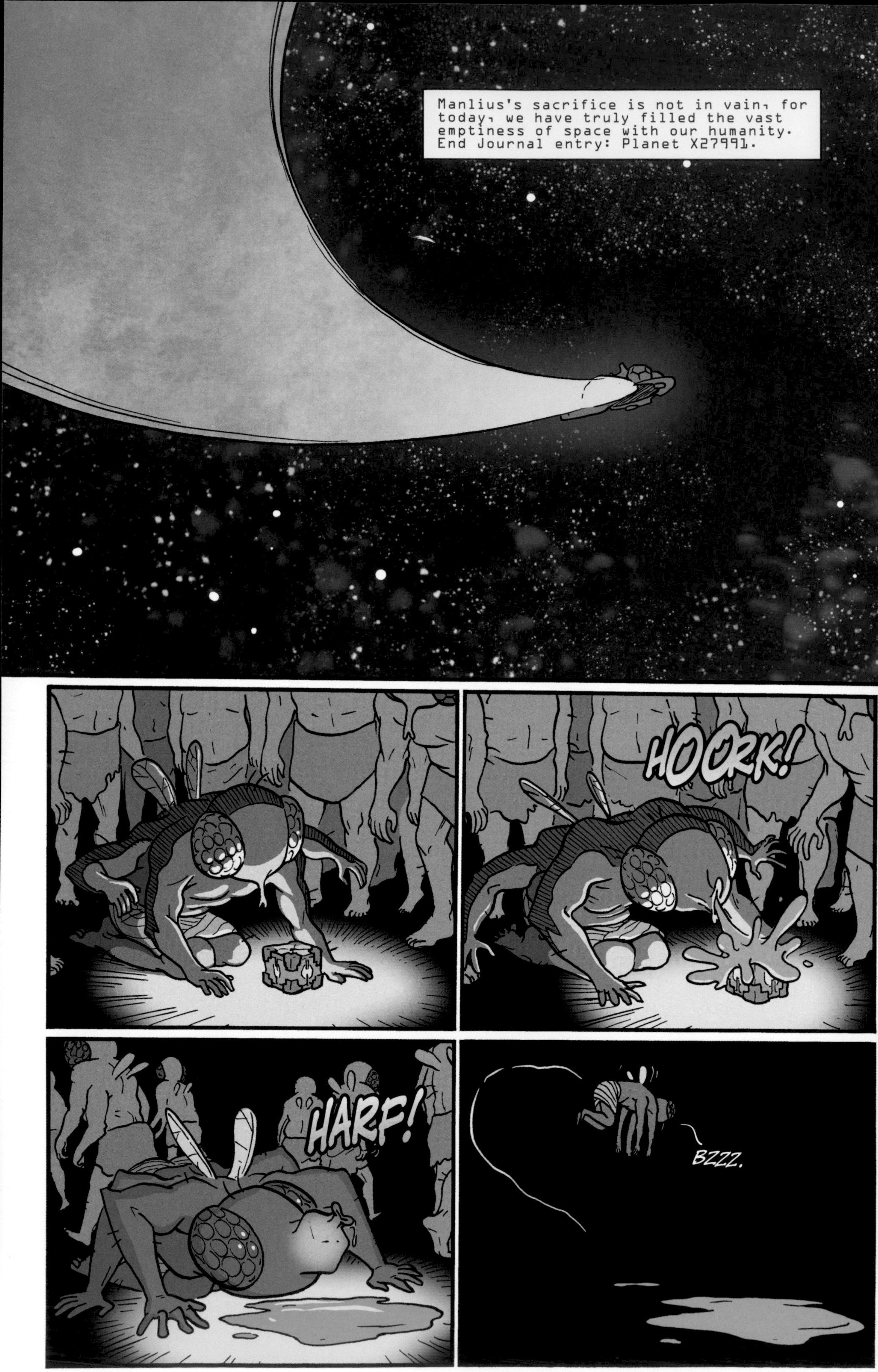
Manlius's sacrifice is not in vain, for today, we have truly filled the vast emptiness of space with our humanity. End Journal entry: Planet X27991.
HOORK!
HARF!
BZZZ.

A tale from America's golden age in which a millionaire renounces his riches and becomes a vagrant in a quest to deserve his one true love, The Hobo Princess, in her home the fabled vagrant's paradise...

# MOONSHINE HOLLER

Brought to you by WORKJUICE COMICS GROUP

What man cannot relate to that? Only a man who has never loved.

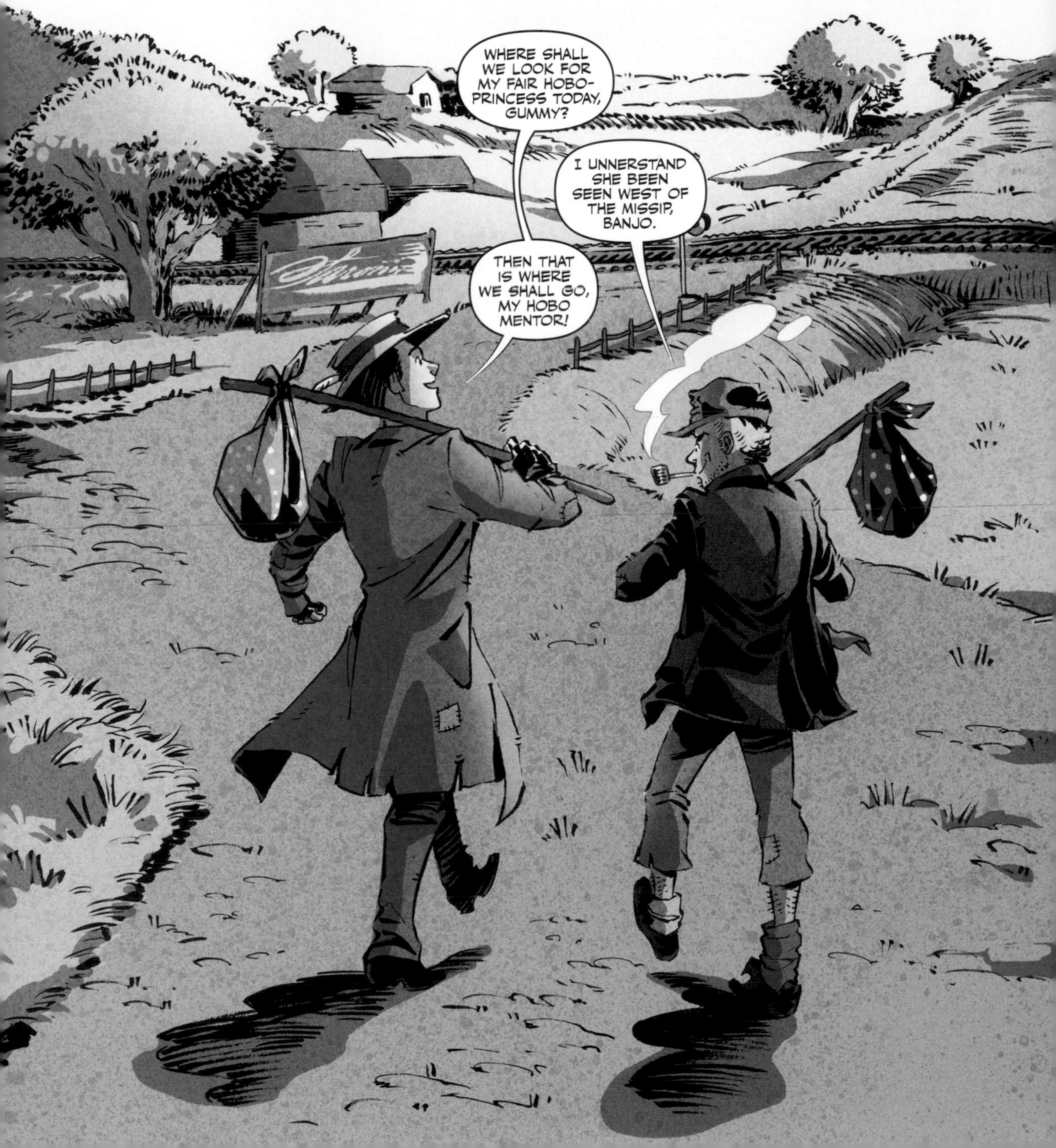

WHERE SHALL WE LOOK FOR MY FAIR HOBO-PRINCESS TODAY, GUMMY?
I UNNERSTAND SHE BEEN SEEN WEST OF THE MISSIP, BANJO.
THEN THAT IS WHERE WE SHALL GO, MY HOBO MENTOR!

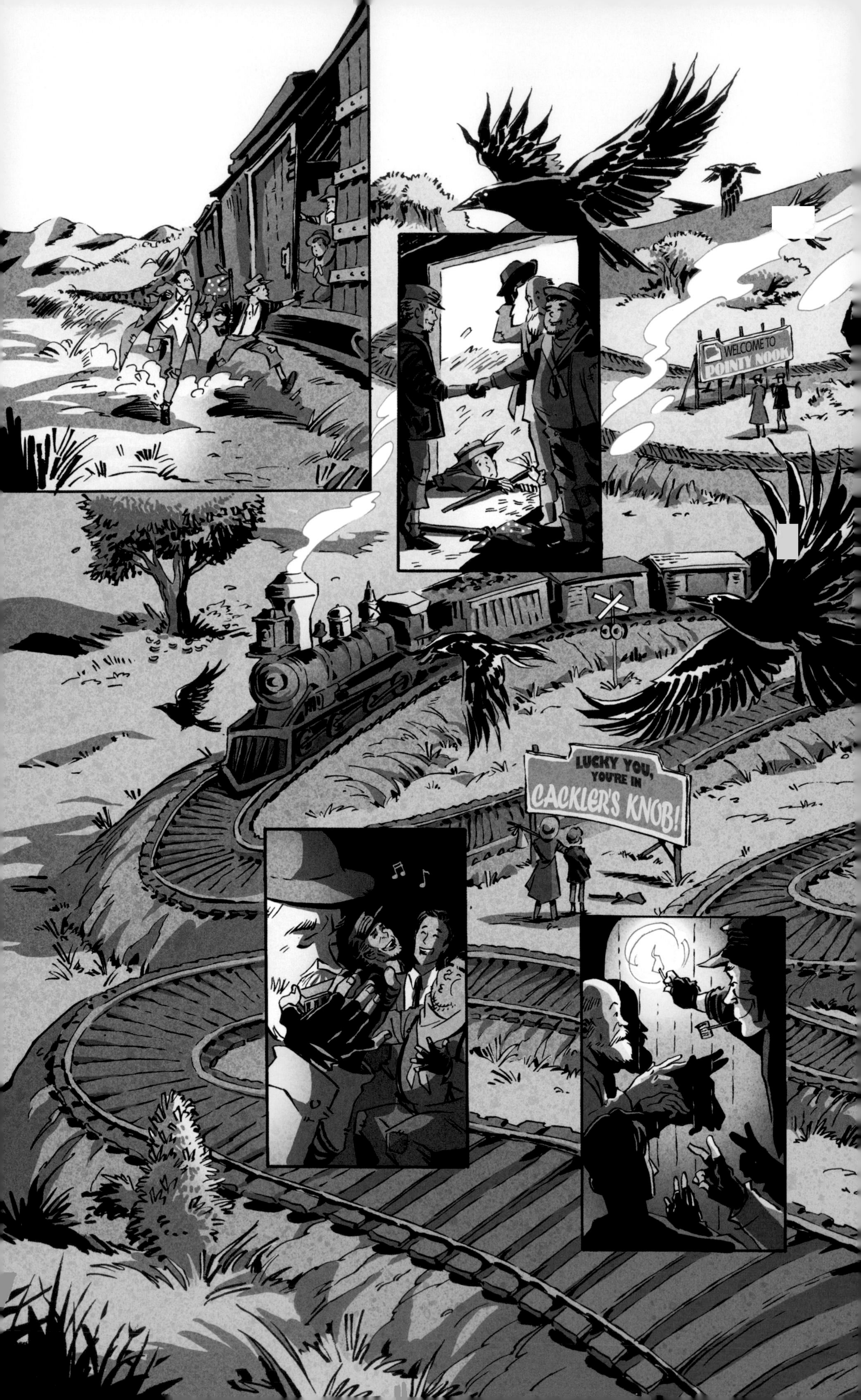
WELCOME TO
POINTY NOOK
LUCKY YOU,
YOU'RE IN
CACKLER'S KNOB!

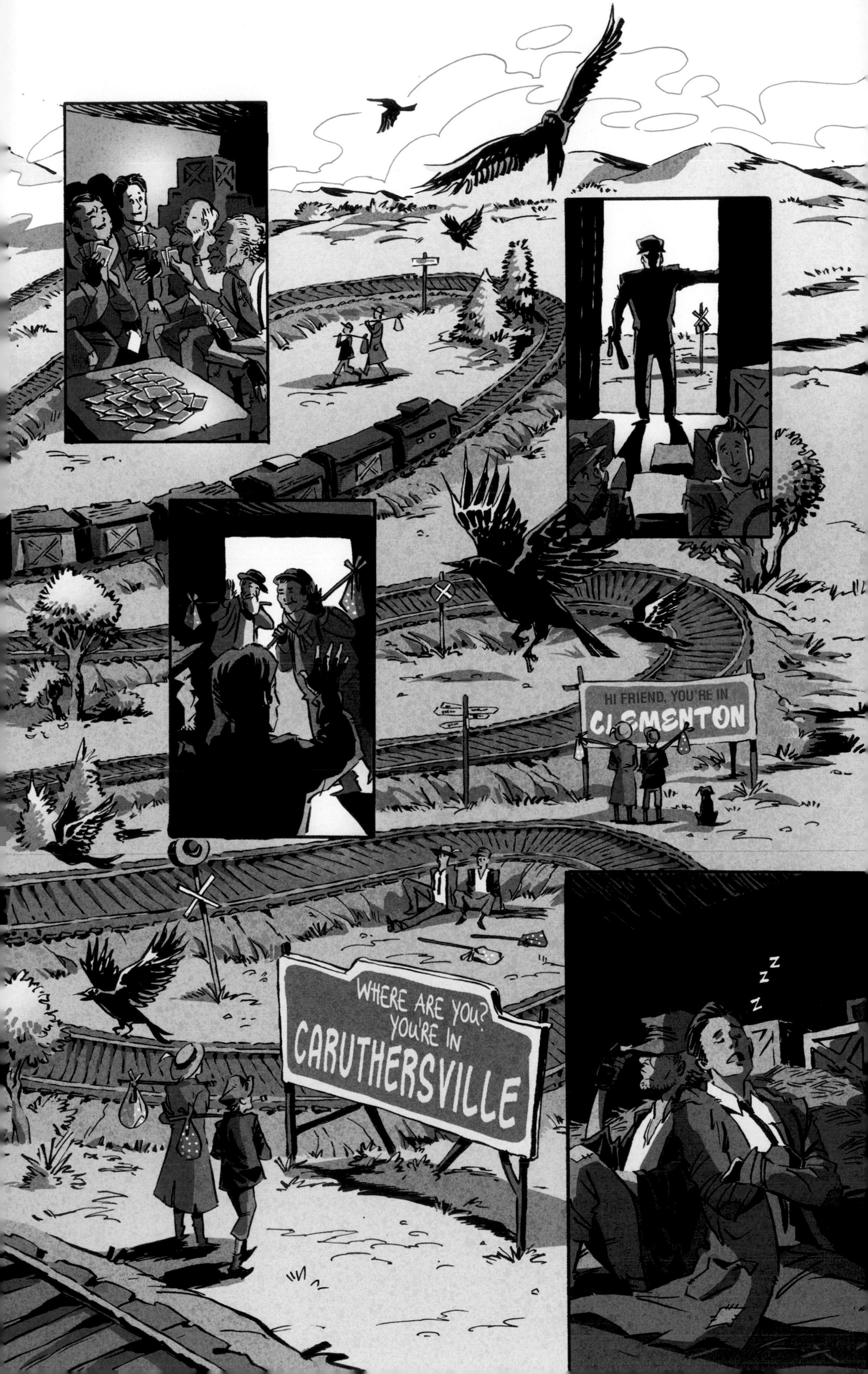
HI FRIEND, YOU'RE IN
CLEMENTON
WHERE ARE YOU? YOU'RE IN
CARUTHERSVILLE
Z Z Z

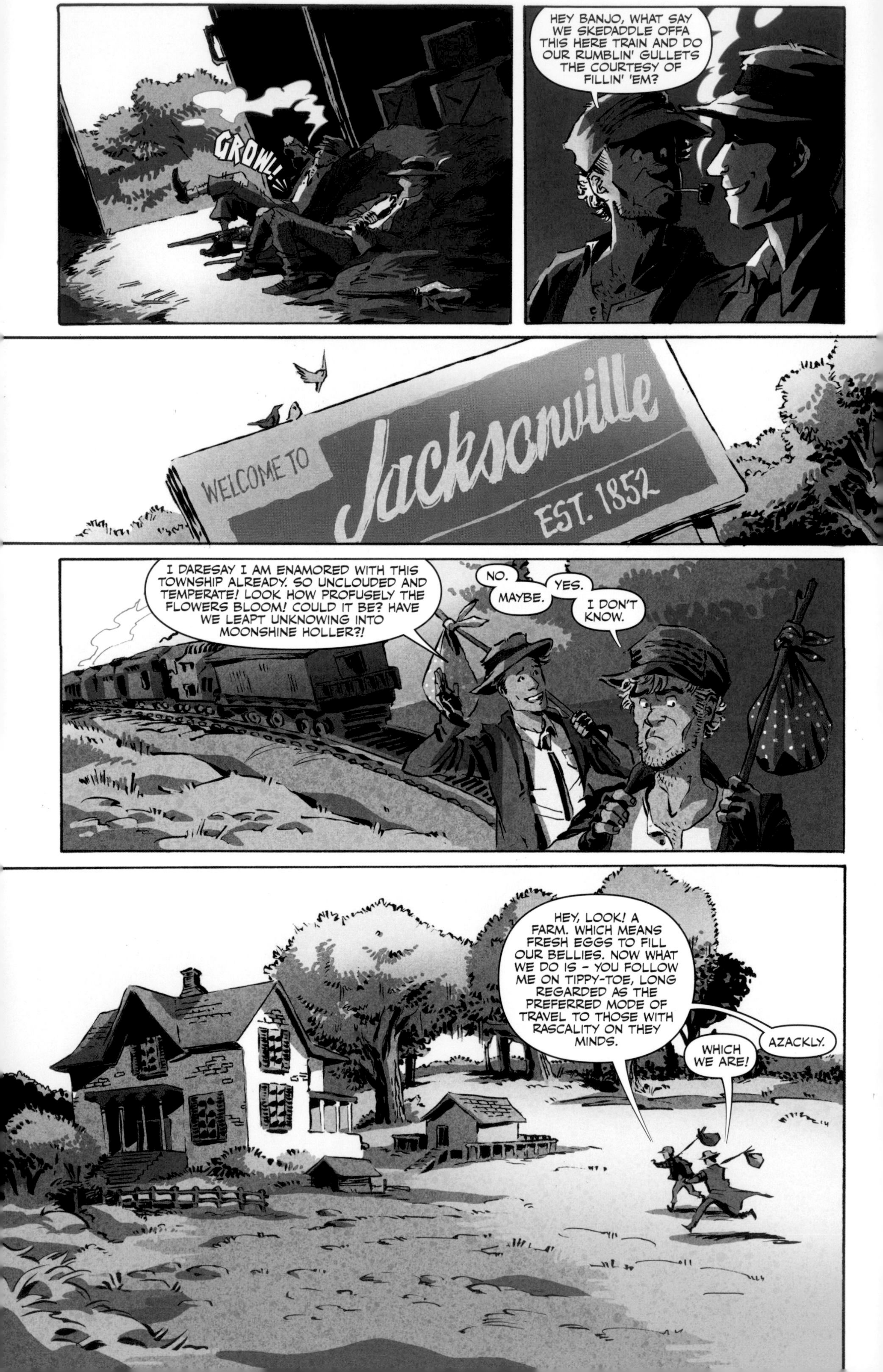
GROWL!
HEY BANJO, WHAT SAY WE SKEDADDLE OFFA THIS HERE TRAIN AND DO OUR RUMBLIN' GULLETS THE COURTESY OF FILLIN' 'EM?
WELCOME TO Jacksonville EST. 1852
I DARESAY I AM ENAMORED WITH THIS TOWNSHIP ALREADY. SO UNCLOUDED AND TEMPERATE! LOOK HOW PROFUSELY THE FLOWERS BLOOM! COULD IT BE? HAVE WE LEAPT UNKNOWING INTO MOONSHINE HOLLER?!
NO.
MAYBE.
YES.
I DON'T KNOW.
HEY, LOOK! A FARM. WHICH MEANS FRESH EGGS TO FILL OUR BELLIES. NOW WHAT WE DO IS – YOU FOLLOW ME ON TIPPY-TOE, LONG REGARDED AS THE PREFERRED MODE OF TRAVEL TO THOSE WITH RASCALITY ON THEY MINDS.
WHICH WE ARE!
AZACKLY.

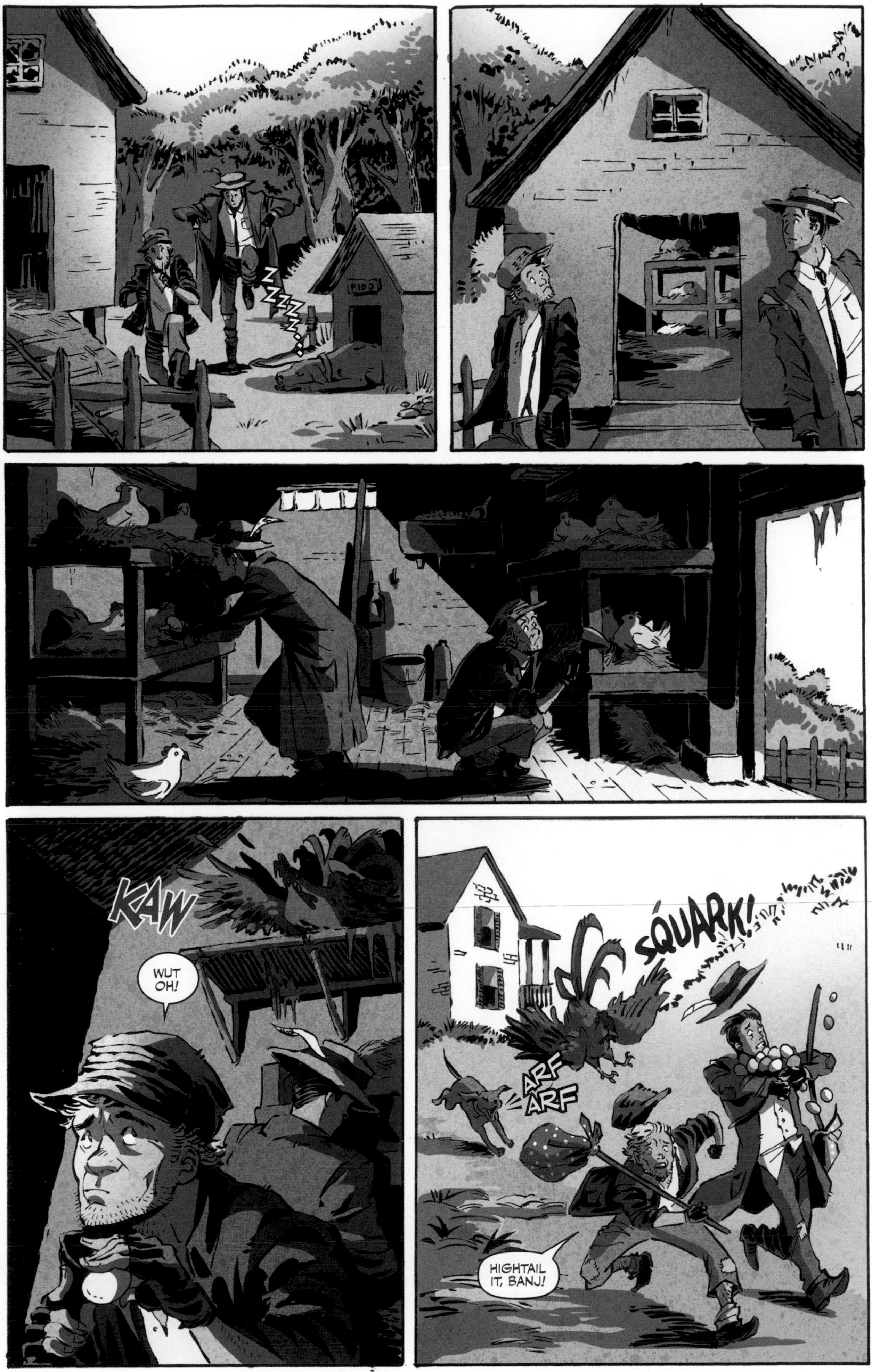
ZZZZZ
FIDO
KAW
WUT OH!
SQUARK!
ARF ARF
HIGHTAIL IT, BANJ!

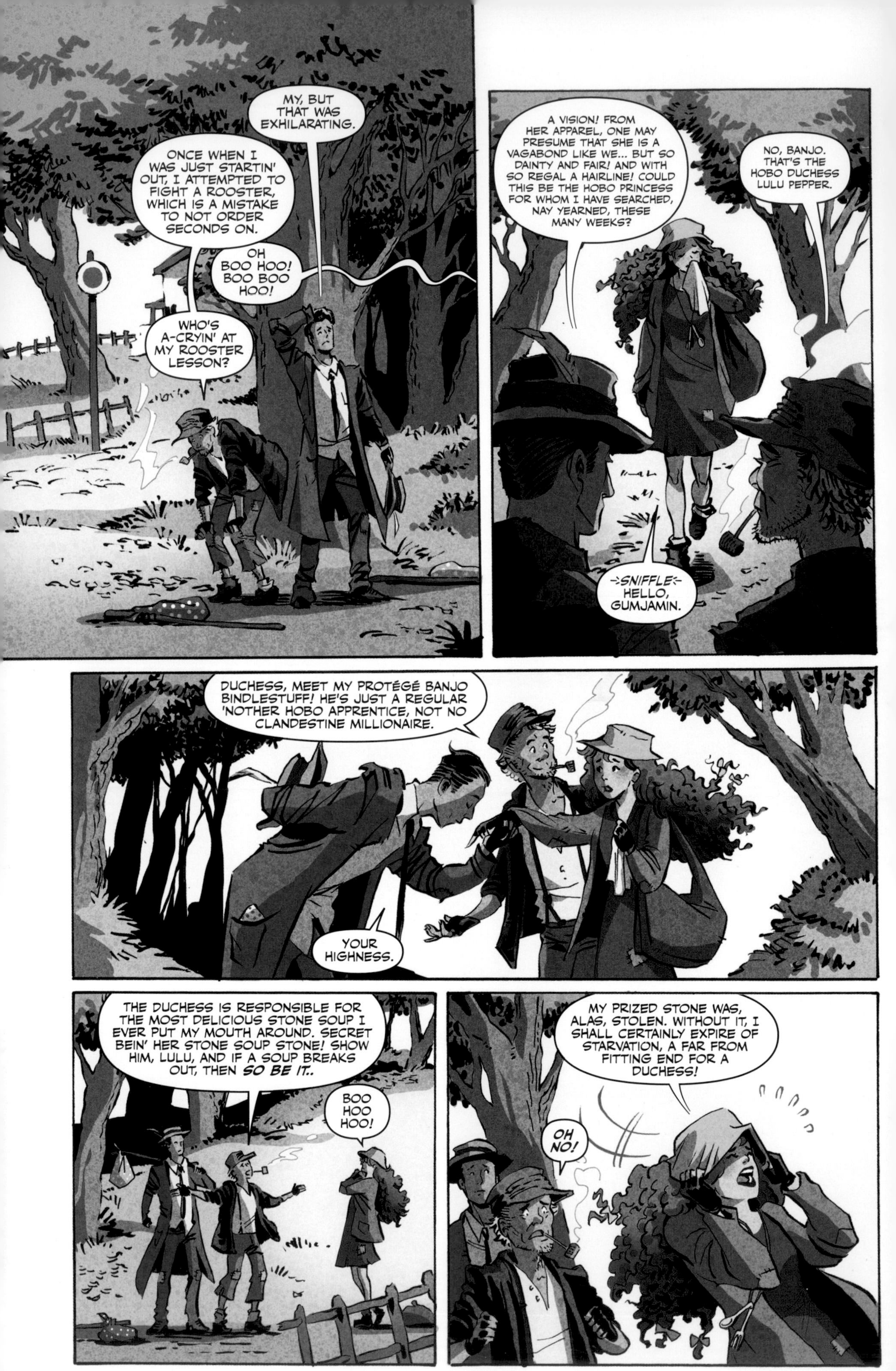
MY, BUT THAT WAS EXHILARATING.
ONCE WHEN I WAS JUST STARTIN' OUT, I ATTEMPTED TO FIGHT A ROOSTER, WHICH IS A MISTAKE TO NOT ORDER SECONDS ON.
OH BOO HOO! BOO BOO HOO!
WHO'S A-CRYIN' AT MY ROOSTER LESSON?
A VISION! FROM HER APPAREL, ONE MAY PRESUME THAT SHE IS A VAGABOND LIKE WE... BUT SO DAINTY AND FAIR! AND WITH SO REGAL A HAIRLINE! COULD THIS BE THE HOBO PRINCESS FOR WHOM I HAVE SEARCHED, NAY YEARNED, THESE MANY WEEKS?
NO, BANJO. THAT'S THE HOBO DUCHESS LULU PEPPER.
-SNIFFLE- HELLO, GUMJAMIN.
DUCHESS, MEET MY PROTÉGÉ BANJO BINDLESTUFF! HE'S JUST A REGULAR 'NOTHER HOBO APPRENTICE, NOT NO CLANDESTINE MILLIONAIRE.
YOUR HIGHNESS.
THE DUCHESS IS RESPONSIBLE FOR THE MOST DELICIOUS STONE SOUP I EVER PUT MY MOUTH AROUND. SECRET BEIN' HER STONE SOUP STONE! SHOW HIM, LULU, AND IF A SOUP BREAKS OUT, THEN SO BE IT..
BOO HOO HOO!
MY PRIZED STONE WAS, ALAS, STOLEN. WITHOUT IT, I SHALL CERTAINLY EXPIRE OF STARVATION, A FAR FROM FITTING END FOR A DUCHESS!
OH NO!

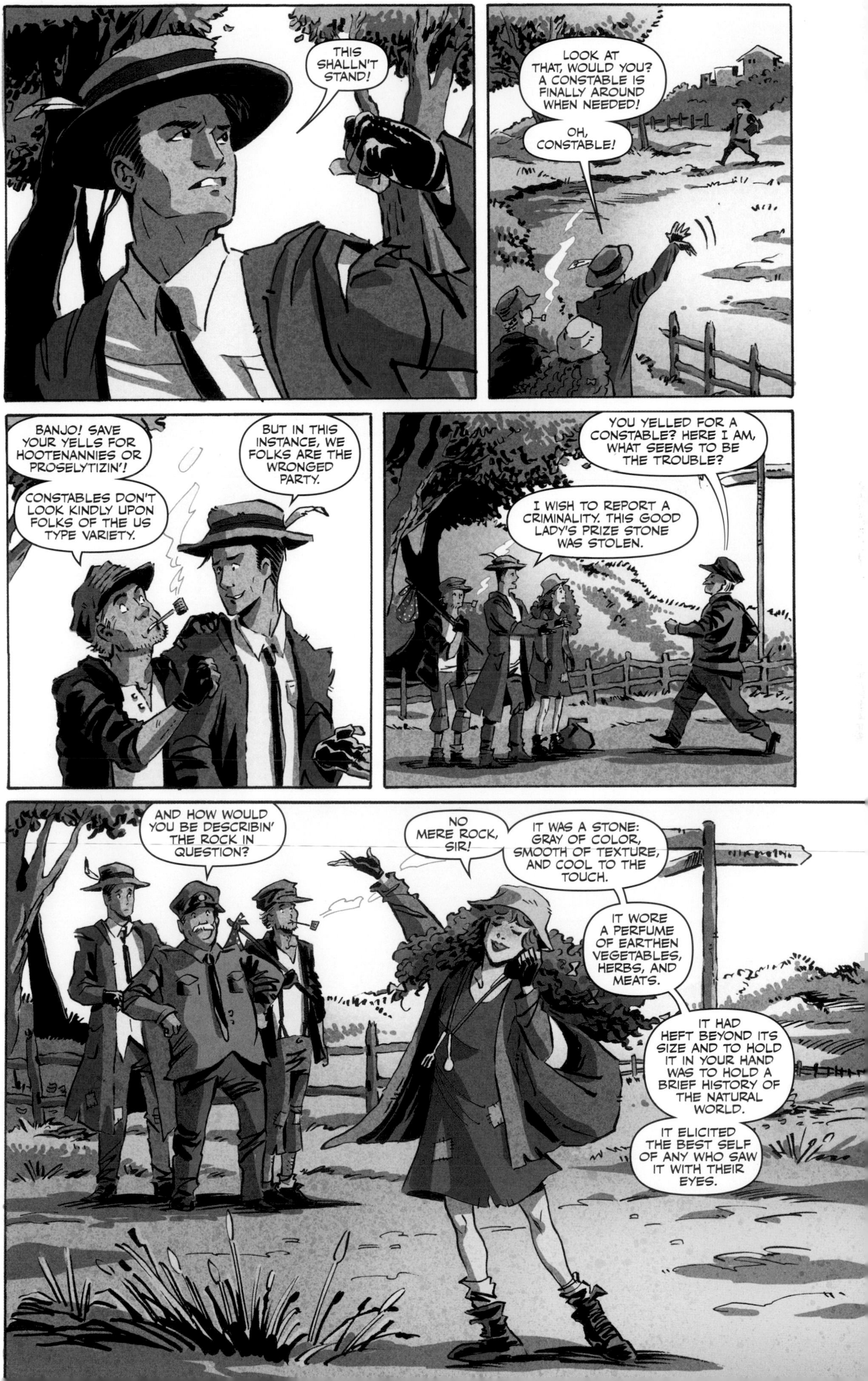
THIS SHALLN'T STAND!
LOOK AT THAT, WOULD YOU? A CONSTABLE IS FINALLY AROUND WHEN NEEDED!
OH, CONSTABLE!
BANJO! SAVE YOUR YELLS FOR HOOTENANNIES OR PROSELYTIZIN'!
CONSTABLES DON'T LOOK KINDLY UPON FOLKS OF THE US TYPE VARIETY.
BUT IN THIS INSTANCE, WE FOLKS ARE THE WRONGED PARTY.
YOU YELLED FOR A CONSTABLE? HERE I AM, WHAT SEEMS TO BE THE TROUBLE?
I WISH TO REPORT A CRIMINALITY. THIS GOOD LADY'S PRIZE STONE WAS STOLEN.
AND HOW WOULD YOU BE DESCRIBIN' THE ROCK IN QUESTION?
NO MERE ROCK, SIR!
IT WAS A STONE: GRAY OF COLOR, SMOOTH OF TEXTURE, AND COOL TO THE TOUCH.
IT WORE A PERFUME OF EARTHEN VEGETABLES, HERBS, AND MEATS.
IT HAD HEFT BEYOND ITS SIZE AND TO HOLD IT IN YOUR HAND WAS TO HOLD A BRIEF HISTORY OF THE NATURAL WORLD.
IT ELICITED THE BEST SELF OF ANY WHO SAW IT WITH THEIR EYES.

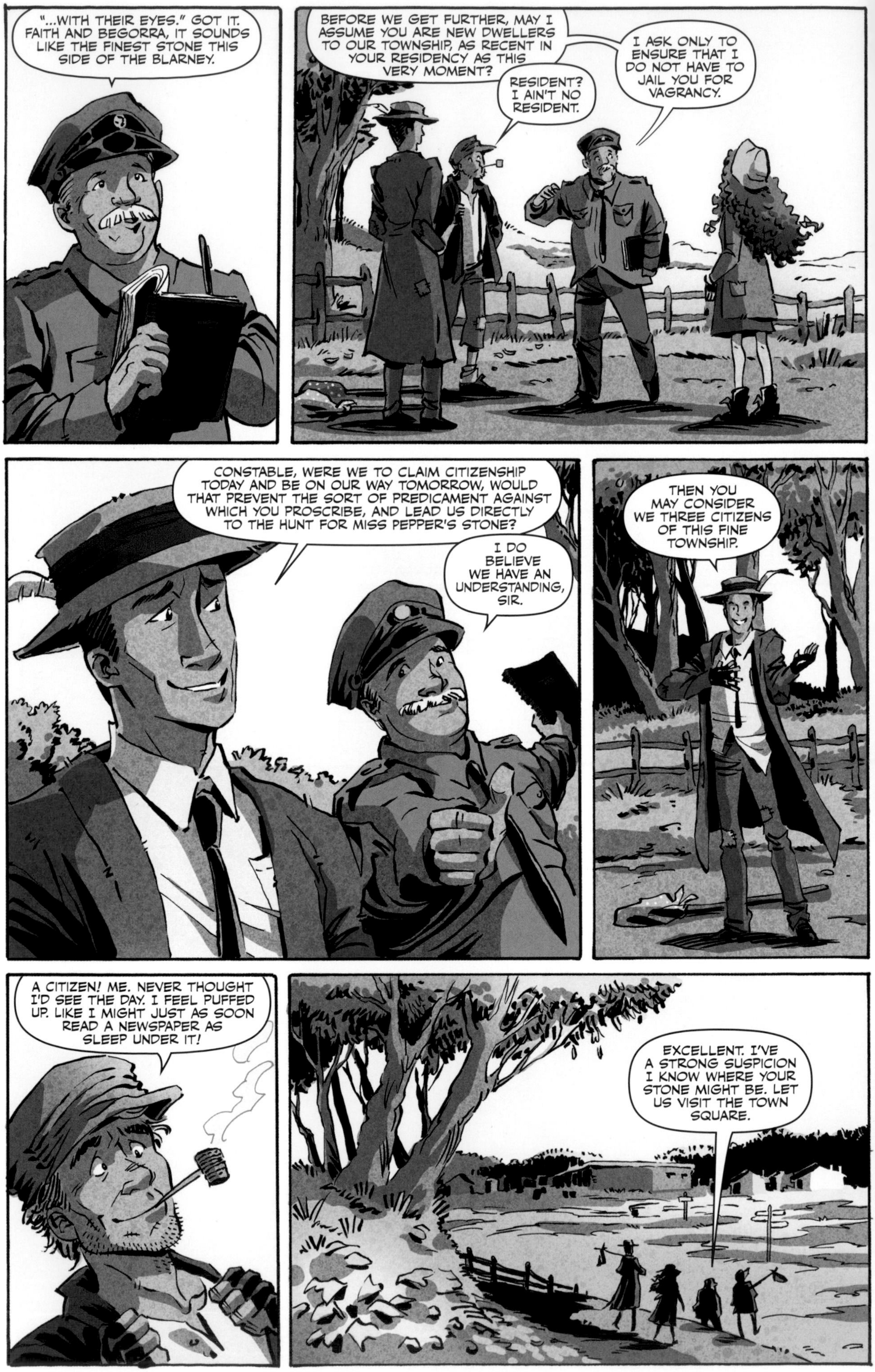
"...WITH THEIR EYES." GOT IT. FAITH AND BEGORRA, IT SOUNDS LIKE THE FINEST STONE THIS SIDE OF THE BLARNEY.
BEFORE WE GET FURTHER, MAY I ASSUME YOU ARE NEW DWELLERS TO OUR TOWNSHIP, AS RECENT IN YOUR RESIDENCY AS THIS VERY MOMENT?
I ASK ONLY TO ENSURE THAT I DO NOT HAVE TO JAIL YOU FOR VAGRANCY.
RESIDENT? I AIN'T NO RESIDENT.
CONSTABLE, WERE WE TO CLAIM CITIZENSHIP TODAY AND BE ON OUR WAY TOMORROW, WOULD THAT PREVENT THE SORT OF PREDICAMENT AGAINST WHICH YOU PROSCRIBE, AND LEAD US DIRECTLY TO THE HUNT FOR MISS PEPPER'S STONE?
I DO BELIEVE WE HAVE AN UNDERSTANDING, SIR.
THEN YOU MAY CONSIDER WE THREE CITIZENS OF THIS FINE TOWNSHIP.
A CITIZEN! ME. NEVER THOUGHT I'D SEE THE DAY. I FEEL PUFFED UP. LIKE I MIGHT JUST AS SOON READ A NEWSPAPER AS SLEEP UNDER IT!
EXCELLENT. I'VE A STRONG SUSPICION I KNOW WHERE YOUR STONE MIGHT BE. LET US VISIT THE TOWN SQUARE.

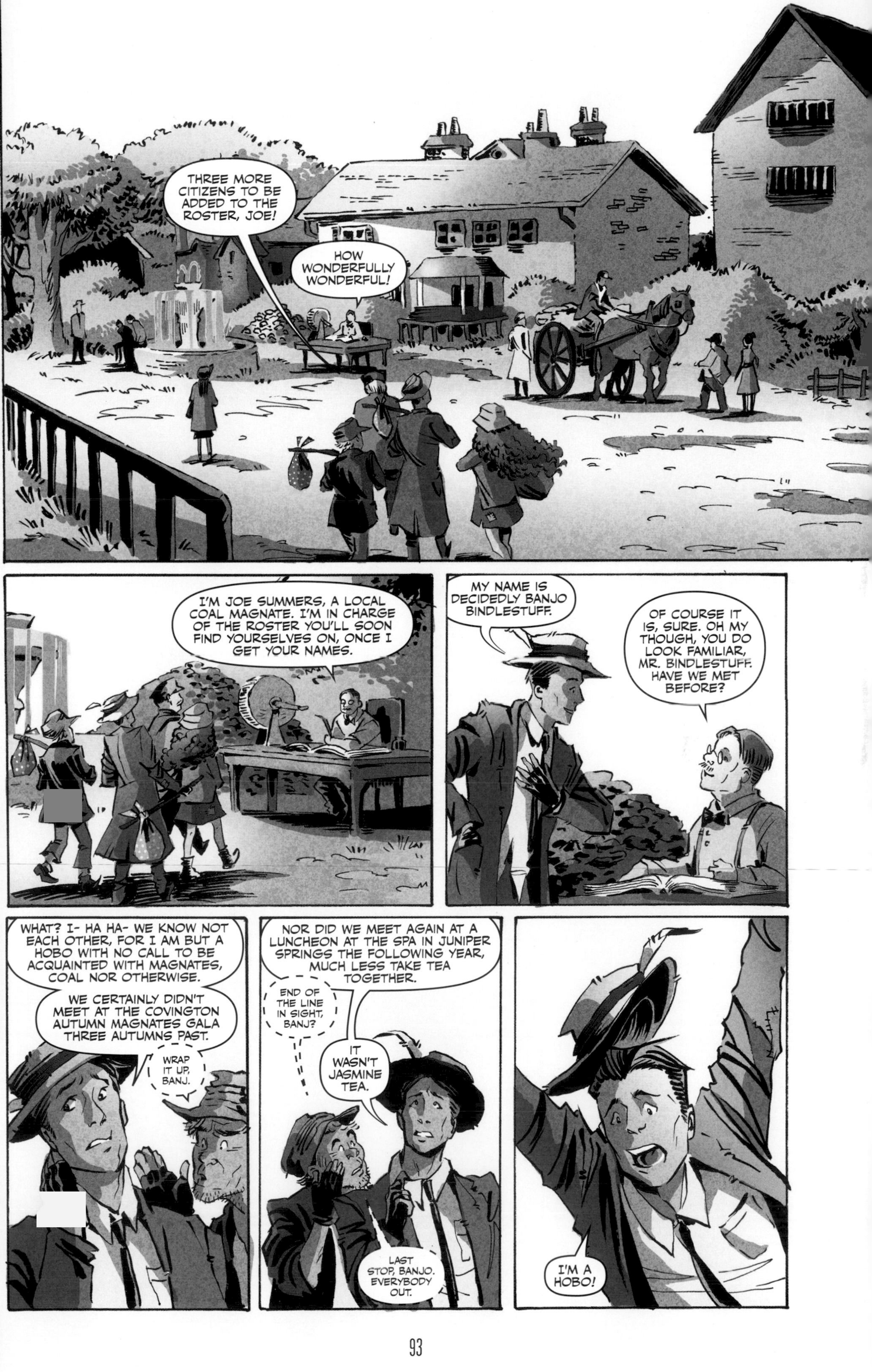
THREE MORE CITIZENS TO BE ADDED TO THE ROSTER, JOE!
HOW WONDERFULLY WONDERFUL!
I'M JOE SUMMERS, A LOCAL COAL MAGNATE. I'M IN CHARGE OF THE ROSTER YOU'LL SOON FIND YOURSELVES ON, ONCE I GET YOUR NAMES.
MY NAME IS DECIDEDLY BANJO BINDLESTUFF.
OF COURSE IT IS, SURE. OH MY THOUGH, YOU DO LOOK FAMILIAR, MR. BINDLESTUFF. HAVE WE MET BEFORE?
WHAT? I- HA HA- WE KNOW NOT EACH OTHER, FOR I AM BUT A HOBO WITH NO CALL TO BE ACQUAINTED WITH MAGNATES, COAL NOR OTHERWISE.
WE CERTAINLY DIDN'T MEET AT THE COVINGTON AUTUMN MAGNATES GALA THREE AUTUMNS PAST.
WRAP IT UP, BANJ.
NOR DID WE MEET AGAIN AT A LUNCHEON AT THE SPA IN JUNIPER SPRINGS THE FOLLOWING YEAR, MUCH LESS TAKE TEA TOGETHER.
END OF THE LINE IN SIGHT, BANJ?
IT WASN'T JASMINE TEA.
LAST STOP, BANJO. EVERYBODY OUT.
I'M A HOBO!

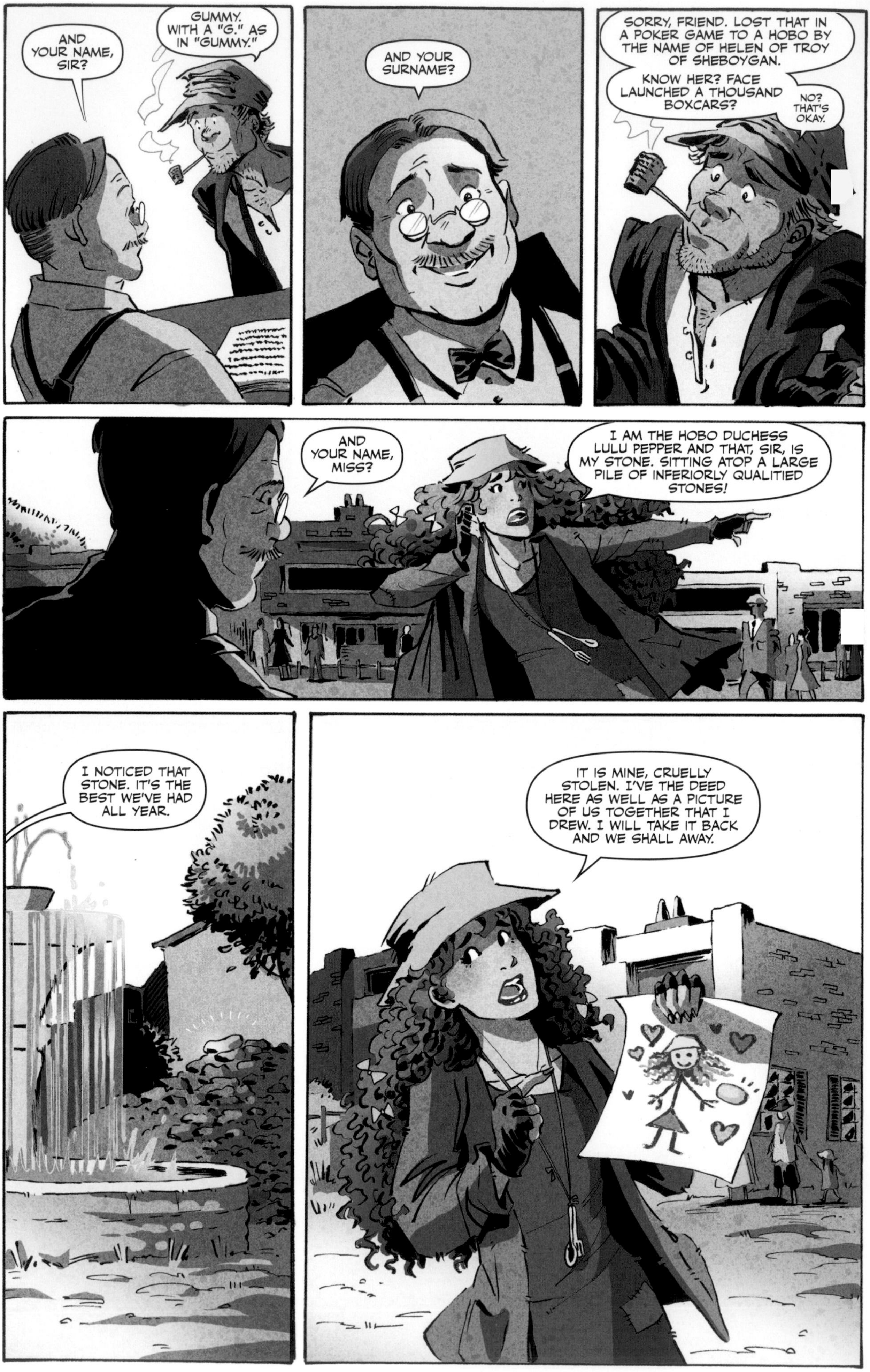
AND YOUR NAME, SIR?
GUMMY. WITH A "G." AS IN "GUMMY."
AND YOUR SURNAME?
SORRY, FRIEND. LOST THAT IN A POKER GAME TO A HOBO BY THE NAME OF HELEN OF TROY OF SHEBOYGAN.
KNOW HER? FACE LAUNCHED A THOUSAND BOXCARS?
NO? THAT'S OKAY.
AND YOUR NAME, MISS?
I AM THE HOBO DUCHESS LULU PEPPER AND THAT, SIR, IS MY STONE. SITTING ATOP A LARGE PILE OF INFERIORLY QUALITIED STONES!
I NOTICED THAT STONE. IT'S THE BEST WE'VE HAD ALL YEAR.
IT IS MINE, CRUELLY STOLEN. I'VE THE DEED HERE AS WELL AS A PICTURE OF US TOGETHER THAT I DREW. I WILL TAKE IT BACK AND WE SHALL AWAY.

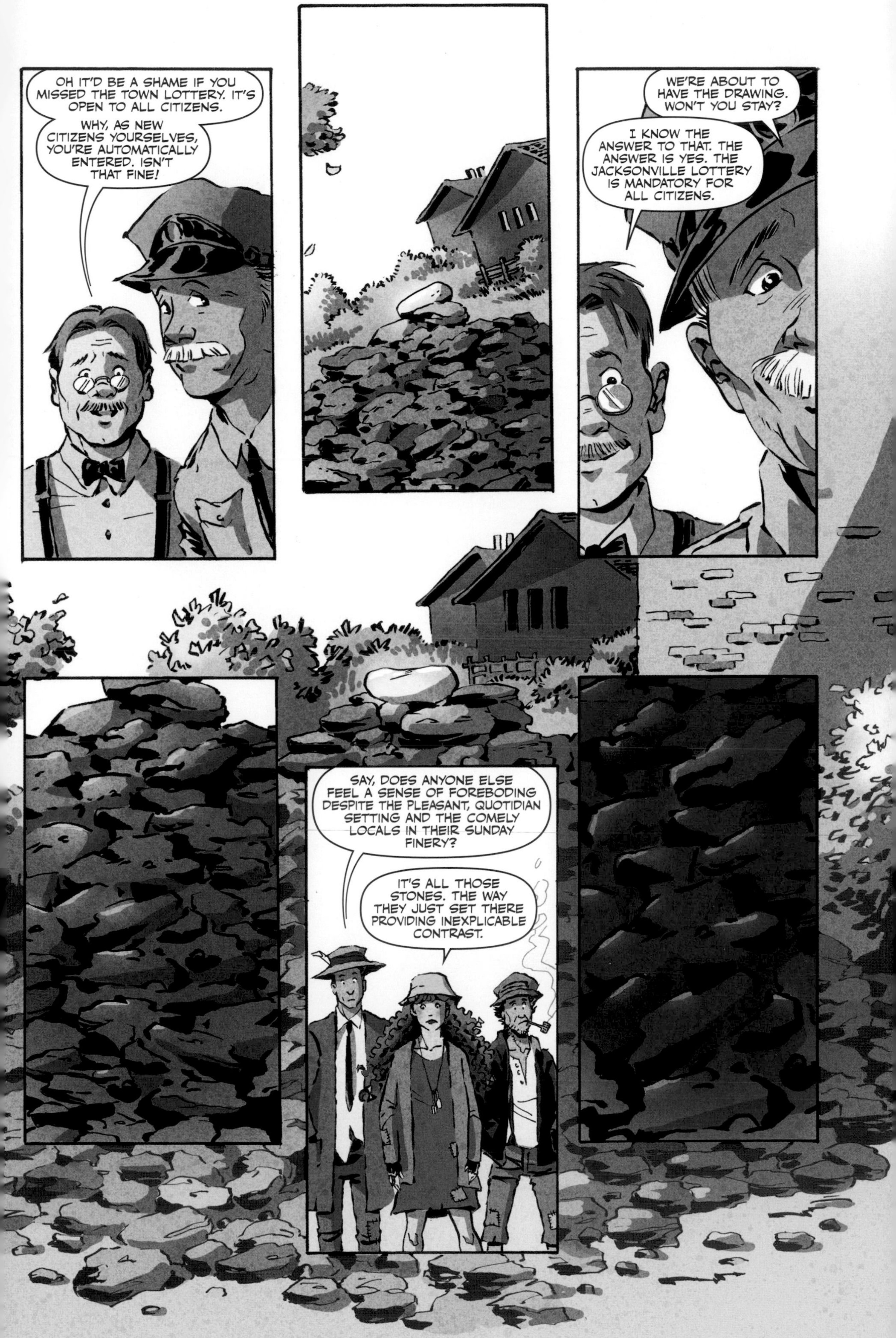
OH IT'D BE A SHAME IF YOU MISSED THE TOWN LOTTERY. IT'S OPEN TO ALL CITIZENS.
WHY, AS NEW CITIZENS YOURSELVES, YOU'RE AUTOMATICALLY ENTERED. ISN'T THAT FINE!
WE'RE ABOUT TO HAVE THE DRAWING. WON'T YOU STAY?
I KNOW THE ANSWER TO THAT. THE ANSWER IS YES. THE JACKSONVILLE LOTTERY IS MANDATORY FOR ALL CITIZENS.
SAY, DOES ANYONE ELSE FEEL A SENSE OF FOREBODING DESPITE THE PLEASANT, QUOTIDIAN SETTING AND THE COMELY LOCALS IN THEIR SUNDAY FINERY?
IT'S ALL THOSE STONES. THE WAY THEY JUST SET THERE PROVIDING INEXPLICABLE CONTRAST.

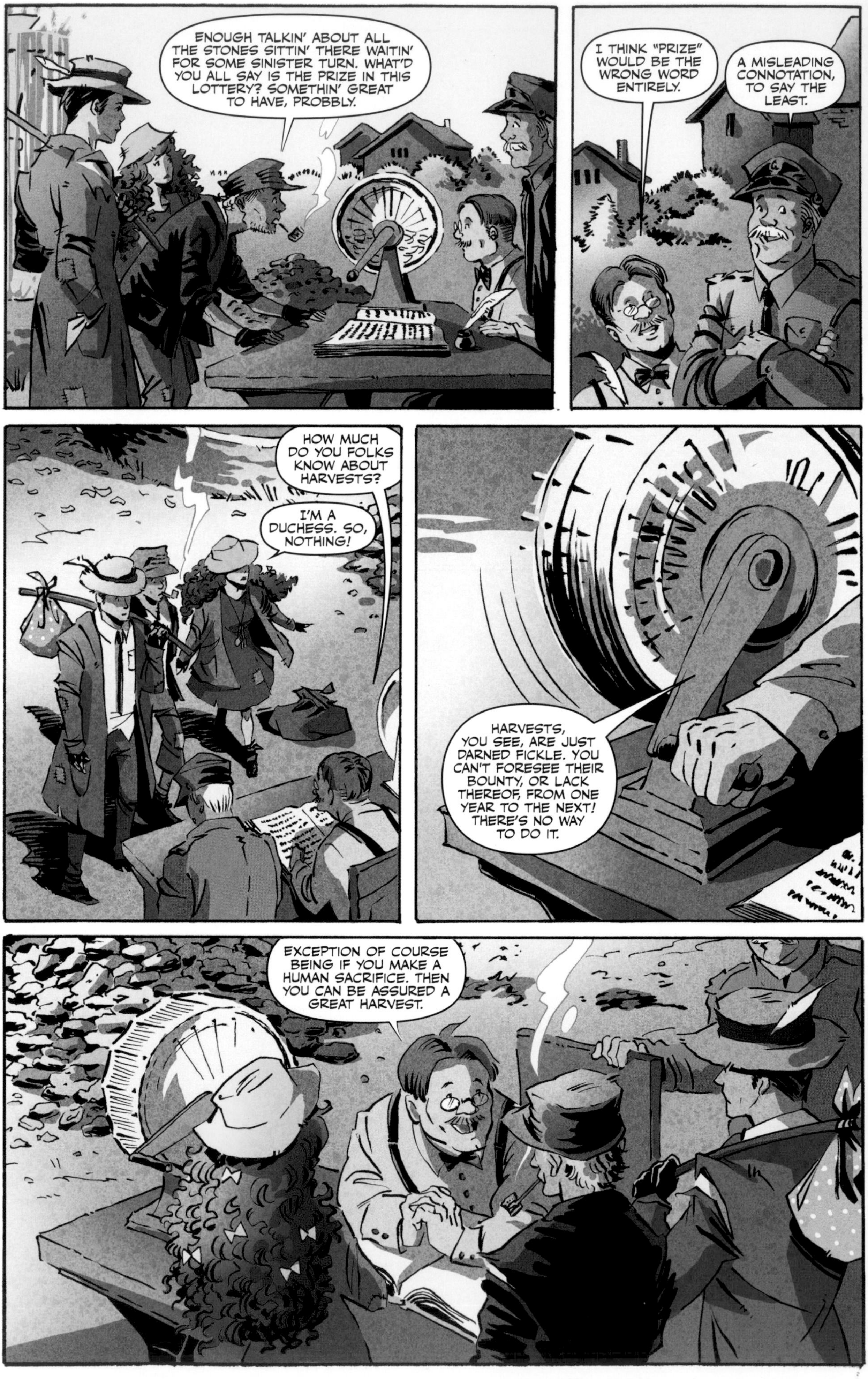
ENOUGH TALKIN' ABOUT ALL THE STONES SITTIN' THERE WAITIN' FOR SOME SINISTER TURN. WHAT'D YOU ALL SAY IS THE PRIZE IN THIS LOTTERY? SOMETHIN' GREAT TO HAVE, PROBBLY.
I THINK "PRIZE" WOULD BE THE WRONG WORD ENTIRELY.
A MISLEADING CONNOTATION, TO SAY THE LEAST.
HOW MUCH DO YOU FOLKS KNOW ABOUT HARVESTS?
I'M A DUCHESS. SO, NOTHING!
HARVESTS, YOU SEE, ARE JUST DARNED FICKLE. YOU CAN'T FORESEE THEIR BOUNTY, OR LACK THEREOF, FROM ONE YEAR TO THE NEXT! THERE'S NO WAY TO DO IT.
EXCEPTION OF COURSE BEING IF YOU MAKE A HUMAN SACRIFICE. THEN YOU CAN BE ASSURED A GREAT HARVEST.

THE LOTTERY SYSTEM IS IN PLACE TO SELECT WHO'LL SERVE AS THE SACRIFICE.

WHUT OH!

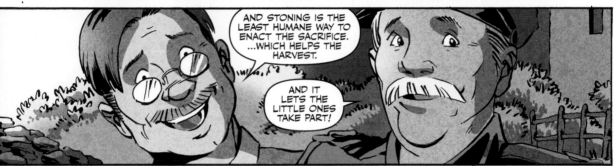

AND STONING IS THE LEAST HUMANE WAY TO ENACT THE SACRIFICE. ...WHICH HELPS THE HARVEST.

AND IT LETS THE LITTLE ONES TAKE PART!

I SUSPECT IT'S TIMMY HANSEN WHO STOLE YOUR ROCK MA'AM. THE HANSEN FAMILY IS WELL KNOWN TO HAVE THE EYE FOR QUALITY MINERALOIDS.

I DID STEAL THE LADY'S ROCK, WHILE SHE WAS JUST A-SLEEPIN'!

HO HO! NOW IT'S THE CARMICHAELS YOU GOTTA WATCH OUT FOR ONCE THE STONING COMMENCES.

GOT ARMS JUST BORN TO THROW.

HA HA HA.

HE'S RIGHT!

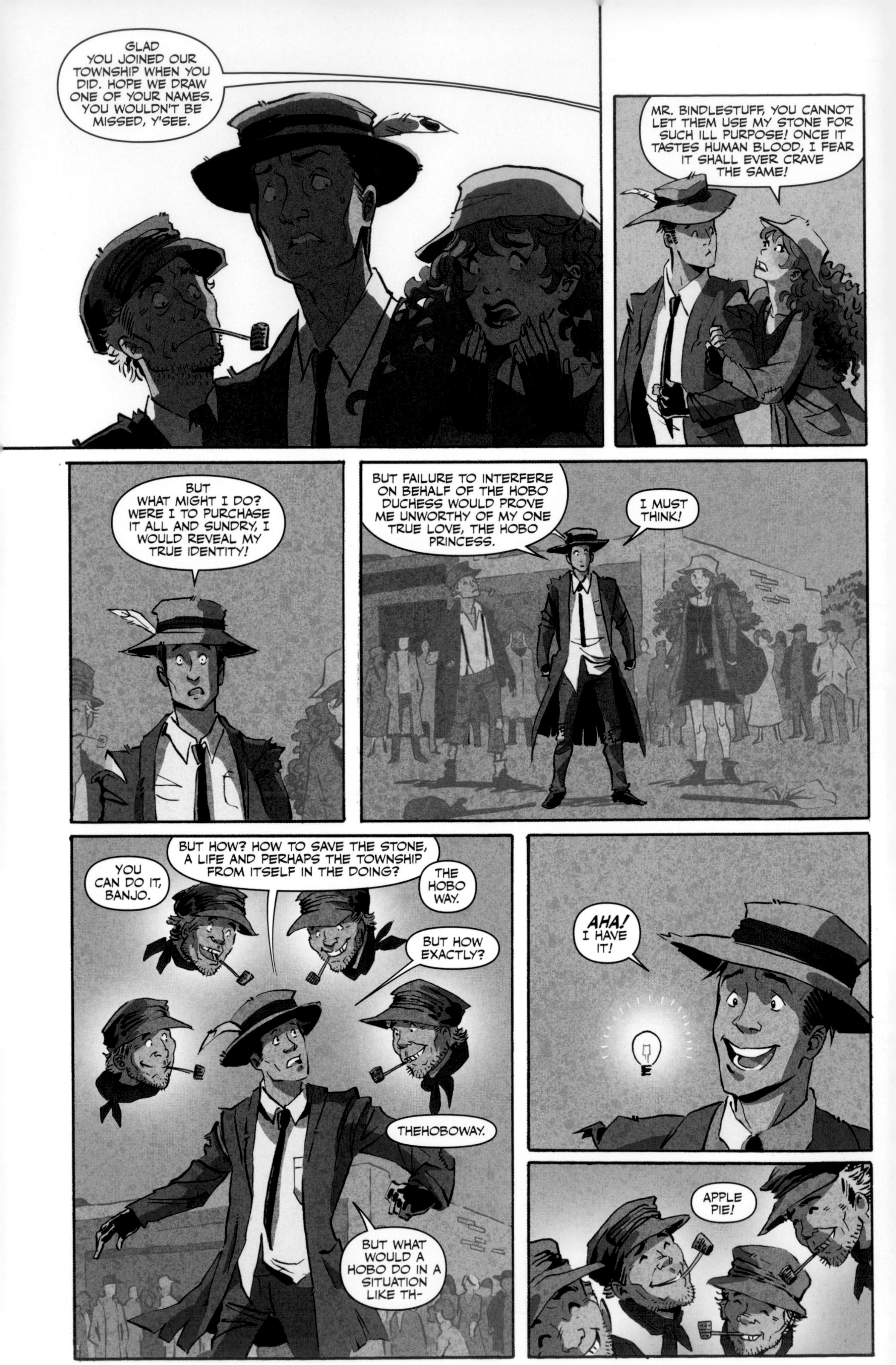
GLAD YOU JOINED OUR TOWNSHIP WHEN YOU DID. HOPE WE DRAW ONE OF YOUR NAMES. YOU WOULDN'T BE MISSED, Y'SEE.
MR. BINDLESTUFF, YOU CANNOT LET THEM USE MY STONE FOR SUCH ILL PURPOSE! ONCE IT TASTES HUMAN BLOOD, I FEAR IT SHALL EVER CRAVE THE SAME!
BUT WHAT MIGHT I DO? WERE I TO PURCHASE IT ALL AND SUNDRY, I WOULD REVEAL MY TRUE IDENTITY!
BUT FAILURE TO INTERFERE ON BEHALF OF THE HOBO DUCHESS WOULD PROVE ME UNWORTHY OF MY ONE TRUE LOVE, THE HOBO PRINCESS.
I MUST THINK!
BUT HOW? HOW TO SAVE THE STONE, A LIFE AND PERHAPS THE TOWNSHIP FROM ITSELF IN THE DOING?
YOU CAN DO IT, BANJO.
THE HOBO WAY.
BUT HOW EXACTLY?
THEHOBOWAY.
BUT WHAT WOULD A HOBO DO IN A SITUATION LIKE TH-
AHA! I HAVE IT!
APPLE PIE!

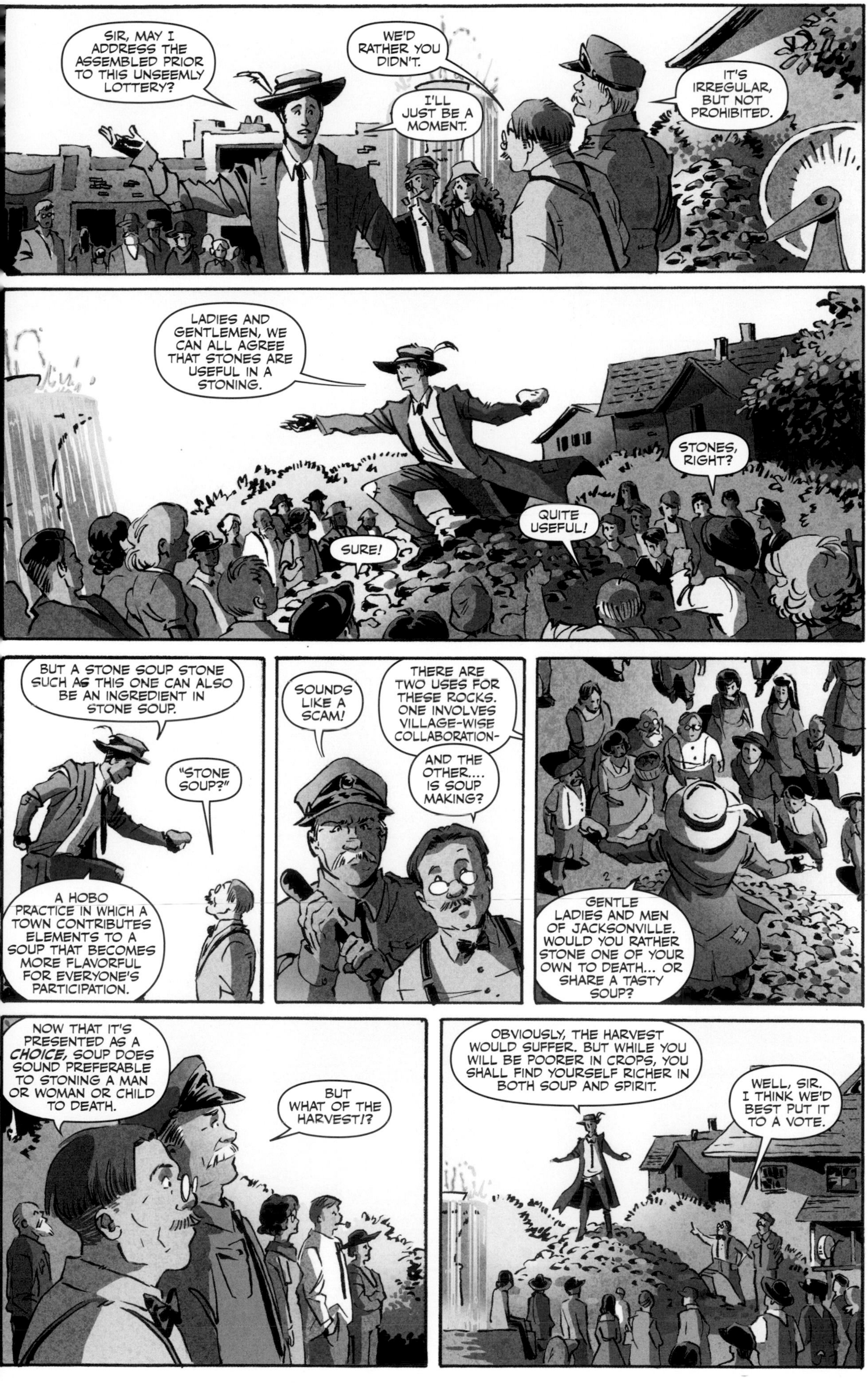
SIR, MAY I ADDRESS THE ASSEMBLED PRIOR TO THIS UNSEEMLY LOTTERY?
WE'D RATHER YOU DIDN'T.
I'LL JUST BE A MOMENT.
IT'S IRREGULAR, BUT NOT PROHIBITED.
LADIES AND GENTLEMEN, WE CAN ALL AGREE THAT STONES ARE USEFUL IN A STONING.
STONES, RIGHT?
QUITE USEFUL!
SURE!
BUT A STONE SOUP STONE SUCH AS THIS ONE CAN ALSO BE AN INGREDIENT IN STONE SOUP.
"STONE SOUP?"
A HOBO PRACTICE IN WHICH A TOWN CONTRIBUTES ELEMENTS TO A SOUP THAT BECOMES MORE FLAVORFUL FOR EVERYONE'S PARTICIPATION.
SOUNDS LIKE A SCAM!
THERE ARE TWO USES FOR THESE ROCKS. ONE INVOLVES VILLAGE-WISE COLLABORATION-
AND THE OTHER.... IS SOUP MAKING?
GENTLE LADIES AND MEN OF JACKSONVILLE. WOULD YOU RATHER STONE ONE OF YOUR OWN TO DEATH... OR SHARE A TASTY SOUP?
NOW THAT IT'S PRESENTED AS A *CHOICE*, SOUP DOES SOUND PREFERABLE TO STONING A MAN OR WOMAN OR CHILD TO DEATH.
BUT WHAT OF THE HARVEST!?
OBVIOUSLY, THE HARVEST WOULD SUFFER. BUT WHILE YOU WILL BE POORER IN CROPS, YOU SHALL FIND YOURSELF RICHER IN BOTH SOUP AND SPIRIT.
WELL, SIR. I THINK WE'D BEST PUT IT TO A VOTE.

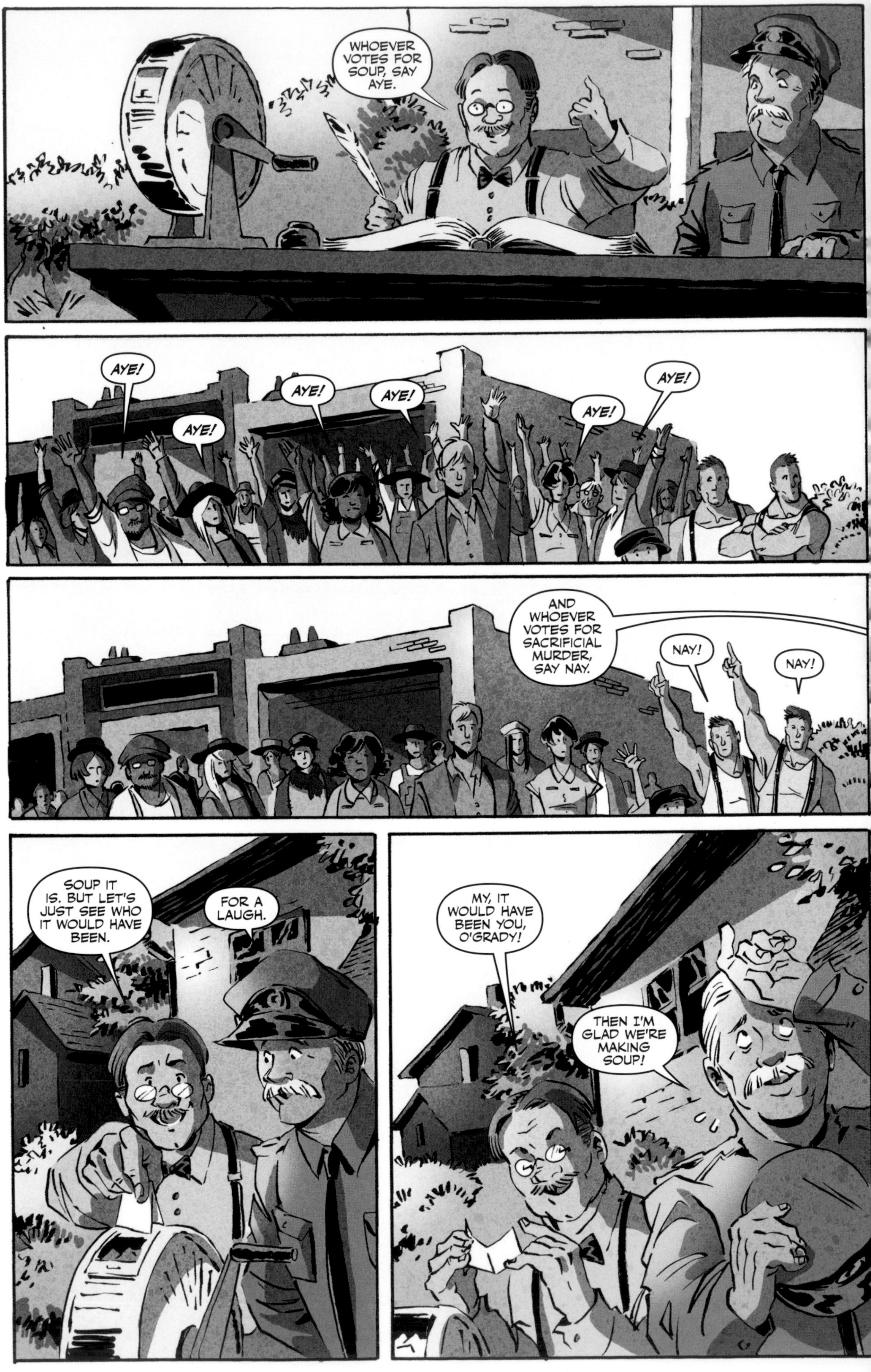
WHOEVER VOTES FOR SOUP, SAY AYE.
AYE!
AYE!
AYE!
AYE!
AYE!
AYE!
AND WHOEVER VOTES FOR SACRIFICIAL MURDER, SAY NAY.
NAY!
NAY!
SOUP IT IS. BUT LET'S JUST SEE WHO IT WOULD HAVE BEEN.
FOR A LAUGH.
MY, IT WOULD HAVE BEEN YOU, O'GRADY!
THEN I'M GLAD WE'RE MAKING SOUP!

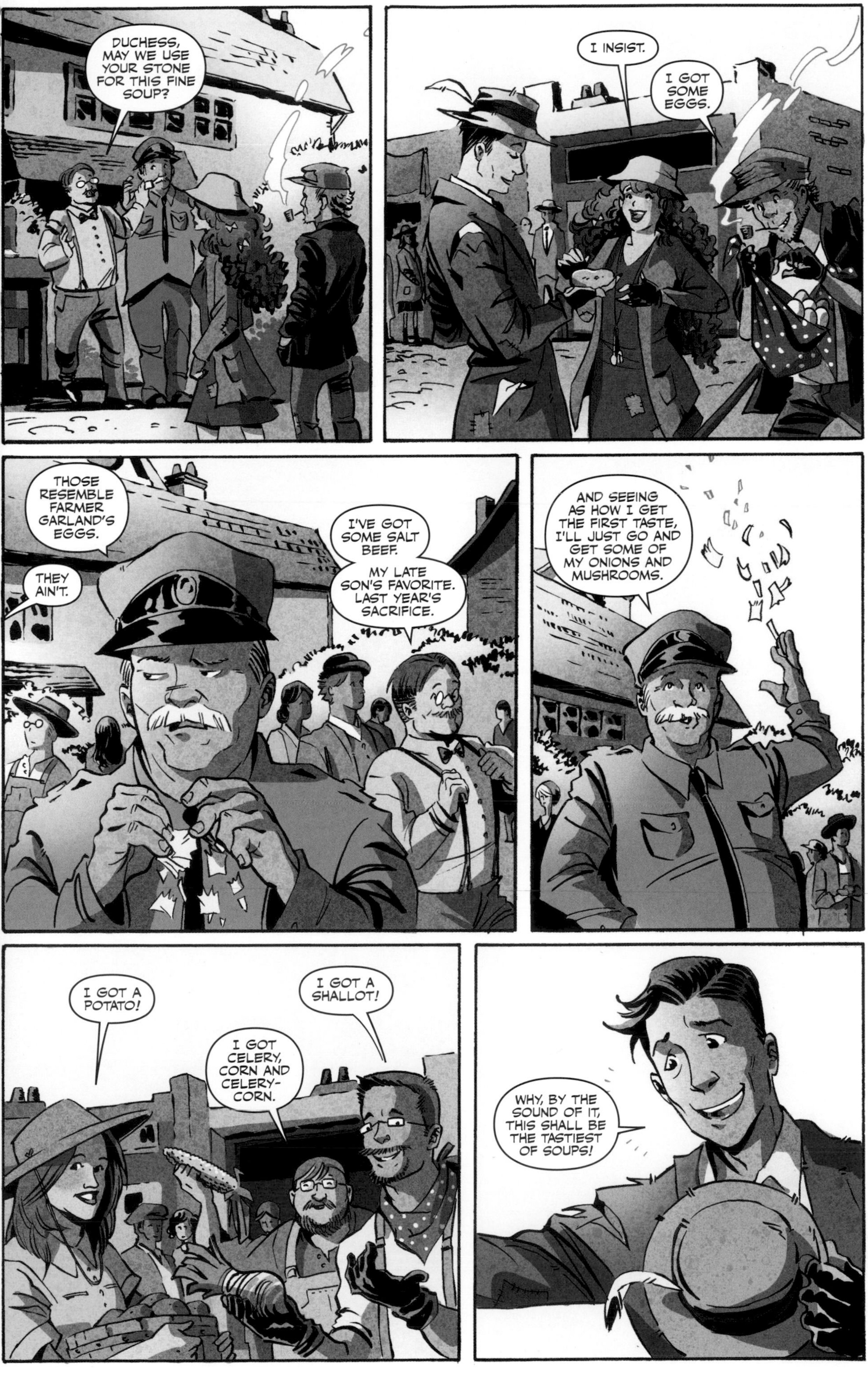
DUCHESS, MAY WE USE YOUR STONE FOR THIS FINE SOUP?
I INSIST.
I GOT SOME EGGS.
THOSE RESEMBLE FARMER GARLAND'S EGGS.
THEY AIN'T.
I'VE GOT SOME SALT BEEF.
MY LATE SON'S FAVORITE. LAST YEAR'S SACRIFICE.
AND SEEING AS HOW I GET THE FIRST TASTE, I'LL JUST GO AND GET SOME OF MY ONIONS AND MUSHROOMS.
I GOT A POTATO!
I GOT A SHALLOT!
I GOT CELERY, CORN AND CELERY-CORN.
WHY, BY THE SOUND OF IT, THIS SHALL BE THE TASTIEST OF SOUPS!

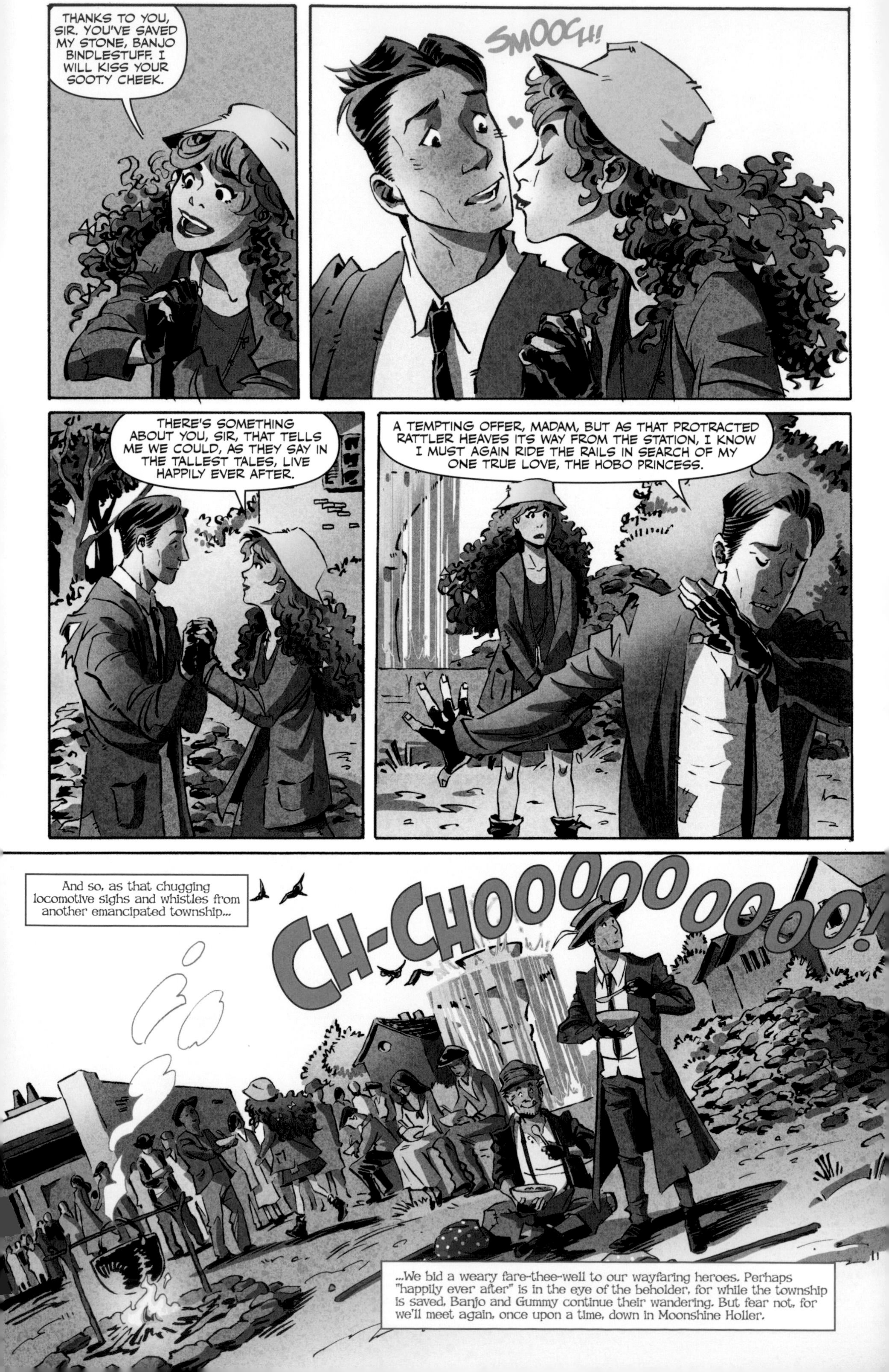
THANKS TO YOU, SIR. YOU'VE SAVED MY STONE, BANJO BINDLESTUFF. I WILL KISS YOUR SOOTY CHEEK.
SMOOCH!
THERE'S SOMETHING ABOUT YOU, SIR, THAT TELLS ME WE COULD, AS THEY SAY IN THE TALLEST TALES, LIVE HAPPILY EVER AFTER.
A TEMPTING OFFER, MADAM, BUT AS THAT PROTRACTED RATTLER HEAVES ITS WAY FROM THE STATION, I KNOW I MUST AGAIN RIDE THE RAILS IN SEARCH OF MY ONE TRUE LOVE, THE HOBO PRINCESS.
And so, as that chugging locomotive sighs and whistles from another emancipated township...
CH-CHOOOOOOOOOO!
...We bid a weary fare-thee-well to our wayfaring heroes. Perhaps "happily ever after" is in the eye of the beholder, for while the township is saved, Banjo and Gummy continue their wandering. But fear not, for we'll meet again, once upon a time, down in Moonshine Holler.

**Amelia EARHART**
FEARLESS FLYER!

WHERE WILL SHE GO NEXT?

Only On The Thrilling Adventure Hour

~BUY~
PATRIOT BRAND
CIGARETTES
~EARN~
PATRIOT POINTS

SEE YOUR LOCAL PATRIOT BRAND CIGARETTE
RETAILER FOR MORE DETAILS.

**Quixotic** TRANSMEDIA
"Entertainment is a meal best served."

DRINK COFFEE

## Patriot Brand Cigarettes Proudly Presents

# ★ BETSY ROSS ★

*America's Founding Mother*

ENJOY THE BRAND
THAT SPARKED A REVOLUTION!

PROUD TO BE AN
AMERICAN ORIGINAL

★★★★★★★★★★★★

When I sewed the stars and stripes, I thought to myself "Betsy, you've nearly peaked. You've got one design left in you old girl, so make it a doozy!"

My doctor agreed. He said if I designed one more thing, my poor heart would give out from the strain. Seconds later, President George Washington phoned and asked me to design the packaging for his new tobacco company, which he founded with Thomas Jefferson and John Quincy Adams! I couldn't say no!

So I designed that one last design and then I died. At my funeral, old George himself declared that design a doozy, and he couldn't tell a lie! So my death was worthwhile after all!

★★★★★★★★★★★★

**TRY PATRIOT BRAND CIGARETTES**

**PATRIOT BRAND** CIGARETTES

THEY'RE GOOD...
FOR YOUR CONSTITUTION.

Patriot Brand Cigarettes is a proud sponsor of Jefferson Reid: Ace American and The Thrilling Adventure Hour.

# COFFINWOOD WHISKEY
EST. 1860

*A Proud Co-Sponsor of The Thrilling Adventure Hour's Beyond Belief*

**❝** I read this repeatedly, laughing all over again. It's that flat-out wonderful and hilarious. Crossing from one medium to another is a ten for difficulty but luckily **Acker and Blacker** have made whole new dimensions in narrative their next frontier. It's *The Thrilling Adventure Hour's* planet and we're lucky to live in it. Like so many others in this book, I'm glad that, after all, we're making soup. **❞**

## Glen David Gold

{Award-worthy author of *Carter Beats the Devil* and *Sunnyside*}

Justice Rides A Rocket Steed

**SPARKS NEVADA**
Marshal on Mars

OUT OF THE THRILLING ADVENTURE HOUR

Brought to you by

# AMELIA EARHART FEARLESS FLIER

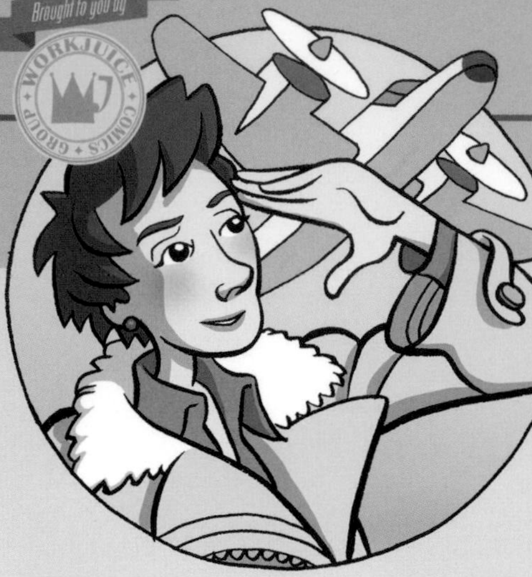

## NEWS ON PARADE!

DATELINE: The wild blue yonder! The question on everyone's lips: What ever happened to Amelia Earhart? The answer in nobody's ears: In 1938 America's soaring sweetheart faked her disappearance at sea in order t serve as the American Victory Commission's covert one-woman air forc

Now, thanks to classified chrono-engineering, Amelia Earhart - the fearless flier - traverses time in her Lockheed Electra in the name of truth, liberty, and the American way!

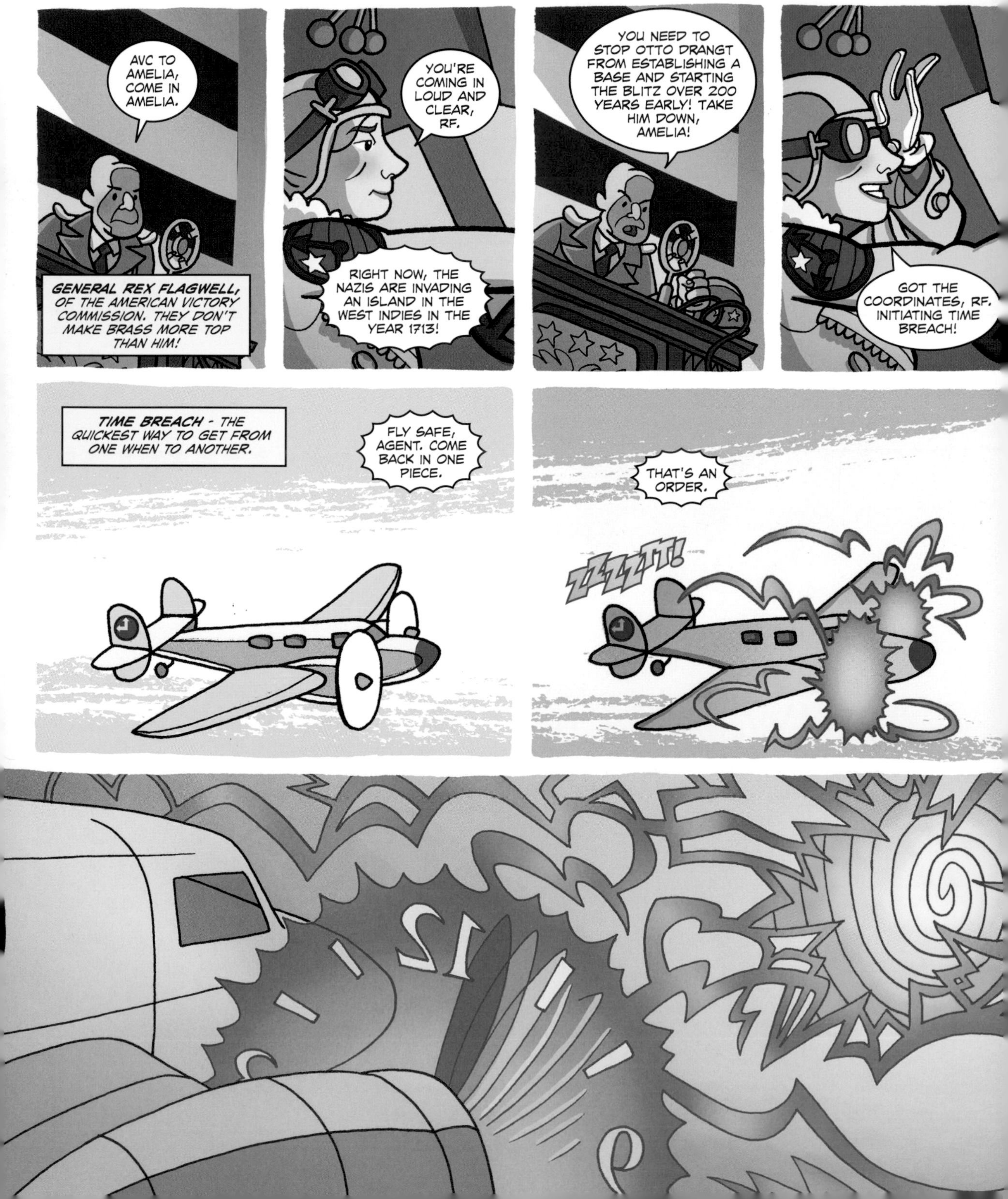

AVC TO AMELIA, COME IN AMELIA.
GENERAL REX FLAGWELL, OF THE AMERICAN VICTORY COMMISSION. THEY DON'T MAKE BRASS MORE TOP THAN HIM!
YOU'RE COMING IN LOUD AND CLEAR, RF.
RIGHT NOW, THE NAZIS ARE INVADING AN ISLAND IN THE WEST INDIES IN THE YEAR 1713!
YOU NEED TO STOP OTTO DRANGT FROM ESTABLISHING A BASE AND STARTING THE BLITZ OVER 200 YEARS EARLY! TAKE HIM DOWN, AMELIA!
GOT THE COORDINATES, RF. INITIATING TIME BREACH!
TIME BREACH - THE QUICKEST WAY TO GET FROM ONE WHEN TO ANOTHER.
FLY SAFE, AGENT. COME BACK IN ONE PIECE.
THAT'S AN ORDER.
ZZZZT!

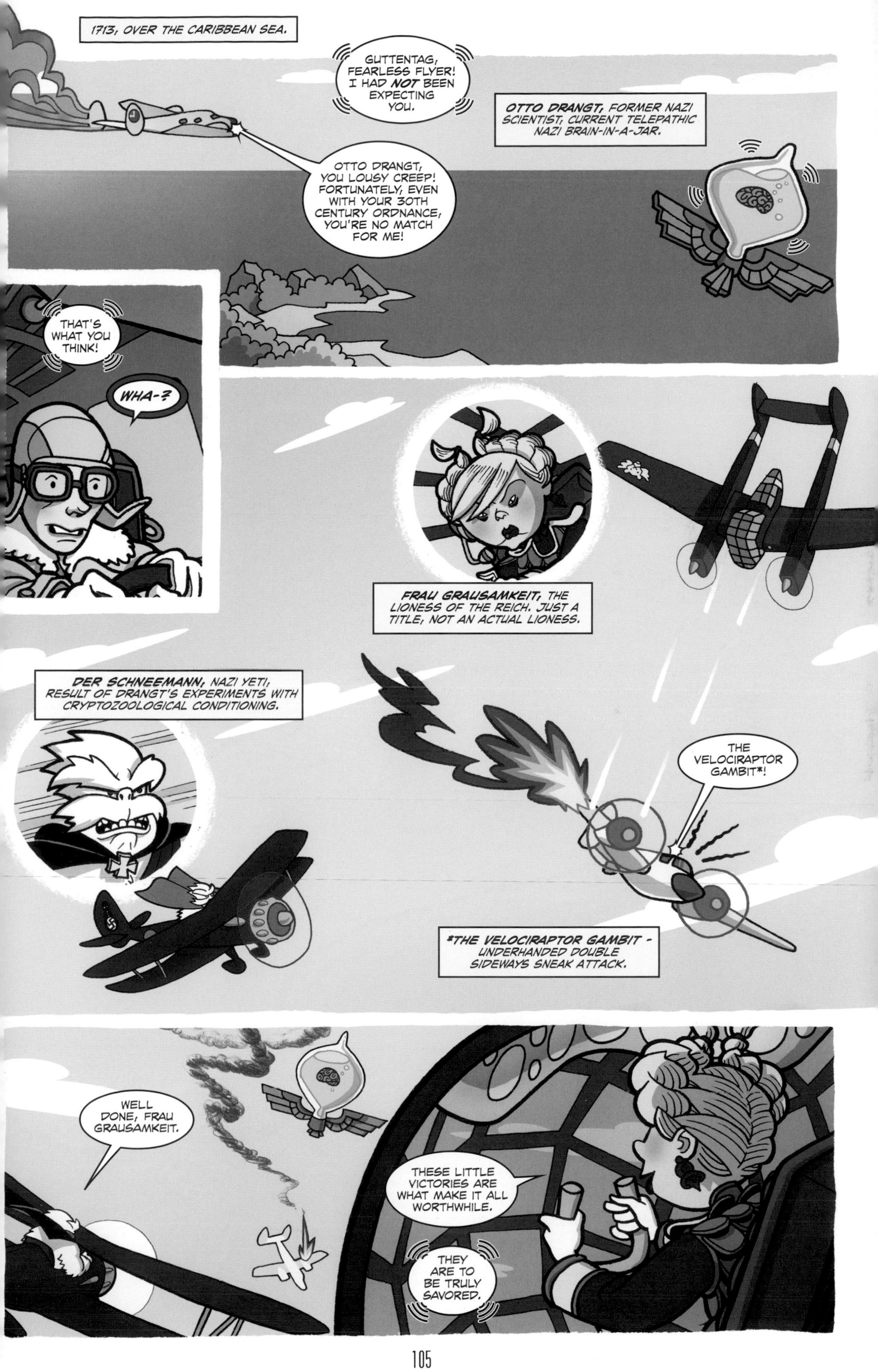
1713, OVER THE CARIBBEAN SEA.
GUTTENTAG, FEARLESS FLYER! I HAD NOT BEEN EXPECTING YOU.
OTTO DRANGT, FORMER NAZI SCIENTIST, CURRENT TELEPATHIC NAZI BRAIN-IN-A-JAR.
OTTO DRANGT, YOU LOUSY CREEP! FORTUNATELY, EVEN WITH YOUR 30TH CENTURY ORDNANCE, YOU'RE NO MATCH FOR ME!
THAT'S WHAT YOU THINK!
WHA-?
FRAU GRAUSAMKEIT, THE LIONESS OF THE REICH. JUST A TITLE, NOT AN ACTUAL LIONESS.
DER SCHNEEMANN, NAZI YETI, RESULT OF DRANGT'S EXPERIMENTS WITH CRYPTOZOOLOGICAL CONDITIONING.
THE VELOCIRAPTOR GAMBIT*!
*THE VELOCIRAPTOR GAMBIT - UNDERHANDED DOUBLE SIDEWAYS SNEAK ATTACK.
WELL DONE, FRAU GRAUSAMKEIT.
THESE LITTLE VICTORIES ARE WHAT MAKE IT ALL WORTHWHILE.
THEY ARE TO BE TRULY SAVORED.

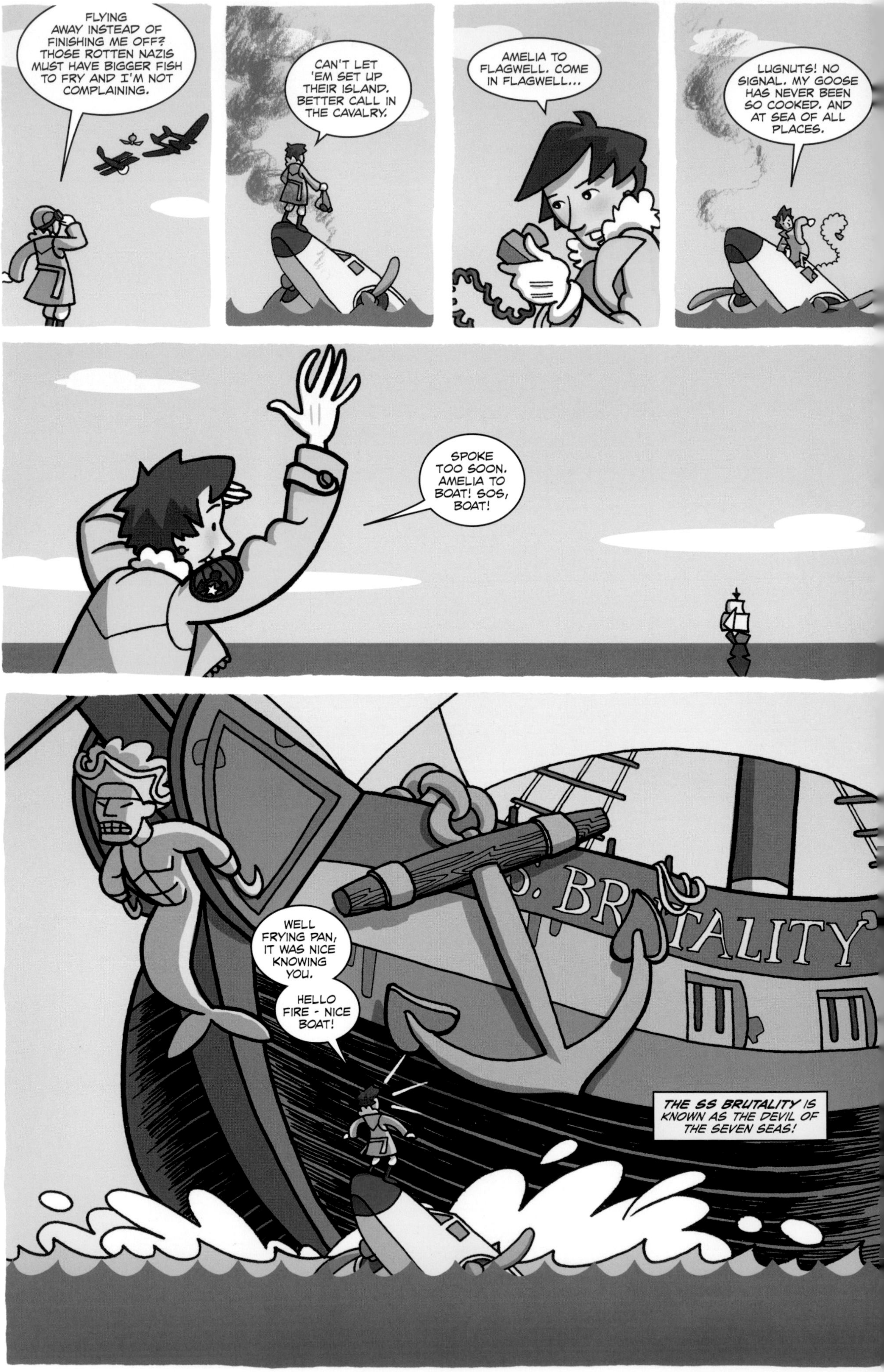
FLYING AWAY INSTEAD OF FINISHING ME OFF? THOSE ROTTEN NAZIS MUST HAVE BIGGER FISH TO FRY AND I'M NOT COMPLAINING.
CAN'T LET 'EM SET UP THEIR ISLAND. BETTER CALL IN THE CAVALRY.
AMELIA TO FLAGWELL. COME IN FLAGWELL...
LUGNUTS! NO SIGNAL. MY GOOSE HAS NEVER BEEN SO COOKED. AND AT SEA OF ALL PLACES.
SPOKE TOO SOON. AMELIA TO BOAT! SOS, BOAT!
WELL FRYING PAN, IT WAS NICE KNOWING YOU.
HELLO FIRE - NICE BOAT!
*THE SS BRUTALITY* IS KNOWN AS THE DEVIL OF THE SEVEN SEAS!

AHOY! I'M AMELIA EARHART, FEARLESS FLYER.

AND YOU MUST BE PIRATES.

YO HO?

ARRR?

THIS BOAT BE MINE AND WHILE YOU'RE UPON HER, YOU BE MINE AS WELL, FOR I BE CAPTAIN—

BAM!

CAPT... LOATHED PI... CAPTAIN EVE... TO COMMAND A SHIP.

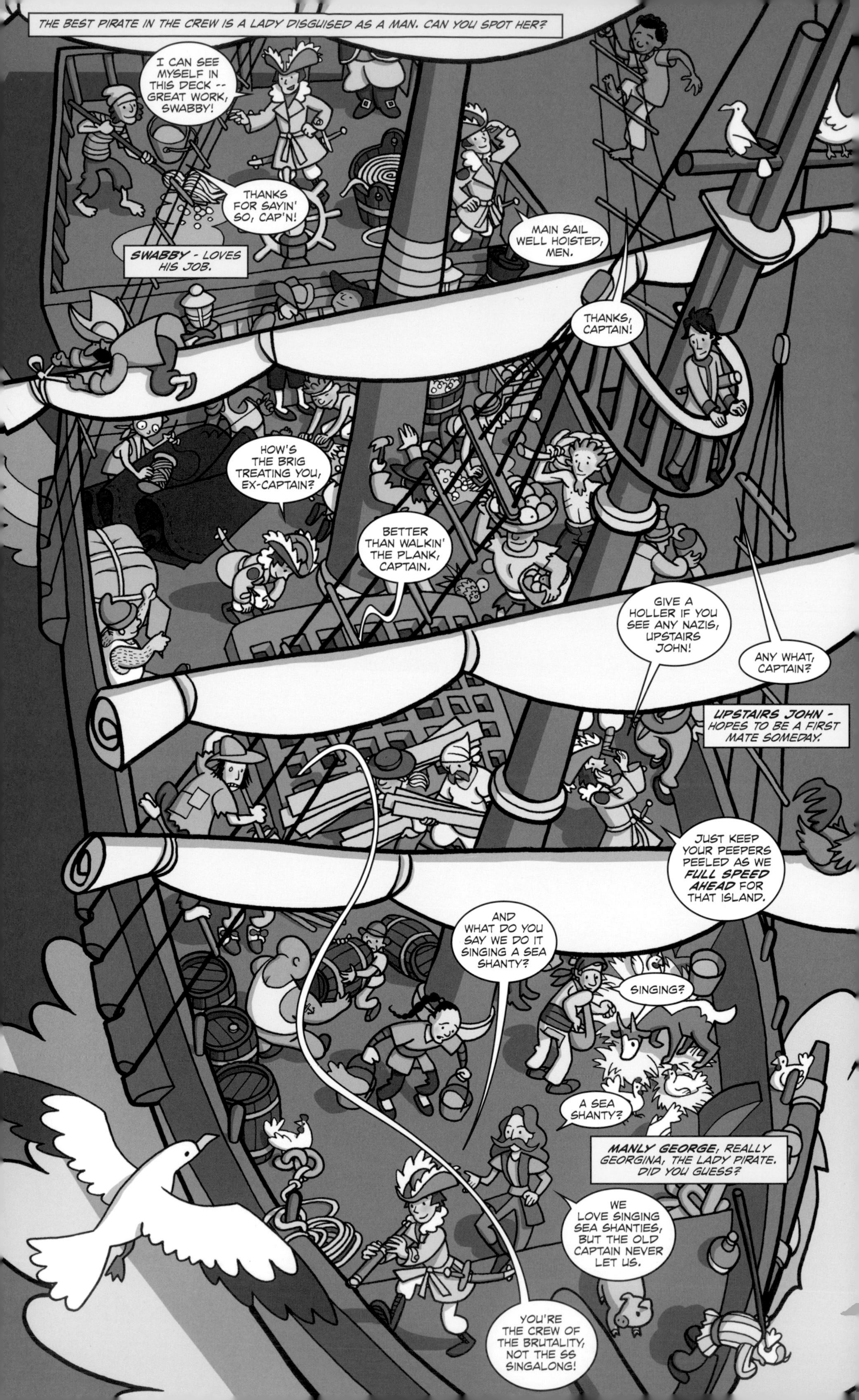
THE BEST PIRATE IN THE CREW IS A LADY DISGUISED AS A MAN. CAN YOU SPOT HER?
I CAN SEE MYSELF IN THIS DECK -- GREAT WORK, SWABBY!
THANKS FOR SAYIN' SO, CAP'N!
SWABBY - LOVES HIS JOB.
MAIN SAIL WELL HOISTED, MEN.
THANKS, CAPTAIN!
HOW'S THE BRIG TREATING YOU, EX-CAPTAIN?
BETTER THAN WALKIN' THE PLANK, CAPTAIN.
GIVE A HOLLER IF YOU SEE ANY NAZIS, UPSTAIRS JOHN!
ANY WHAT, CAPTAIN?
UPSTAIRS JOHN - HOPES TO BE A FIRST MATE SOMEDAY.
JUST KEEP YOUR PEEPERS PEELED AS WE FULL SPEED AHEAD FOR THAT ISLAND.
AND WHAT DO YOU SAY WE DO IT SINGING A SEA SHANTY?
SINGING?
A SEA SHANTY?
MANLY GEORGE, REALLY GEORGINA, THE LADY PIRATE. DID YOU GUESS?
WE LOVE SINGING SEA SHANTIES, BUT THE OLD CAPTAIN NEVER LET US.
YOU'RE THE CREW OF THE BRUTALITY, NOT THE SS SINGALONG!

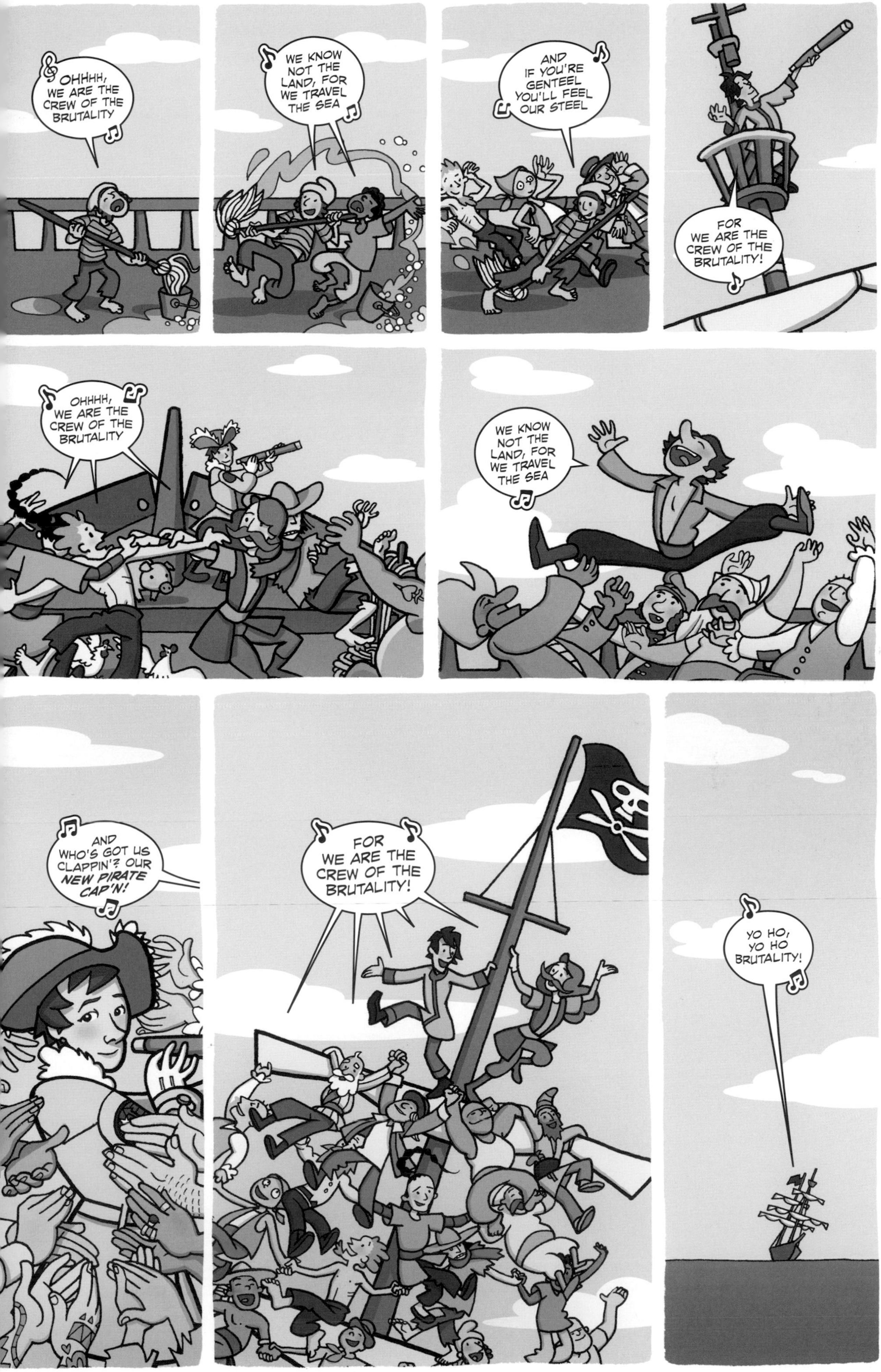
OHHHH, WE ARE THE CREW OF THE BRUTALITY
WE KNOW NOT THE LAND, FOR WE TRAVEL THE SEA
AND IF YOU'RE GENTEEL YOU'LL FEEL OUR STEEL
FOR WE ARE THE CREW OF THE BRUTALITY!
OHHHH, WE ARE THE CREW OF THE BRUTALITY
WE KNOW NOT THE LAND, FOR WE TRAVEL THE SEA
AND WHO'S GOT US CLAPPIN'? OUR NEW PIRATE CAP'N!
FOR WE ARE THE CREW OF THE BRUTALITY!
YO HO, YO HO BRUTALITY!

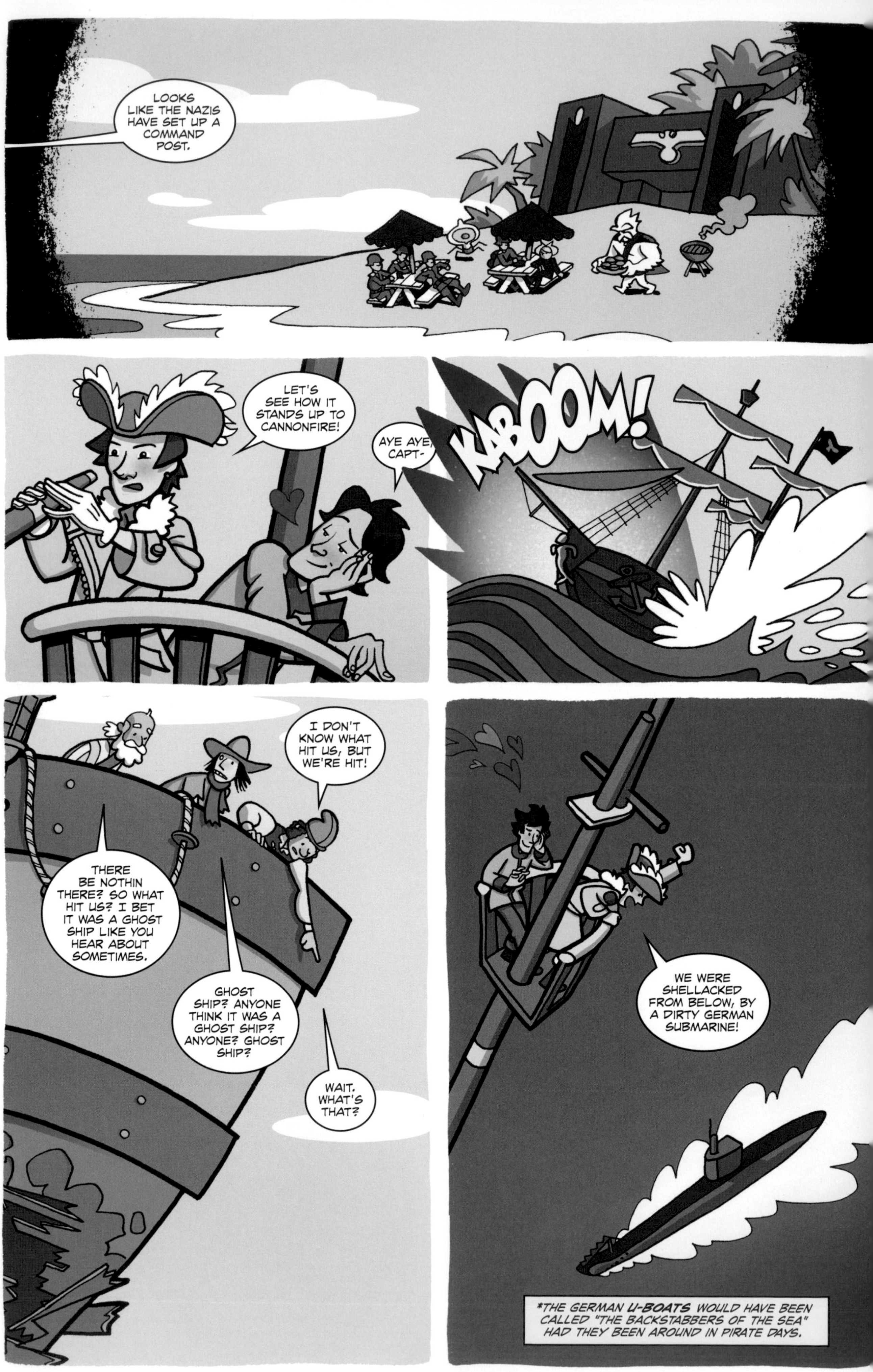
LOOKS LIKE THE NAZIS HAVE SET UP A COMMAND POST.
LET'S SEE HOW IT STANDS UP TO CANNONFIRE!
AYE AYE, CAPT-
KABOOM!
I DON'T KNOW WHAT HIT US, BUT WE'RE HIT!
THERE BE NOTHIN THERE? SO WHAT HIT US? I BET IT WAS A GHOST SHIP LIKE YOU HEAR ABOUT SOMETIMES.
GHOST SHIP? ANYONE THINK IT WAS A GHOST SHIP? ANYONE? GHOST SHIP?
WAIT. WHAT'S THAT?
WE WERE SHELLACKED FROM BELOW, BY A DIRTY GERMAN SUBMARINE!
*THE GERMAN U-BOATS WOULD HAVE BEEN CALLED "THE BACKSTABBERS OF THE SEA" HAD THEY BEEN AROUND IN PIRATE DAYS.

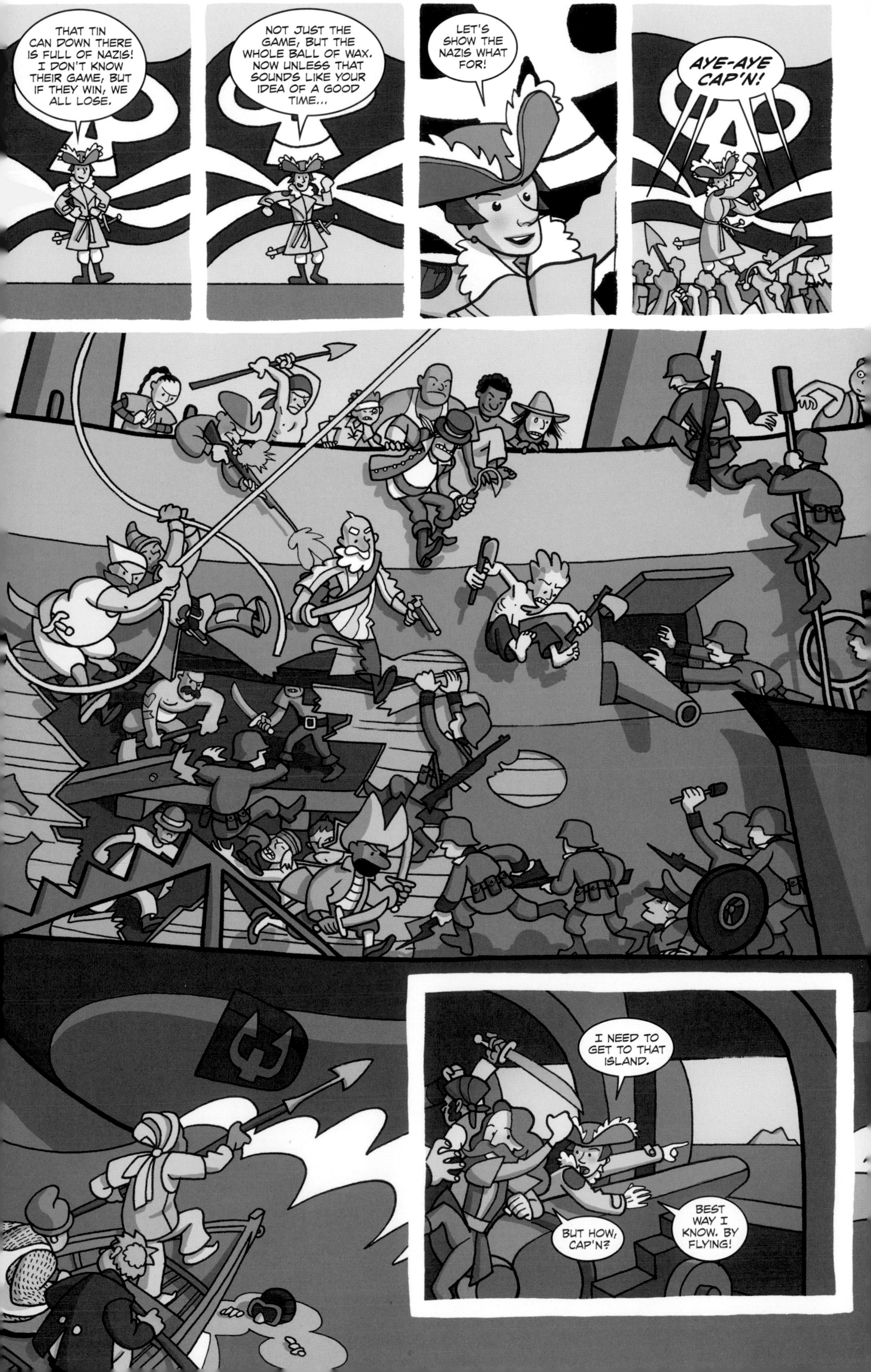
THAT TIN CAN DOWN THERE IS FULL OF NAZIS! I DON'T KNOW THEIR GAME, BUT IF THEY WIN, WE ALL LOSE.
NOT JUST THE GAME, BUT THE WHOLE BALL OF WAX. NOW UNLESS THAT SOUNDS LIKE YOUR IDEA OF A GOOD TIME...
LET'S SHOW THE NAZIS WHAT FOR!
AYE-AYE CAP'N!
I NEED TO GET TO THAT ISLAND.
BUT HOW, CAP'N?
BEST WAY I KNOW. BY FLYING!

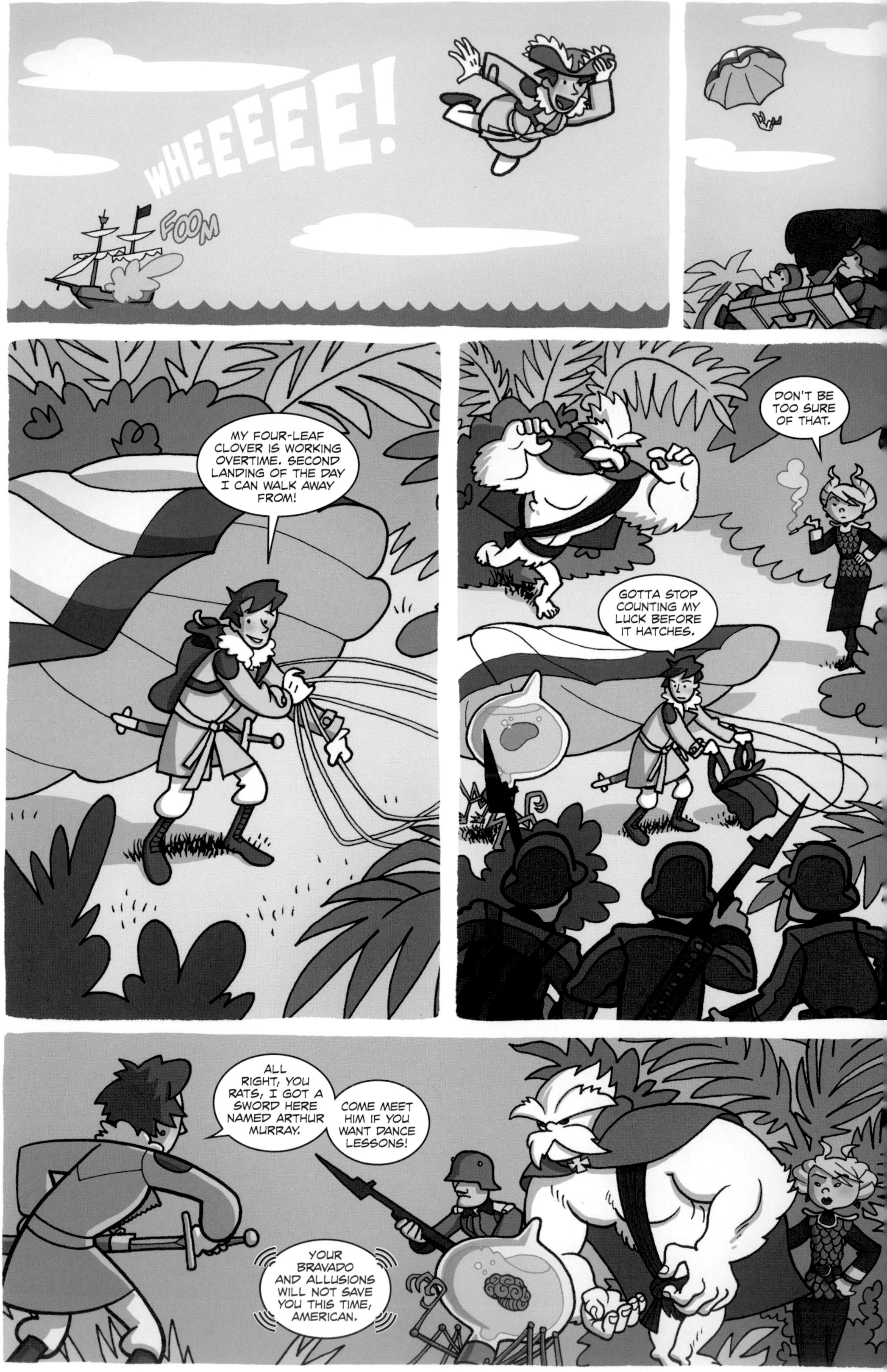
WHEEEEEE!
FOOM
MY FOUR-LEAF CLOVER IS WORKING OVERTIME. SECOND LANDING OF THE DAY I CAN WALK AWAY FROM!
DON'T BE TOO SURE OF THAT.
GOTTA STOP COUNTING MY LUCK BEFORE IT HATCHES.
ALL RIGHT, YOU RATS, I GOT A SWORD HERE NAMED ARTHUR MURRAY.
COME MEET HIM IF YOU WANT DANCE LESSONS!
YOUR BRAVADO AND ALLUSIONS WILL NOT SAVE YOU THIS TIME, AMERICAN.

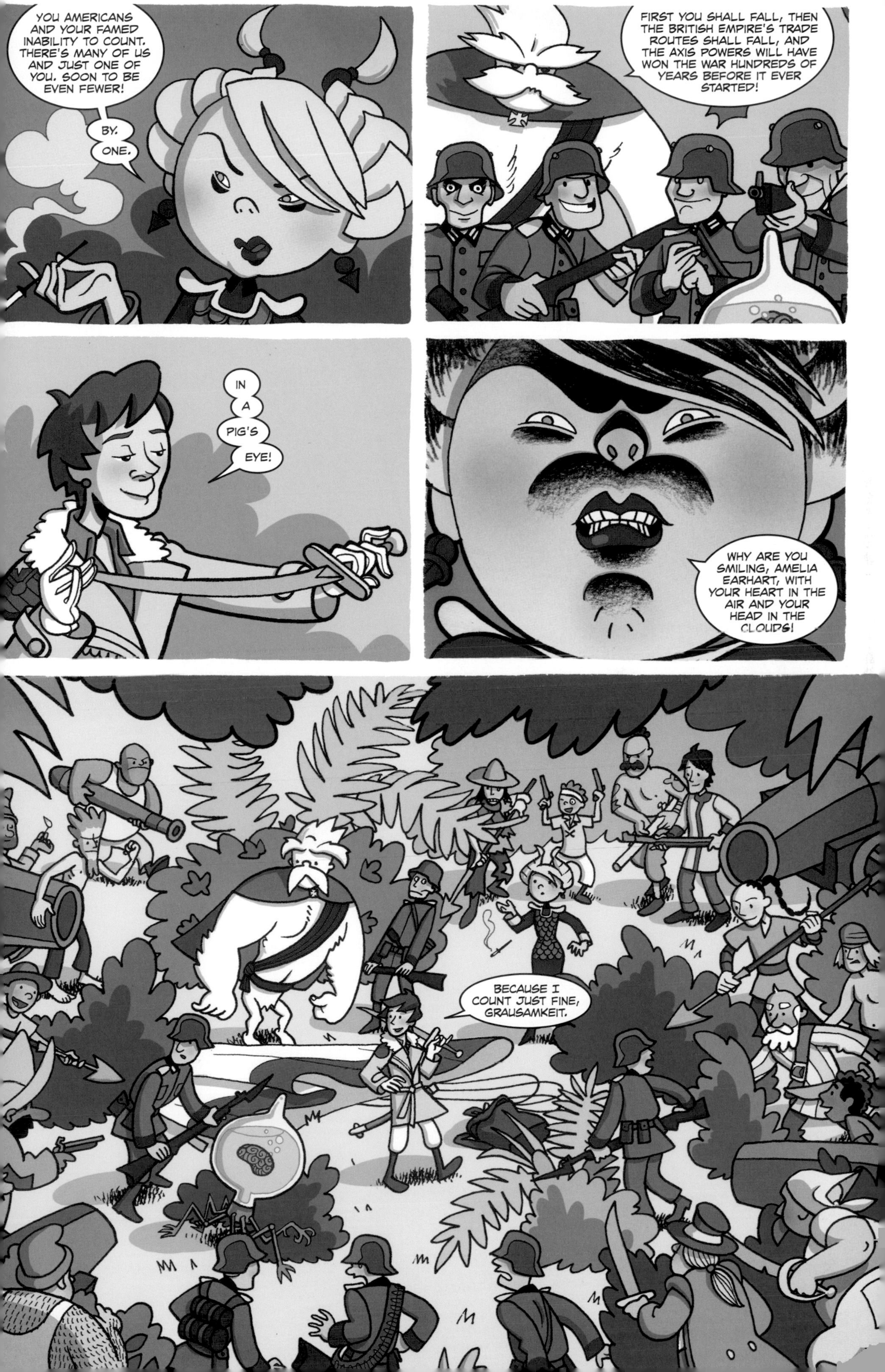
YOU AMERICANS AND YOUR FAMED INABILITY TO COUNT. THERE'S MANY OF US AND JUST ONE OF YOU. SOON TO BE EVEN FEWER!
BY.
ONE.
FIRST YOU SHALL FALL, THEN THE BRITISH EMPIRE'S TRADE ROUTES SHALL FALL, AND THE AXIS POWERS WILL HAVE WON THE WAR HUNDREDS OF YEARS BEFORE IT EVER STARTED!
IN
A
PIG'S
EYE!
WHY ARE YOU SMILING, AMELIA EARHART, WITH YOUR HEART IN THE AIR AND YOUR HEAD IN THE CLOUDS!
BECAUSE I COUNT JUST FINE, GRAUSAMKEIT.

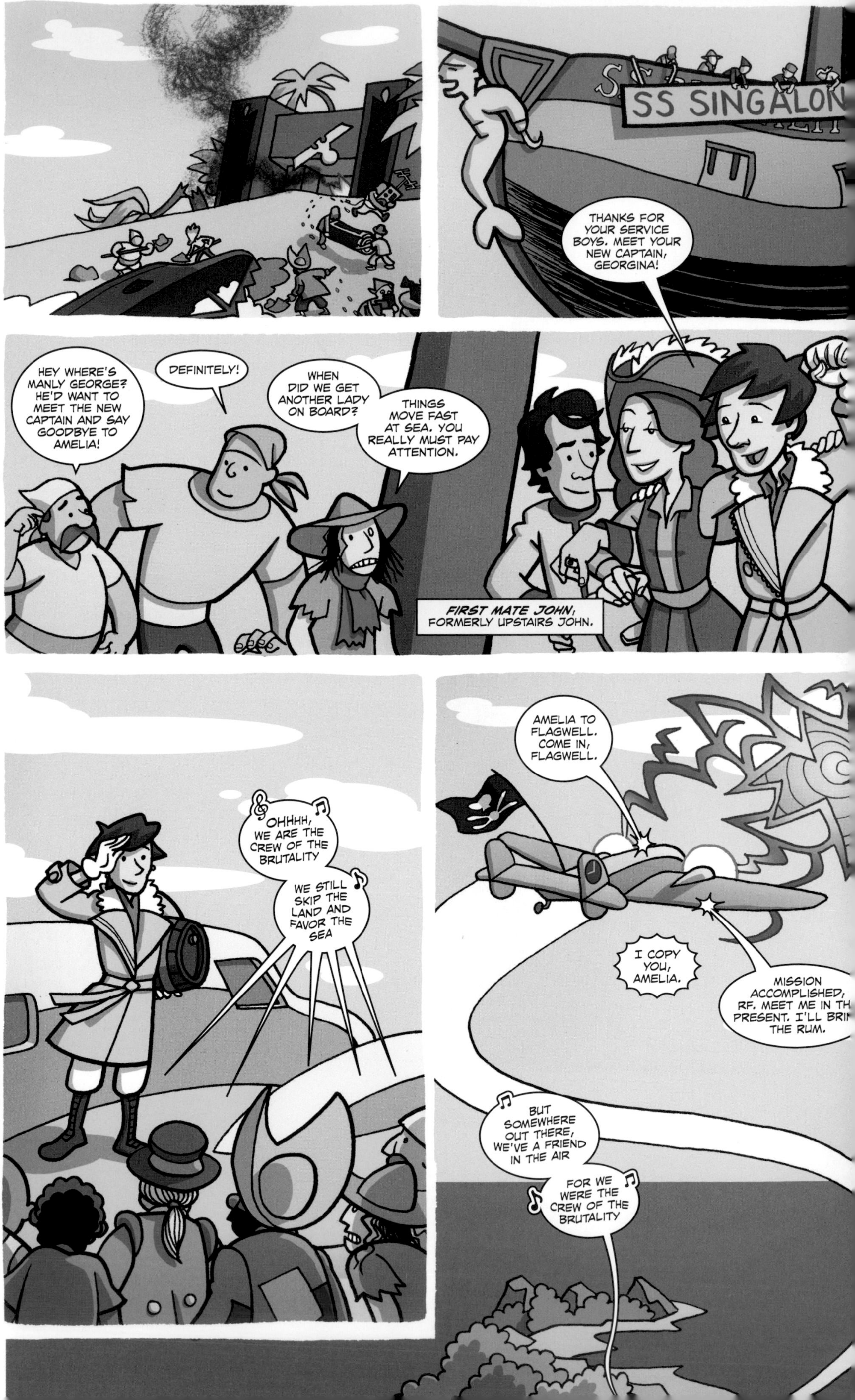
SS SINGALON
THANKS FOR YOUR SERVICE BOYS. MEET YOUR NEW CAPTAIN, GEORGINA!
HEY WHERE'S MANLY GEORGE? HE'D WANT TO MEET THE NEW CAPTAIN AND SAY GOODBYE TO AMELIA!
DEFINITELY!
WHEN DID WE GET ANOTHER LADY ON BOARD?
THINGS MOVE FAST AT SEA. YOU REALLY MUST PAY ATTENTION.
FIRST MATE JOHN; FORMERLY UPSTAIRS JOHN.
OHHHH, WE ARE THE CREW OF THE BRUTALITY
WE STILL SKIP THE LAND AND FAVOR THE SEA
AMELIA TO FLAGWELL. COME IN, FLAGWELL.
I COPY YOU, AMELIA.
MISSION ACCOMPLISHED, RF. MEET ME IN TH PRESENT. I'LL BRI THE RUM.
BUT SOMEWHERE OUT THERE, WE'VE A FRIEND IN THE AIR
FOR WE WERE THE CREW OF THE BRUTALITY

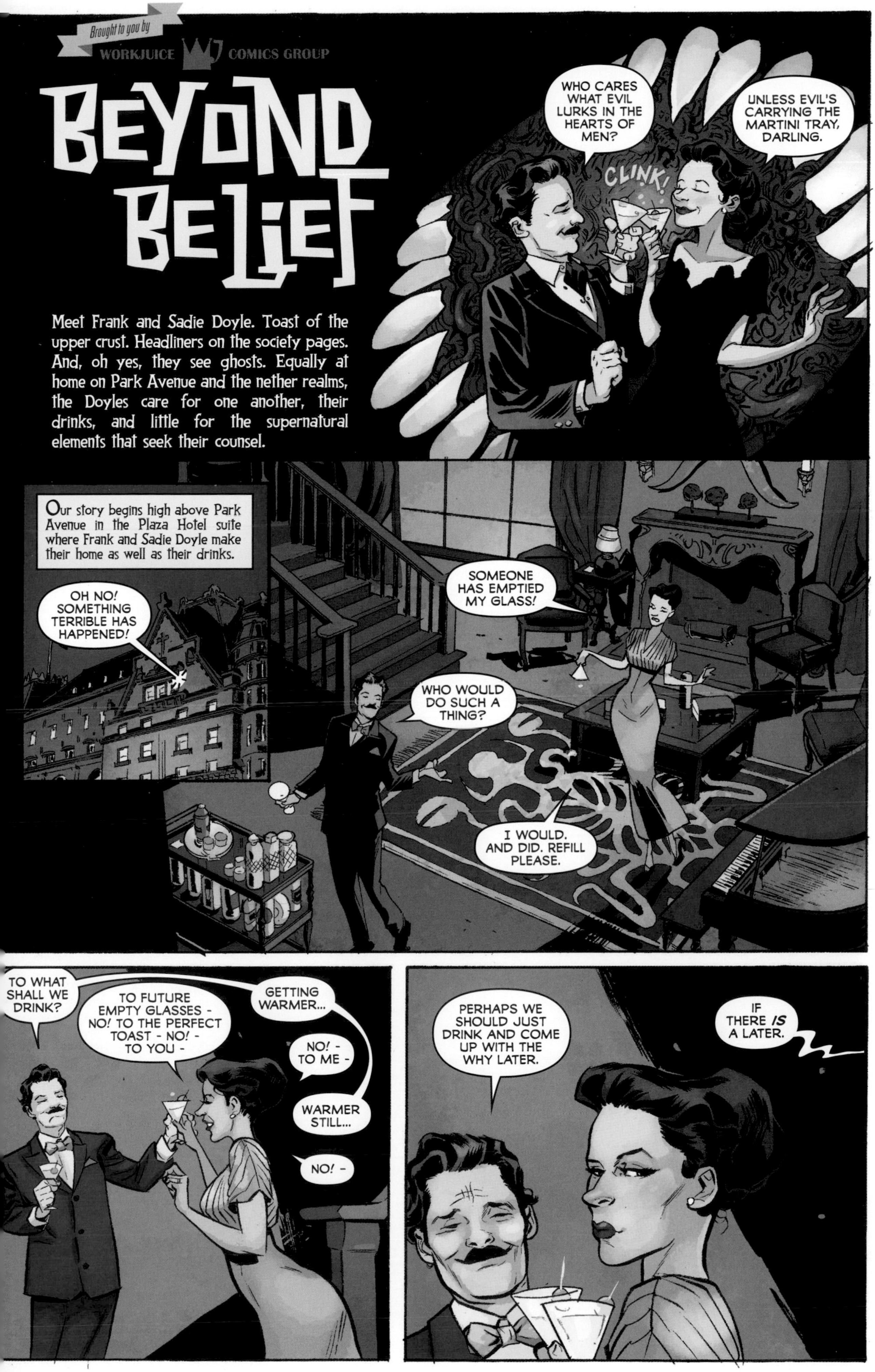
Brought to you by
WORKJUICE COMICS GROUP
BEYOND BELIEF
Meet Frank and Sadie Doyle. Toast of the upper crust. Headliners on the society pages. And, oh yes, they see ghosts. Equally at home on Park Avenue and the nether realms, the Doyles care for one another, their drinks, and little for the supernatural elements that seek their counsel.
WHO CARES WHAT EVIL LURKS IN THE HEARTS OF MEN?
CLINK!
UNLESS EVIL'S CARRYING THE MARTINI TRAY, DARLING.
Our story begins high above Park Avenue in the Plaza Hotel suite where Frank and Sadie Doyle make their home as well as their drinks.
OH NO! SOMETHING TERRIBLE HAS HAPPENED!
SOMEONE HAS EMPTIED MY GLASS!
WHO WOULD DO SUCH A THING?
I WOULD. AND DID. REFILL PLEASE.
TO WHAT SHALL WE DRINK?
TO FUTURE EMPTY GLASSES - NO! TO THE PERFECT TOAST - NO! - TO YOU -
GETTING WARMER...
NO! - TO ME -
WARMER STILL...
NO! -
PERHAPS WE SHOULD JUST DRINK AND COME UP WITH THE WHY LATER.
IF THERE *IS* A LATER.

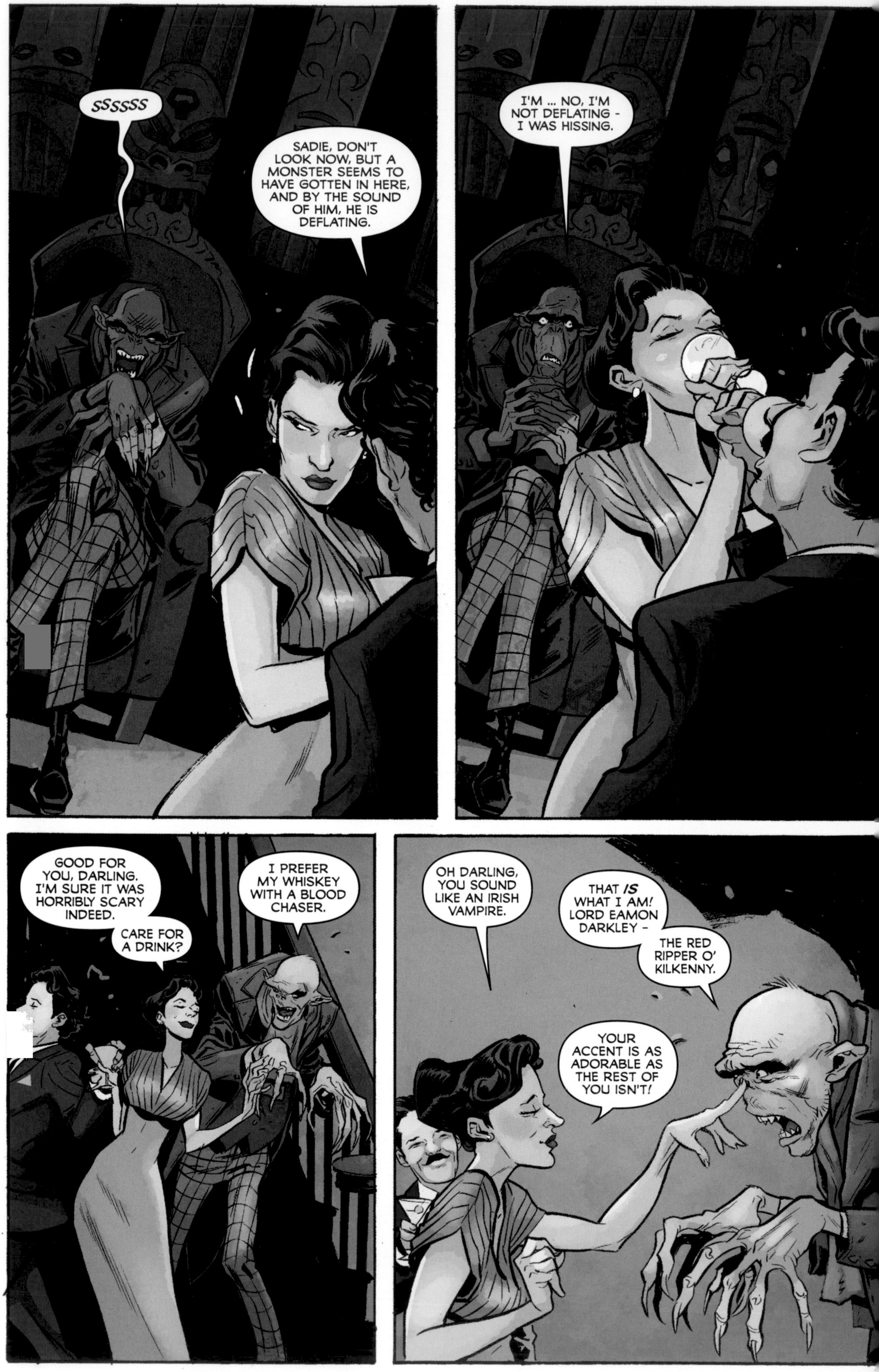
SSSSSS
SADIE, DON'T LOOK NOW, BUT A MONSTER SEEMS TO HAVE GOTTEN IN HERE, AND BY THE SOUND OF HIM, HE IS DEFLATING.
I'M ... NO, I'M NOT DEFLATING - I WAS HISSING.
GOOD FOR YOU, DARLING. I'M SURE IT WAS HORRIBLY SCARY INDEED.
CARE FOR A DRINK?
I PREFER MY WHISKEY WITH A BLOOD CHASER.
OH DARLING, YOU SOUND LIKE AN IRISH VAMPIRE.
THAT *IS* WHAT I AM! LORD EAMON DARKLEY -
THE RED RIPPER O' KILKENNY.
YOUR ACCENT IS AS ADORABLE AS THE REST OF YOU ISN'T!

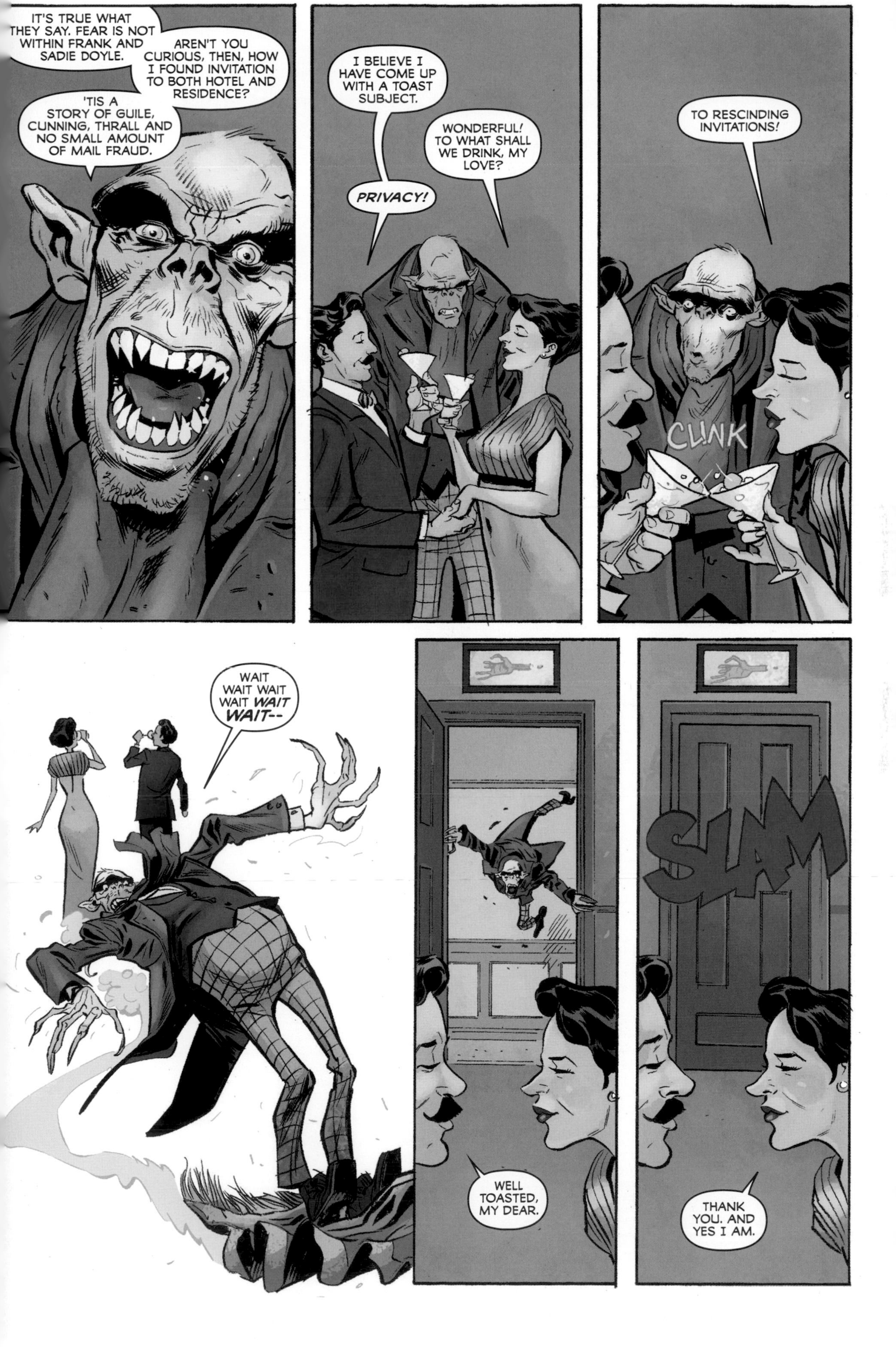
IT'S TRUE WHAT THEY SAY. FEAR IS NOT WITHIN FRANK AND SADIE DOYLE.
AREN'T YOU CURIOUS, THEN, HOW I FOUND INVITATION TO BOTH HOTEL AND RESIDENCE?
'TIS A STORY OF GUILE, CUNNING, THRALL AND NO SMALL AMOUNT OF MAIL FRAUD.
I BELIEVE I HAVE COME UP WITH A TOAST SUBJECT.
WONDERFUL! TO WHAT SHALL WE DRINK, MY LOVE?
PRIVACY!
TO RESCINDING INVITATIONS!
CLINK
WAIT WAIT WAIT WAIT WAIT WAIT--
WELL TOASTED, MY DEAR.
SLAM
THANK YOU. AND YES I AM.

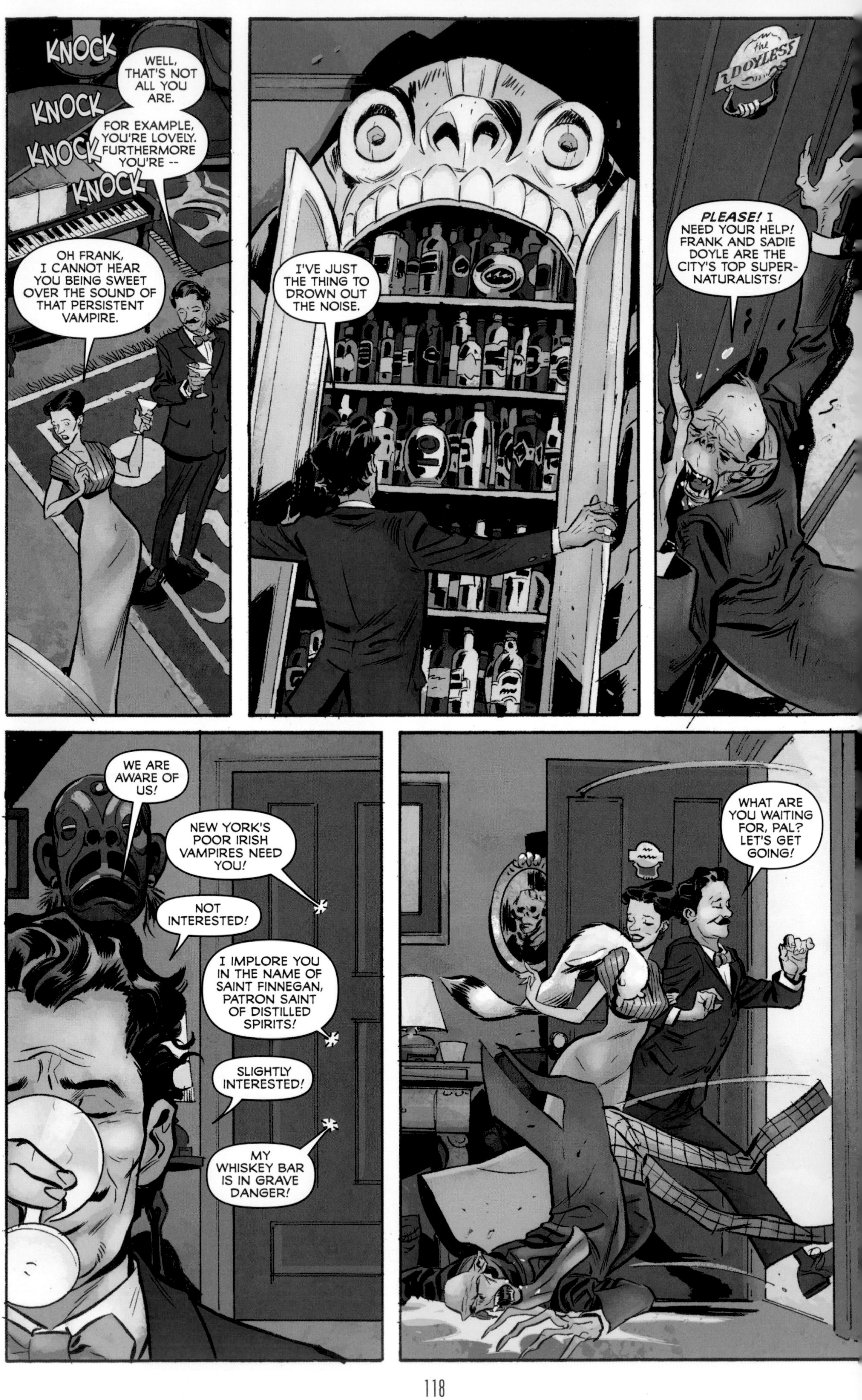
KNOCK
KNOCK
KNOCK
KNOCK
WELL, THAT'S NOT ALL YOU ARE.
FOR EXAMPLE, YOU'RE LOVELY. FURTHERMORE YOU'RE --
OH FRANK, I CANNOT HEAR YOU BEING SWEET OVER THE SOUND OF THAT PERSISTENT VAMPIRE.
I'VE JUST THE THING TO DROWN OUT THE NOISE.
the DOYLES
PLEASE! I NEED YOUR HELP! FRANK AND SADIE DOYLE ARE THE CITY'S TOP SUPER-NATURALISTS!
WE ARE AWARE OF US!
NEW YORK'S POOR IRISH VAMPIRES NEED YOU!
NOT INTERESTED!
I IMPLORE YOU IN THE NAME OF SAINT FINNEGAN, PATRON SAINT OF DISTILLED SPIRITS!
SLIGHTLY INTERESTED!
MY WHISKEY BAR IS IN GRAVE DANGER!
WHAT ARE YOU WAITING FOR, PAL? LET'S GET GOING!

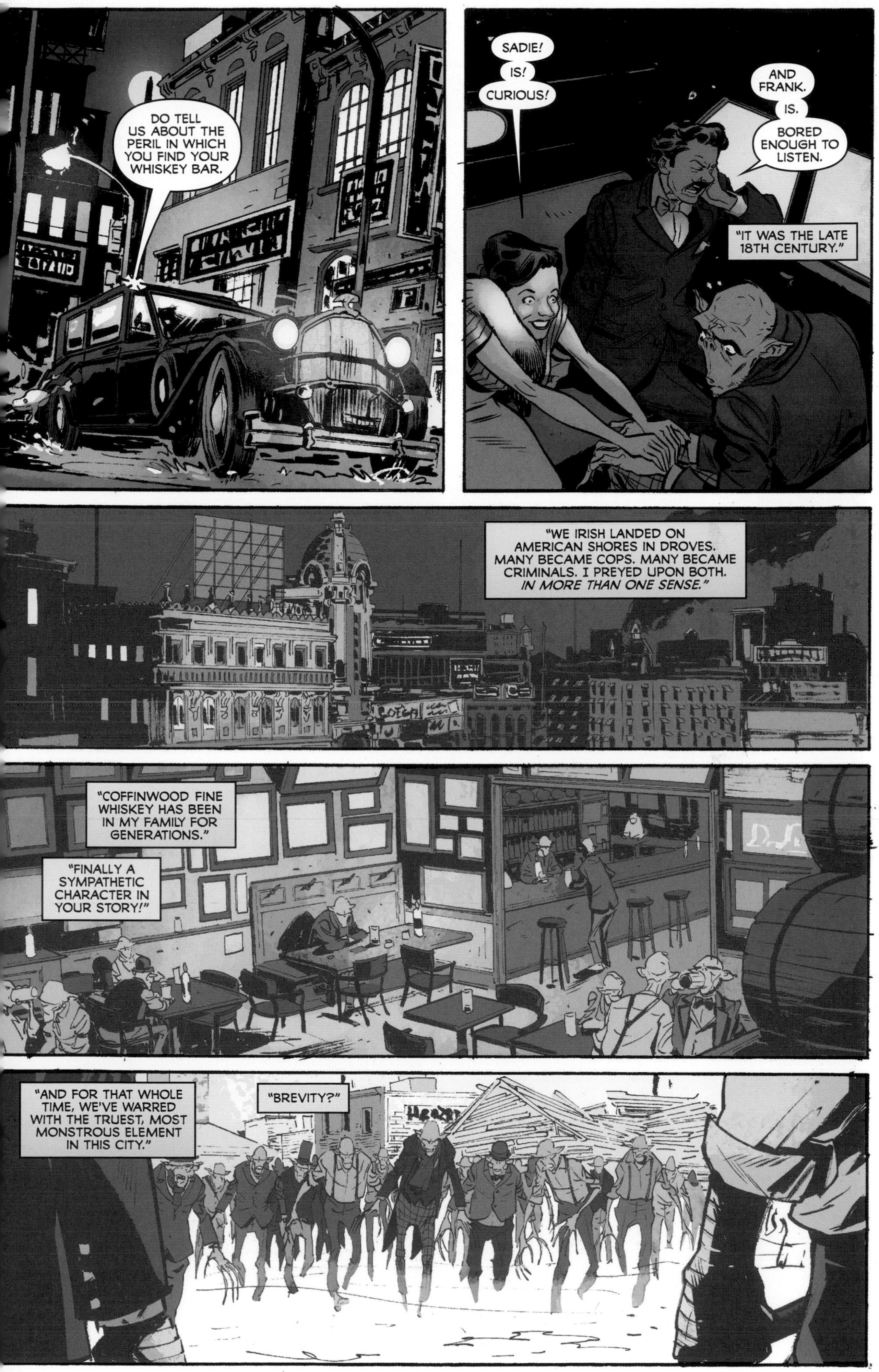
DO TELL US ABOUT THE PERIL IN WHICH YOU FIND YOUR WHISKEY BAR.
SADIE!
IS!
CURIOUS!
AND FRANK.
IS.
BORED ENOUGH TO LISTEN.
"IT WAS THE LATE 18TH CENTURY."
"WE IRISH LANDED ON AMERICAN SHORES IN DROVES. MANY BECAME COPS. MANY BECAME CRIMINALS. I PREYED UPON BOTH. *IN MORE THAN ONE SENSE.*"
"COFFINWOOD FINE WHISKEY HAS BEEN IN MY FAMILY FOR GENERATIONS."
"FINALLY A SYMPATHETIC CHARACTER IN YOUR STORY!"
"AND FOR THAT WHOLE TIME, WE'VE WARRED WITH THE TRUEST, MOST MONSTROUS ELEMENT IN THIS CITY."
"BREVITY?"

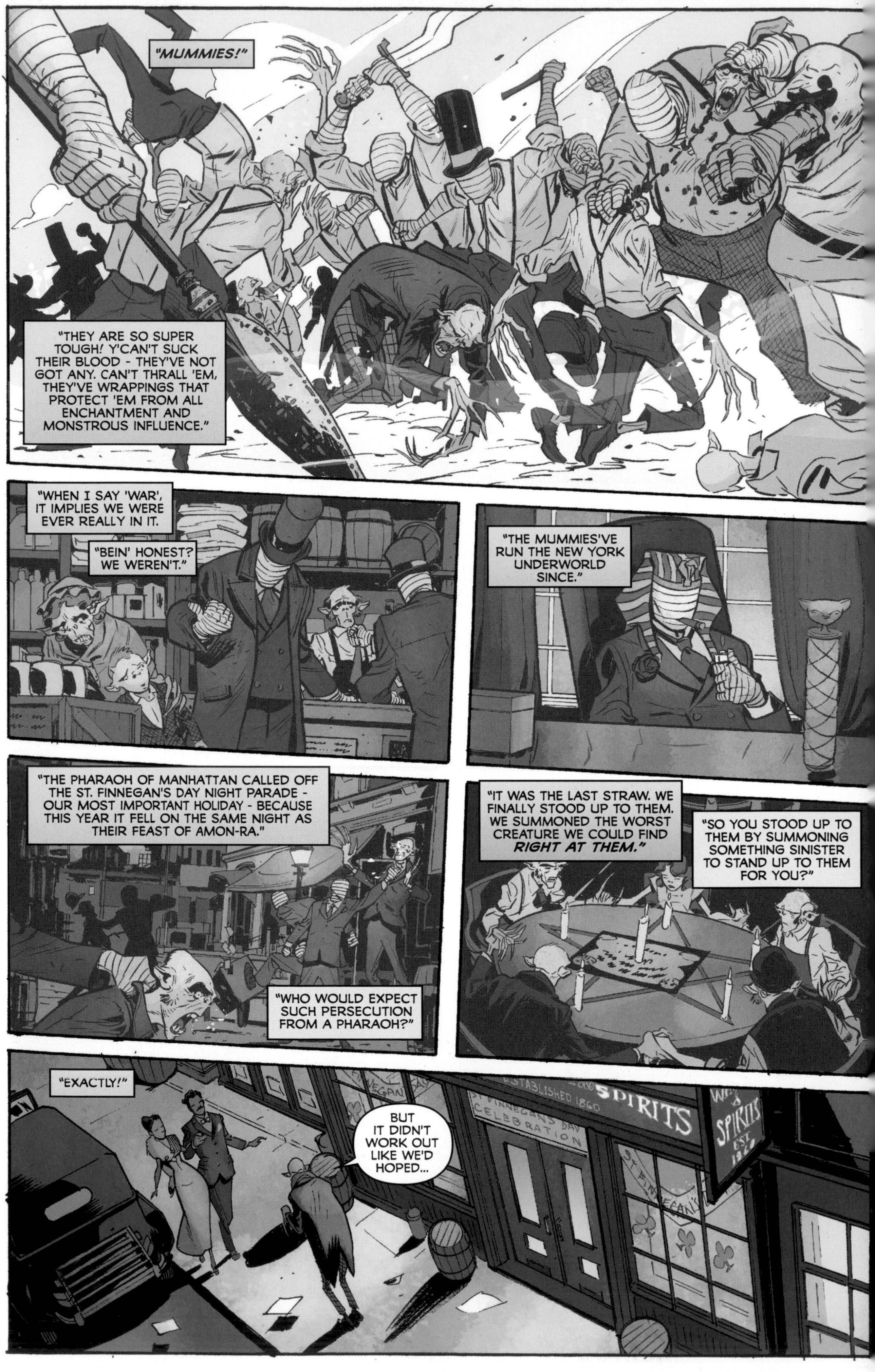
"MUMMIES!"
"THEY ARE SO SUPER TOUGH! Y'CAN'T SUCK THEIR BLOOD - THEY'VE NOT GOT ANY. CAN'T THRALL 'EM, THEY'VE WRAPPINGS THAT PROTECT 'EM FROM ALL ENCHANTMENT AND MONSTROUS INFLUENCE."
"WHEN I SAY 'WAR', IT IMPLIES WE WERE EVER REALLY IN IT.
"BEIN' HONEST? WE WEREN'T."
"THE MUMMIES'VE RUN THE NEW YORK UNDERWORLD SINCE."
"THE PHARAOH OF MANHATTAN CALLED OFF THE ST. FINNEGAN'S DAY NIGHT PARADE - OUR MOST IMPORTANT HOLIDAY - BECAUSE THIS YEAR IT FELL ON THE SAME NIGHT AS THEIR FEAST OF AMON-RA."
"WHO WOULD EXPECT SUCH PERSECUTION FROM A PHARAOH?"
"IT WAS THE LAST STRAW. WE FINALLY STOOD UP TO THEM. WE SUMMONED THE WORST CREATURE WE COULD FIND *RIGHT AT THEM.*"
"SO YOU STOOD UP TO THEM BY SUMMONING SOMETHING SINISTER TO STAND UP TO THEM FOR YOU?"
"EXACTLY!"
ESTABLISHED 1860
SPIRITS
ST FINNEGAN'S DAY CELEBRATION
SPIRITS EST. 1860
BUT IT DIDN'T WORK OUT LIKE WE'D HOPED...

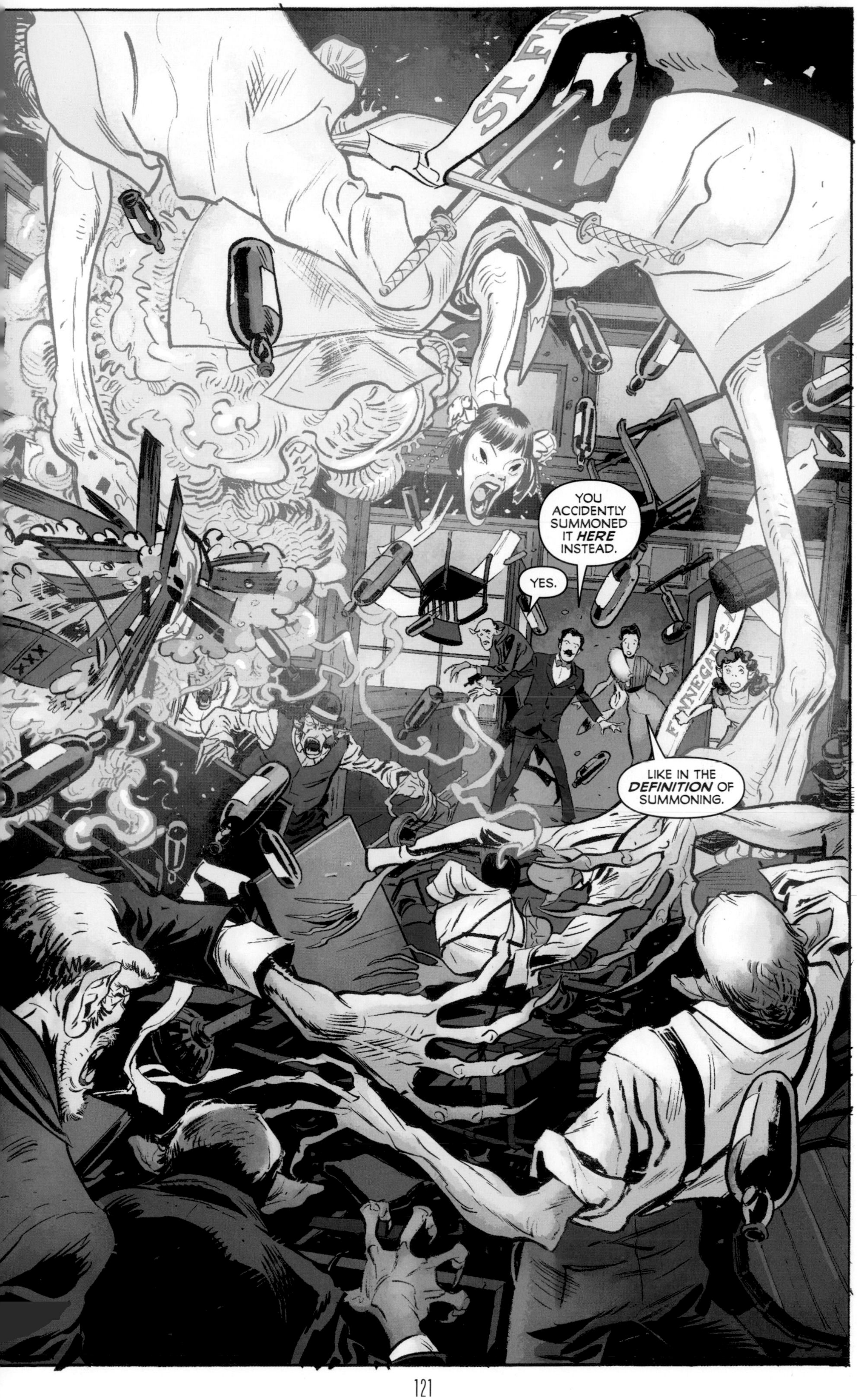
YOU ACCIDENTLY SUMMONED IT *HERE* INSTEAD.
YES.
LIKE IN THE *DEFINITION* OF SUMMONING.

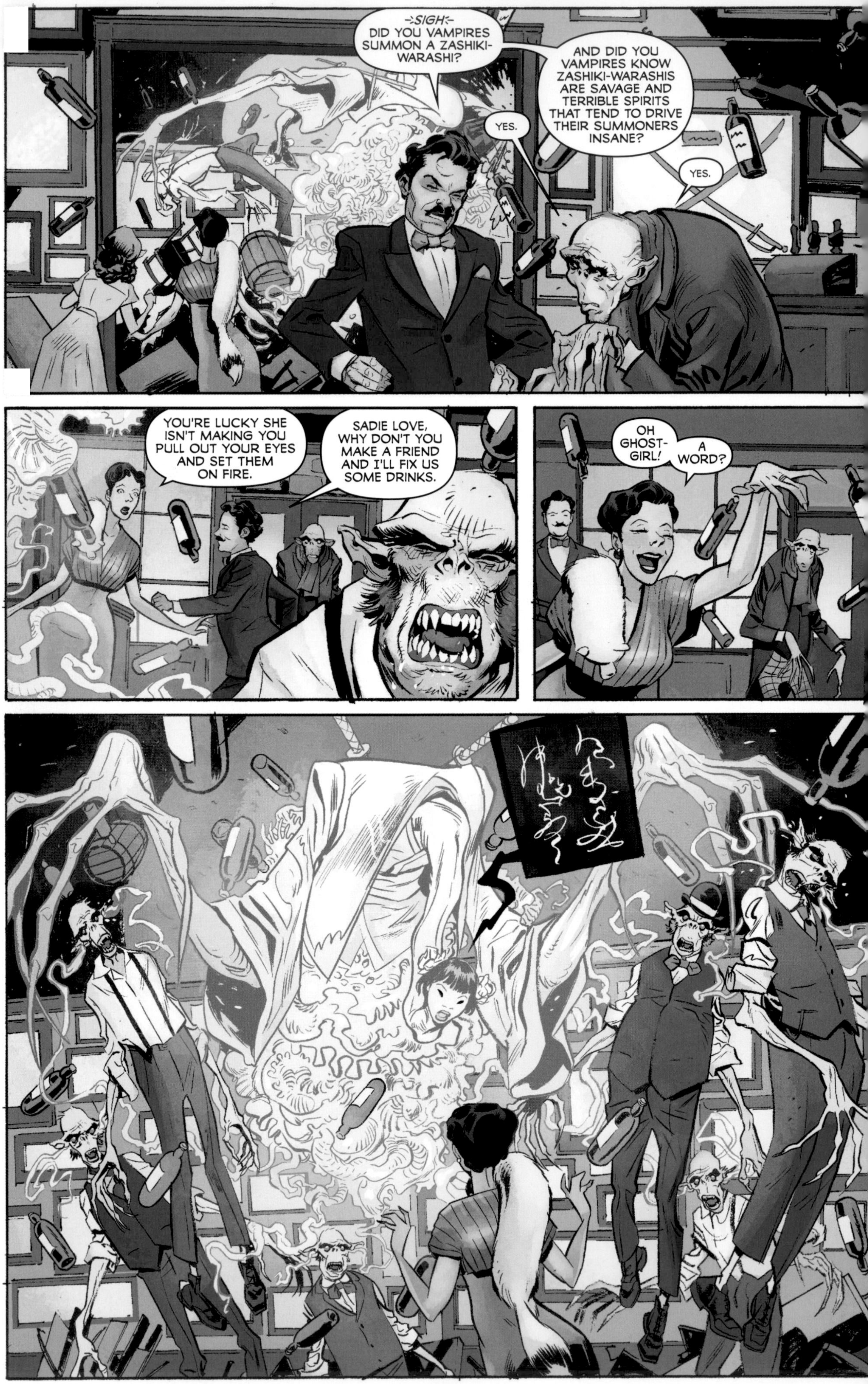
-SIGH-
DID YOU VAMPIRES SUMMON A ZASHIKI-WARASHI?
YES.
AND DID YOU VAMPIRES KNOW ZASHIKI-WARASHIS ARE SAVAGE AND TERRIBLE SPIRITS THAT TEND TO DRIVE THEIR SUMMONERS INSANE?
YES.
YOU'RE LUCKY SHE ISN'T MAKING YOU PULL OUT YOUR EYES AND SET THEM ON FIRE.
SADIE LOVE, WHY DON'T YOU MAKE A FRIEND AND I'LL FIX US SOME DRINKS.
OH GHOST-GIRL!
A WORD?

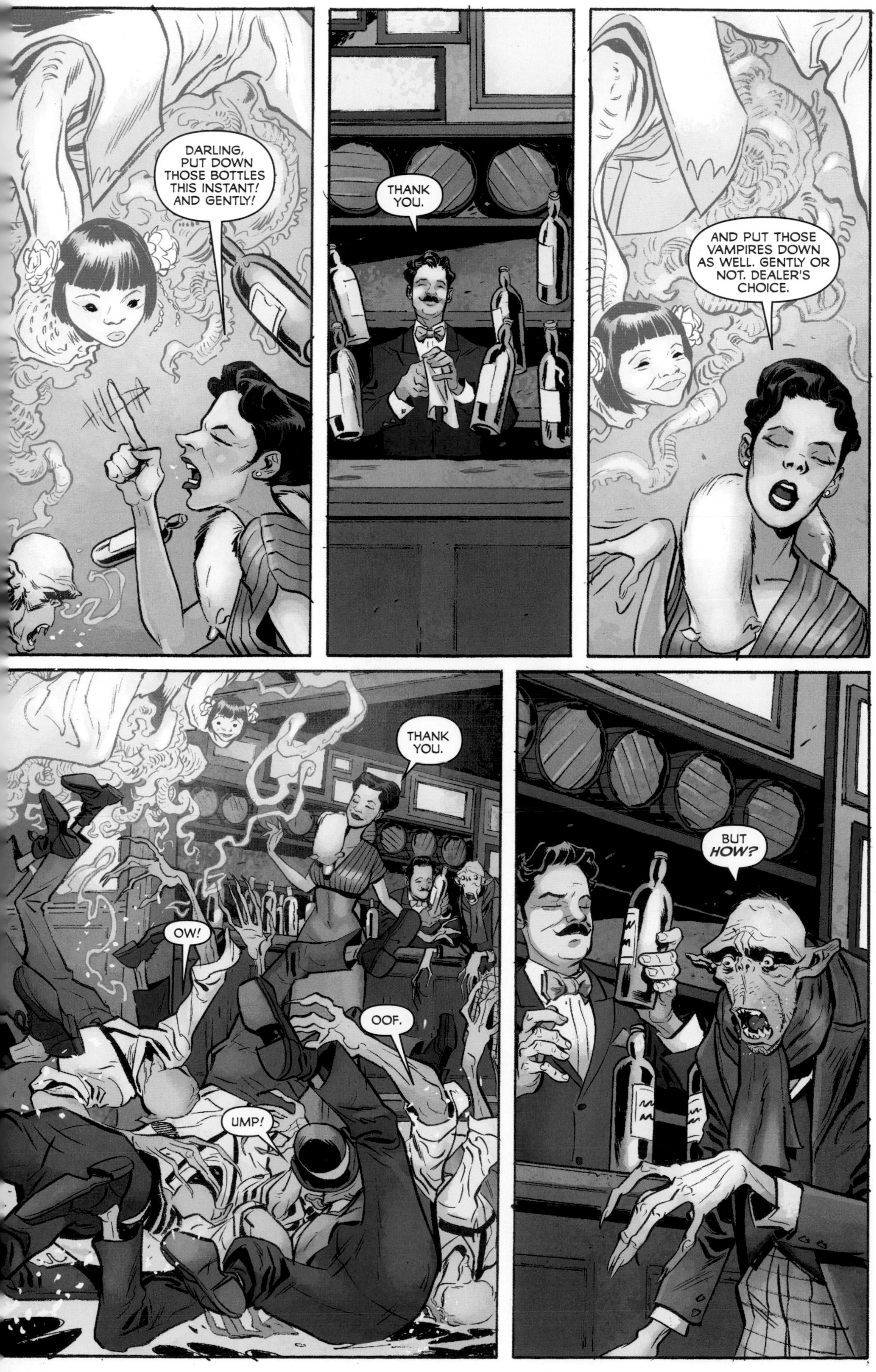
DARLING, PUT DOWN THOSE BOTTLES THIS INSTANT! AND GENTLY!
THANK YOU.
AND PUT THOSE VAMPIRES DOWN AS WELL. GENTLY OR NOT. DEALER'S CHOICE.
THANK YOU.
OW!
OOF.
UMP!
BUT *HOW?*

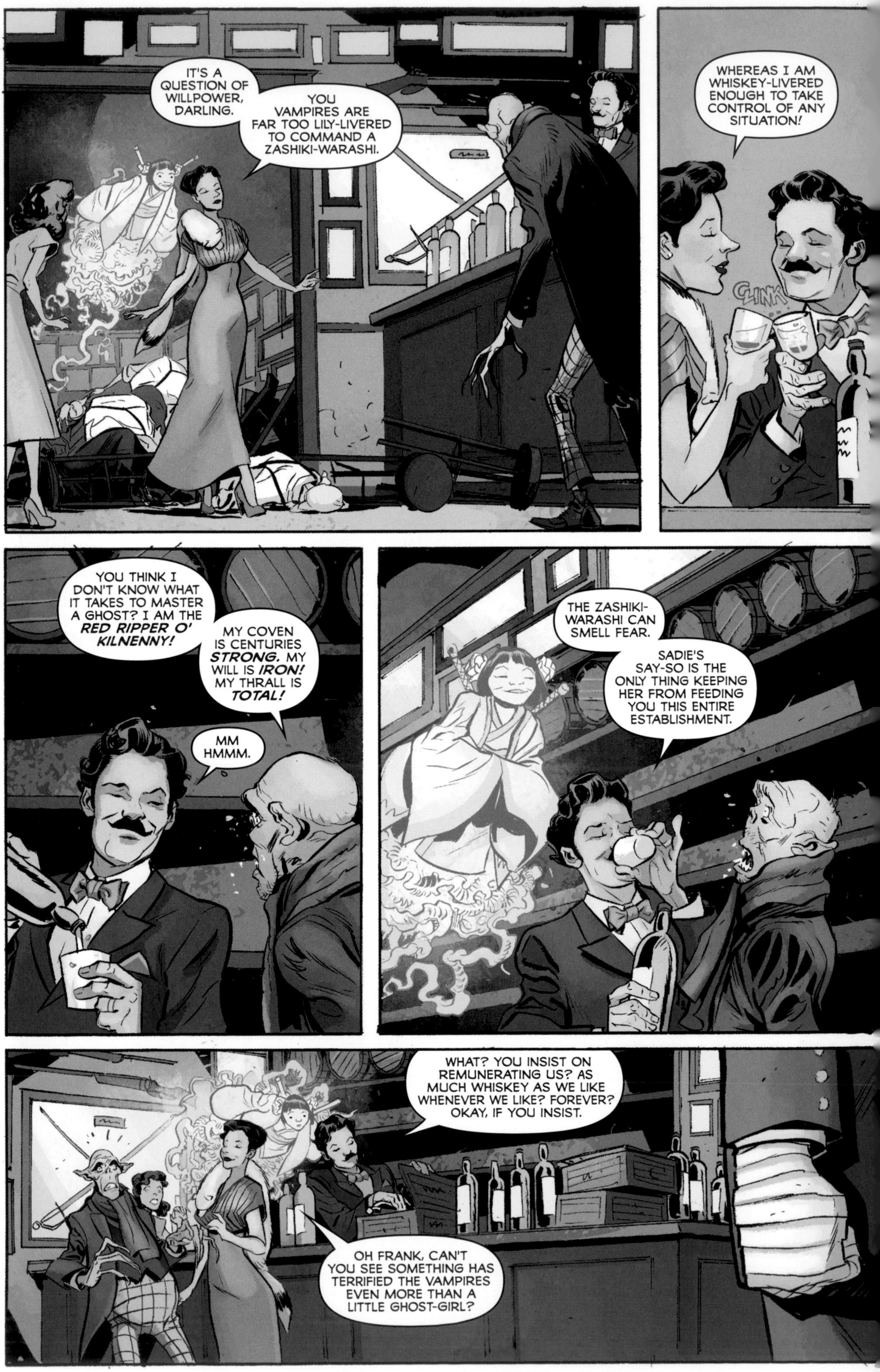

IT'S A QUESTION OF WILLPOWER, DARLING.
YOU VAMPIRES ARE FAR TOO LILY-LIVERED TO COMMAND A ZASHIKI-WARASHI.
WHEREAS I AM WHISKEY-LIVERED ENOUGH TO TAKE CONTROL OF ANY SITUATION!
CLINK
YOU THINK I DON'T KNOW WHAT IT TAKES TO MASTER A GHOST? I AM THE RED RIPPER O' KILNENNY!
MY COVEN IS CENTURIES STRONG. MY WILL IS IRON! MY THRALL IS TOTAL!
MM HMMM.
THE ZASHIKI-WARASHI CAN SMELL FEAR.
SADIE'S SAY-SO IS THE ONLY THING KEEPING HER FROM FEEDING YOU THIS ENTIRE ESTABLISHMENT.
WHAT? YOU INSIST ON REMUNERATING US? AS MUCH WHISKEY AS WE LIKE WHENEVER WE LIKE? FOREVER? OKAY, IF YOU INSIST.
OH FRANK, CAN'T YOU SEE SOMETHING HAS TERRIFIED THE VAMPIRES EVEN MORE THAN A LITTLE GHOST-GIRL?

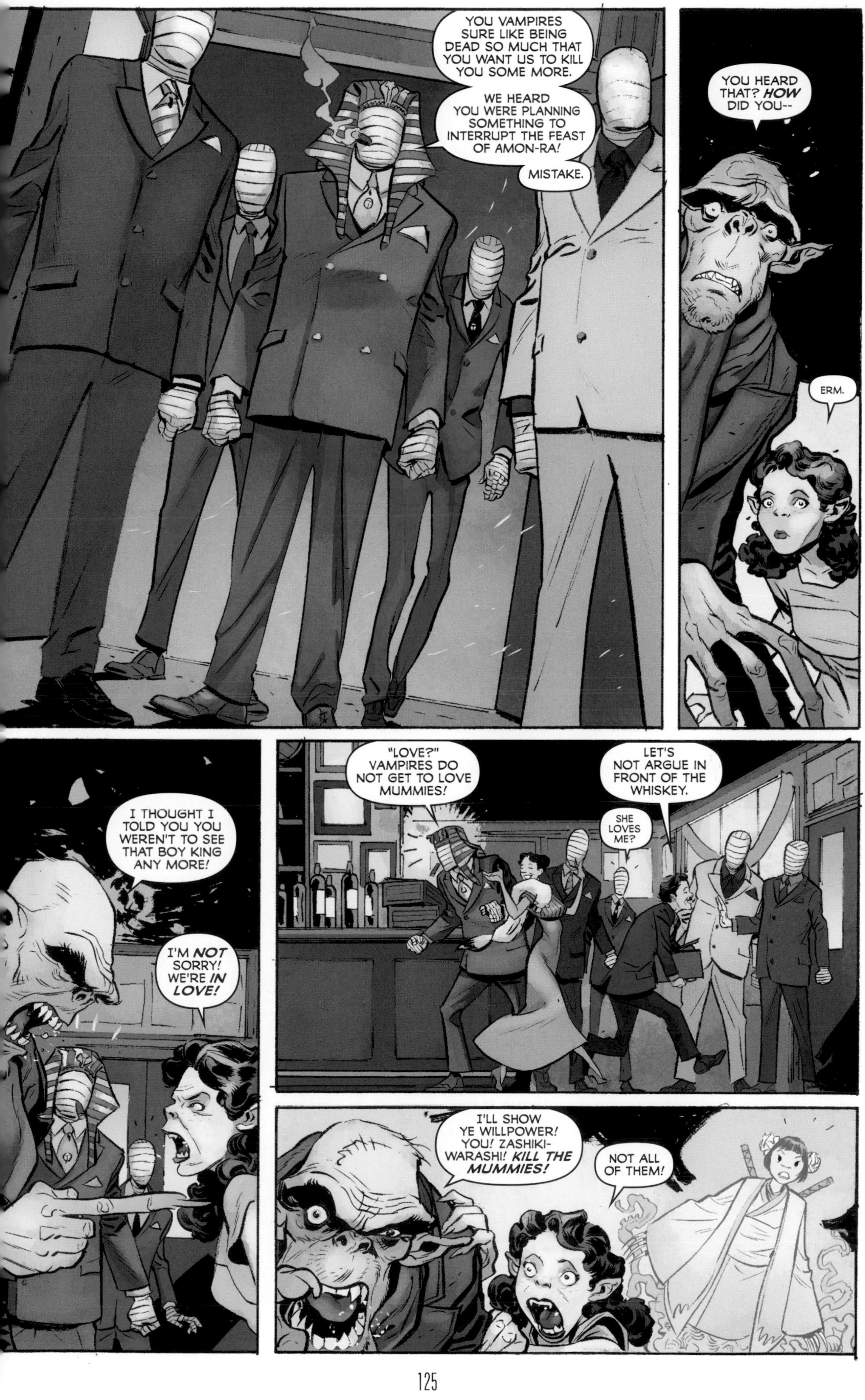
YOU VAMPIRES SURE LIKE BEING DEAD SO MUCH THAT YOU WANT US TO KILL YOU SOME MORE.
WE HEARD YOU WERE PLANNING SOMETHING TO INTERRUPT THE FEAST OF AMON-RA!
MISTAKE.
YOU HEARD THAT? *HOW* DID YOU--
ERM.
I THOUGHT I TOLD YOU YOU WEREN'T TO SEE THAT BOY KING ANY MORE!
I'M *NOT* SORRY! WE'RE *IN LOVE!*
"LOVE?" VAMPIRES DO NOT GET TO LOVE MUMMIES!
SHE LOVES ME?
LET'S NOT ARGUE IN FRONT OF THE WHISKEY.
I'LL SHOW YE WILLPOWER! YOU! ZASHIKI-WARASHI! *KILL THE MUMMIES!*
NOT ALL OF THEM!

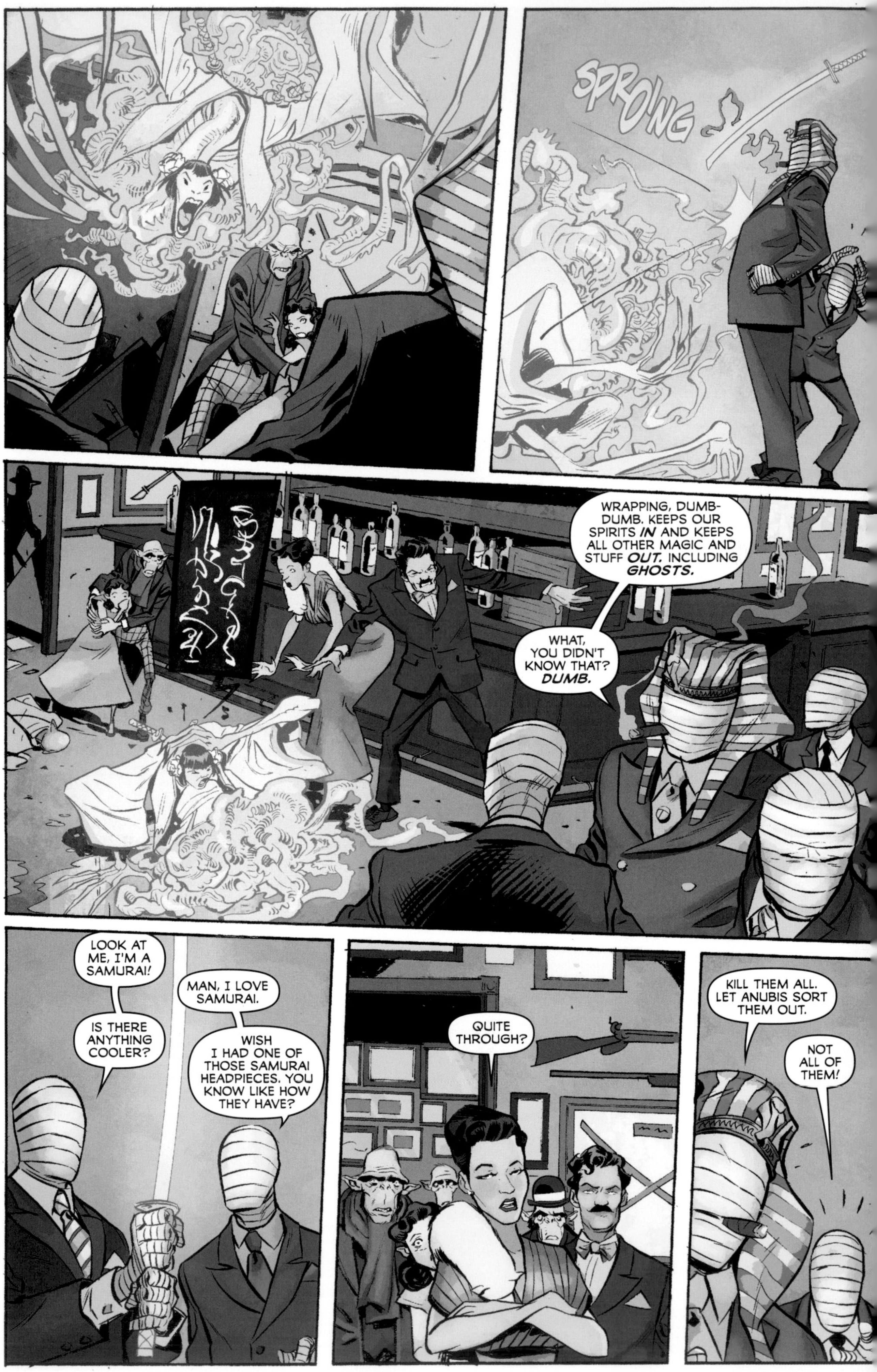
SPROING
WRAPPING, DUMB-DUMB. KEEPS OUR SPIRITS IN AND KEEPS ALL OTHER MAGIC AND STUFF OUT. INCLUDING GHOSTS.
WHAT, YOU DIDN'T KNOW THAT? DUMB.
LOOK AT ME, I'M A SAMURAI!
IS THERE ANYTHING COOLER?
MAN, I LOVE SAMURAI.
WISH I HAD ONE OF THOSE SAMURAI HEADPIECES. YOU KNOW LIKE HOW THEY HAVE?
QUITE THROUGH?
KILL THEM ALL. LET ANUBIS SORT THEM OUT.
NOT ALL OF THEM!

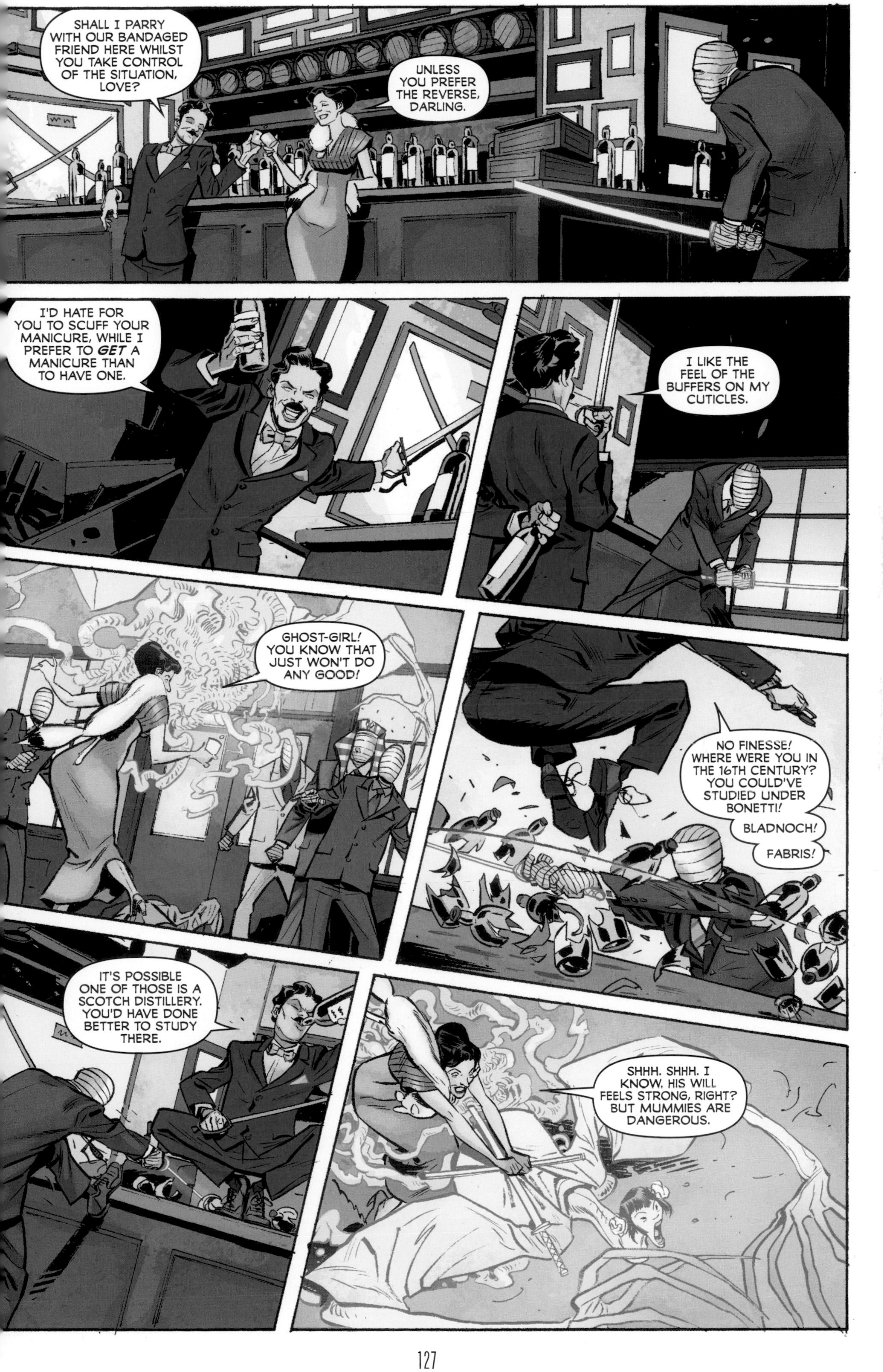
SHALL I PARRY WITH OUR BANDAGED FRIEND HERE WHILST YOU TAKE CONTROL OF THE SITUATION, LOVE?
UNLESS YOU PREFER THE REVERSE, DARLING.
I'D HATE FOR YOU TO SCUFF YOUR MANICURE, WHILE I PREFER TO GET A MANICURE THAN TO HAVE ONE.
I LIKE THE FEEL OF THE BUFFERS ON MY CUTICLES.
GHOST-GIRL! YOU KNOW THAT JUST WON'T DO ANY GOOD!
NO FINESSE! WHERE WERE YOU IN THE 16TH CENTURY? YOU COULD'VE STUDIED UNDER BONETTI!
BLADNOCH!
FABRIS!
IT'S POSSIBLE ONE OF THOSE IS A SCOTCH DISTILLERY. YOU'D HAVE DONE BETTER TO STUDY THERE.
SHHH. SHHH. I KNOW. HIS WILL FEELS STRONG, RIGHT? BUT MUMMIES ARE DANGEROUS.

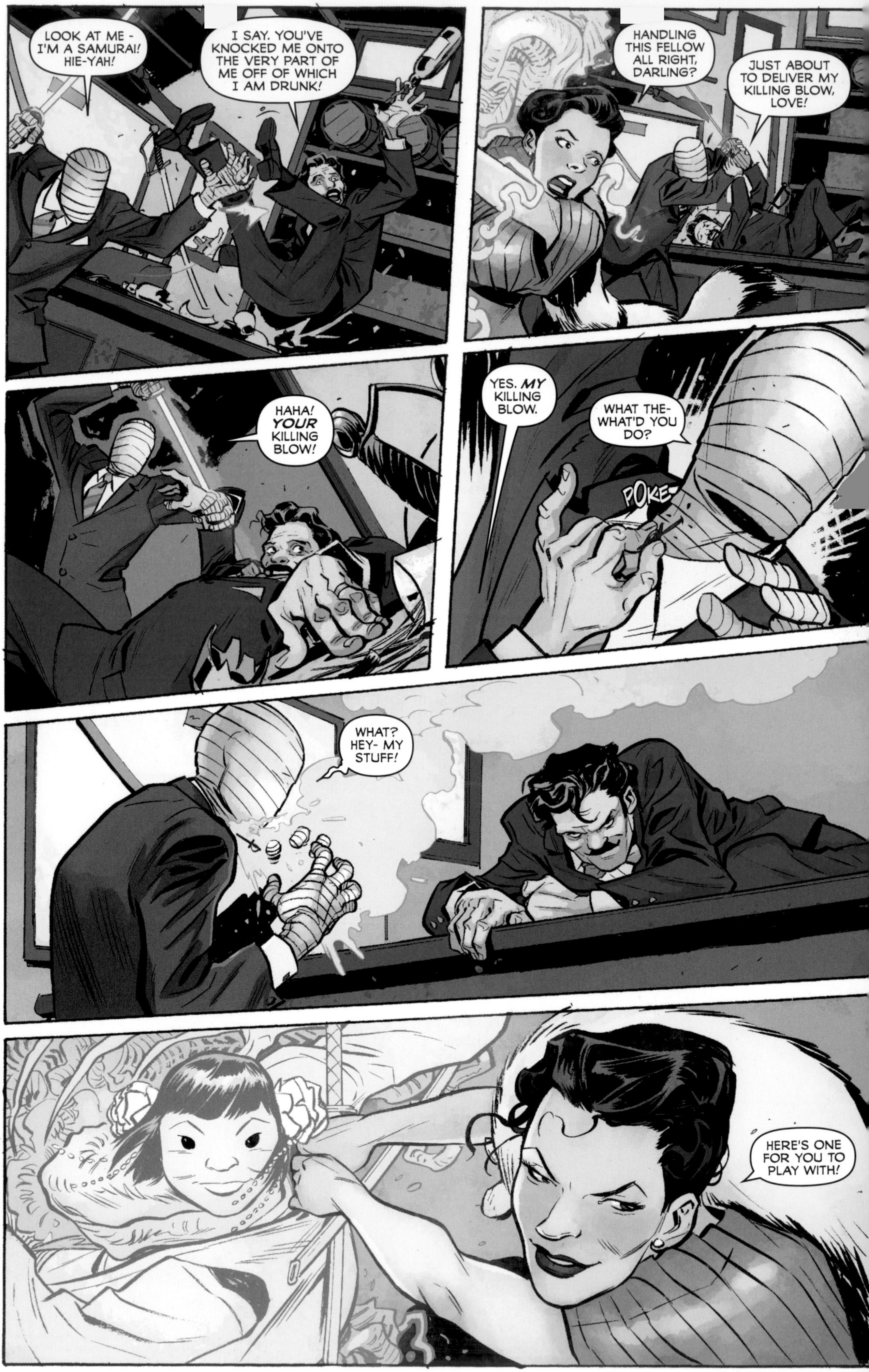
LOOK AT ME - I'M A SAMURAI! HIE-YAH!
I SAY. YOU'VE KNOCKED ME ONTO THE VERY PART OF ME OFF OF WHICH I AM DRUNK!
HANDLING THIS FELLOW ALL RIGHT, DARLING?
JUST ABOUT TO DELIVER MY KILLING BLOW, LOVE!
HAHA! YOUR KILLING BLOW!
YES. MY KILLING BLOW.
WHAT THE- WHAT'D YOU DO?
POKE
WHAT? HEY- MY STUFF!
HERE'S ONE FOR YOU TO PLAY WITH!

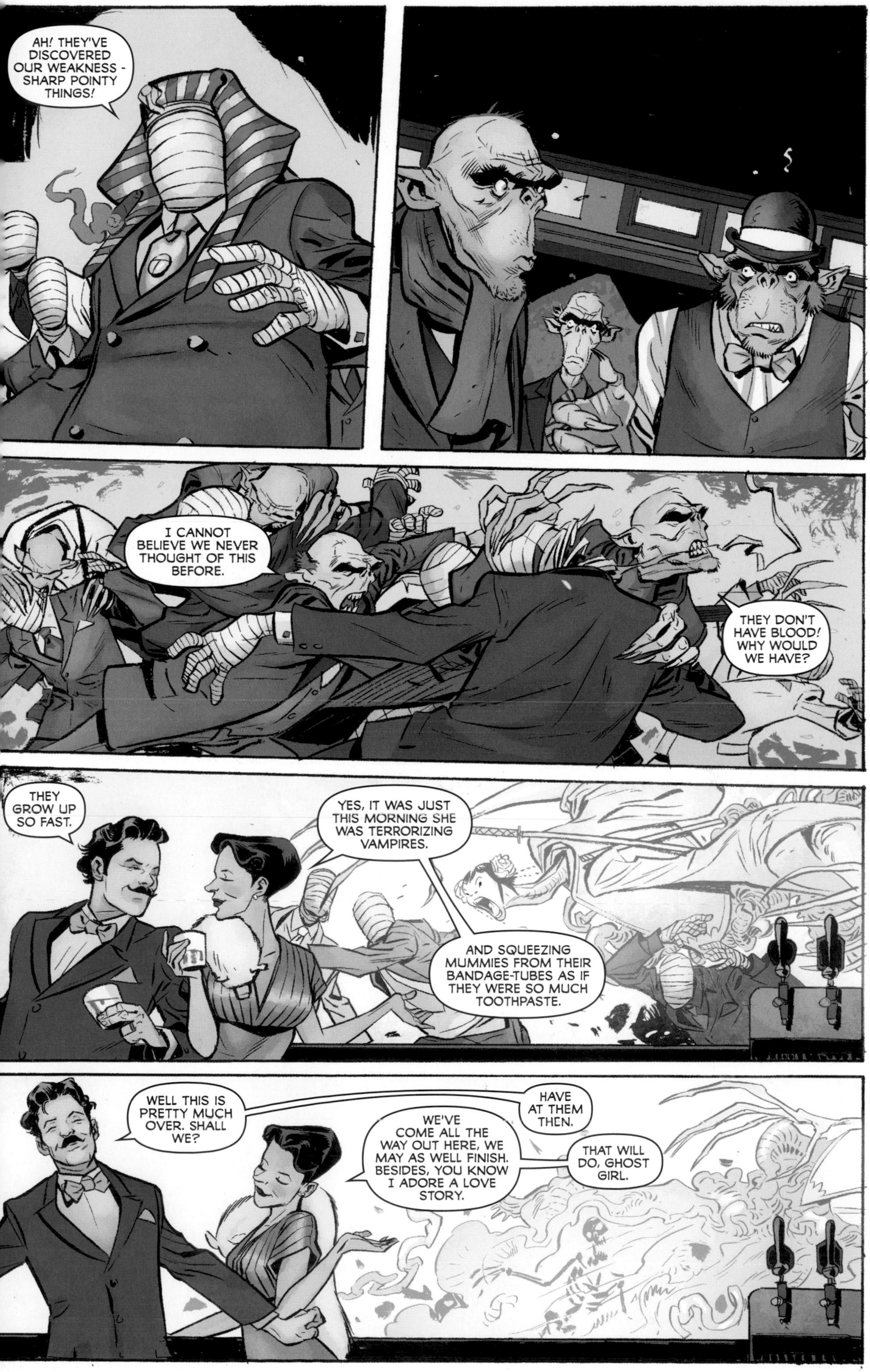
AH! THEY'VE DISCOVERED OUR WEAKNESS - SHARP POINTY THINGS!
I CANNOT BELIEVE WE NEVER THOUGHT OF THIS BEFORE.
THEY DON'T HAVE BLOOD! WHY WOULD WE HAVE?
THEY GROW UP SO FAST.
YES, IT WAS JUST THIS MORNING SHE WAS TERRORIZING VAMPIRES.
AND SQUEEZING MUMMIES FROM THEIR BANDAGE-TUBES AS IF THEY WERE SO MUCH TOOTHPASTE.
WELL THIS IS PRETTY MUCH OVER. SHALL WE?
HAVE AT THEM THEN.
WE'VE COME ALL THE WAY OUT HERE, WE MAY AS WELL FINISH. BESIDES, YOU KNOW I ADORE A LOVE STORY.
THAT WILL DO, GHOST GIRL.

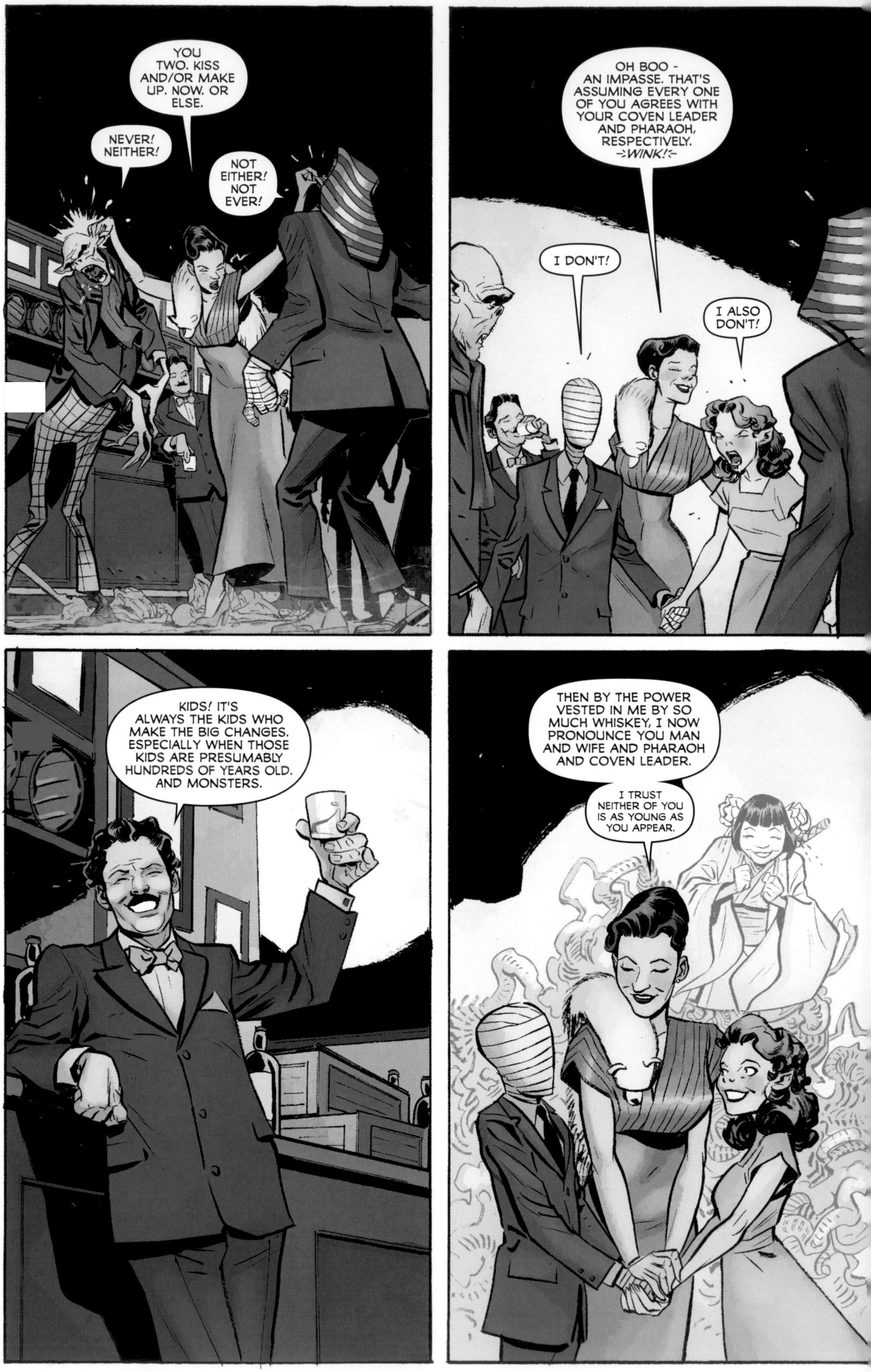
YOU TWO. KISS AND/OR MAKE UP. NOW. OR ELSE.
NEVER! NEITHER!
NOT EITHER! NOT EVER!
OH BOO - AN IMPASSE. THAT'S ASSUMING EVERY ONE OF YOU AGREES WITH YOUR COVEN LEADER AND PHARAOH, RESPECTIVELY. ->WINK!<-
I DON'T!
I ALSO DON'T!
KIDS! IT'S ALWAYS THE KIDS WHO MAKE THE BIG CHANGES. ESPECIALLY WHEN THOSE KIDS ARE PRESUMABLY HUNDREDS OF YEARS OLD. AND MONSTERS.
THEN BY THE POWER VESTED IN ME BY SO MUCH WHISKEY, I NOW PRONOUNCE YOU MAN AND WIFE AND PHARAOH AND COVEN LEADER.
I TRUST NEITHER OF YOU IS AS YOUNG AS YOU APPEAR.

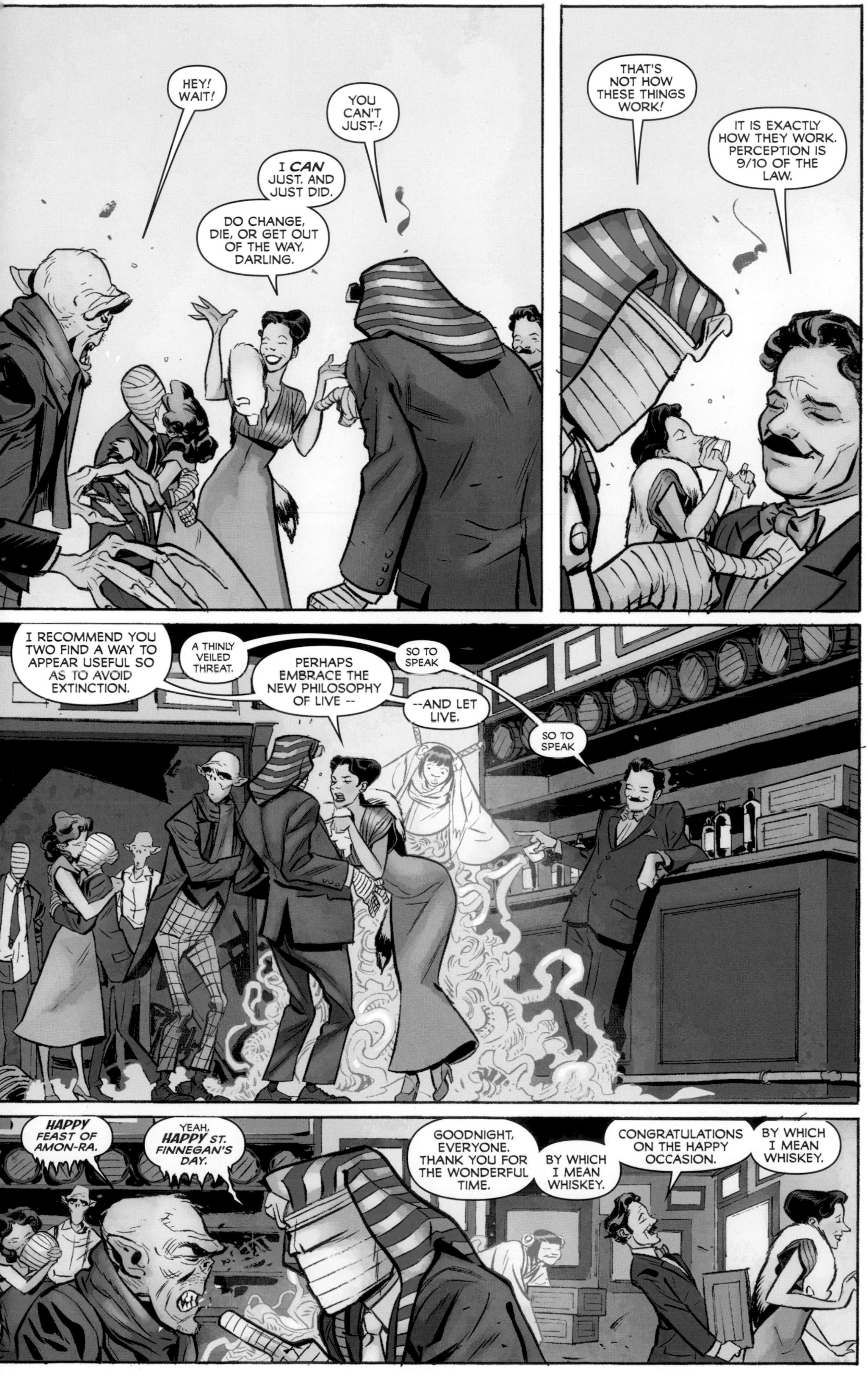
HEY! WAIT!
YOU CAN'T JUST-!
I *CAN* JUST. AND JUST DID.
DO CHANGE, DIE, OR GET OUT OF THE WAY, DARLING.
THAT'S NOT HOW THESE THINGS WORK!
IT IS EXACTLY HOW THEY WORK. PERCEPTION IS 9/10 OF THE LAW.
I RECOMMEND YOU TWO FIND A WAY TO APPEAR USEFUL SO AS TO AVOID EXTINCTION.
A THINLY VEILED THREAT.
PERHAPS EMBRACE THE NEW PHILOSOPHY OF LIVE --
SO TO SPEAK
--AND LET LIVE.
SO TO SPEAK
*HAPPY* FEAST OF AMON-RA.
YEAH, *HAPPY* ST. FINNEGAN'S DAY.
GOODNIGHT, EVERYONE. THANK YOU FOR THE WONDERFUL TIME.
BY WHICH I MEAN WHISKEY.
CONGRATULATIONS ON THE HAPPY OCCASION.
BY WHICH I MEAN WHISKEY.

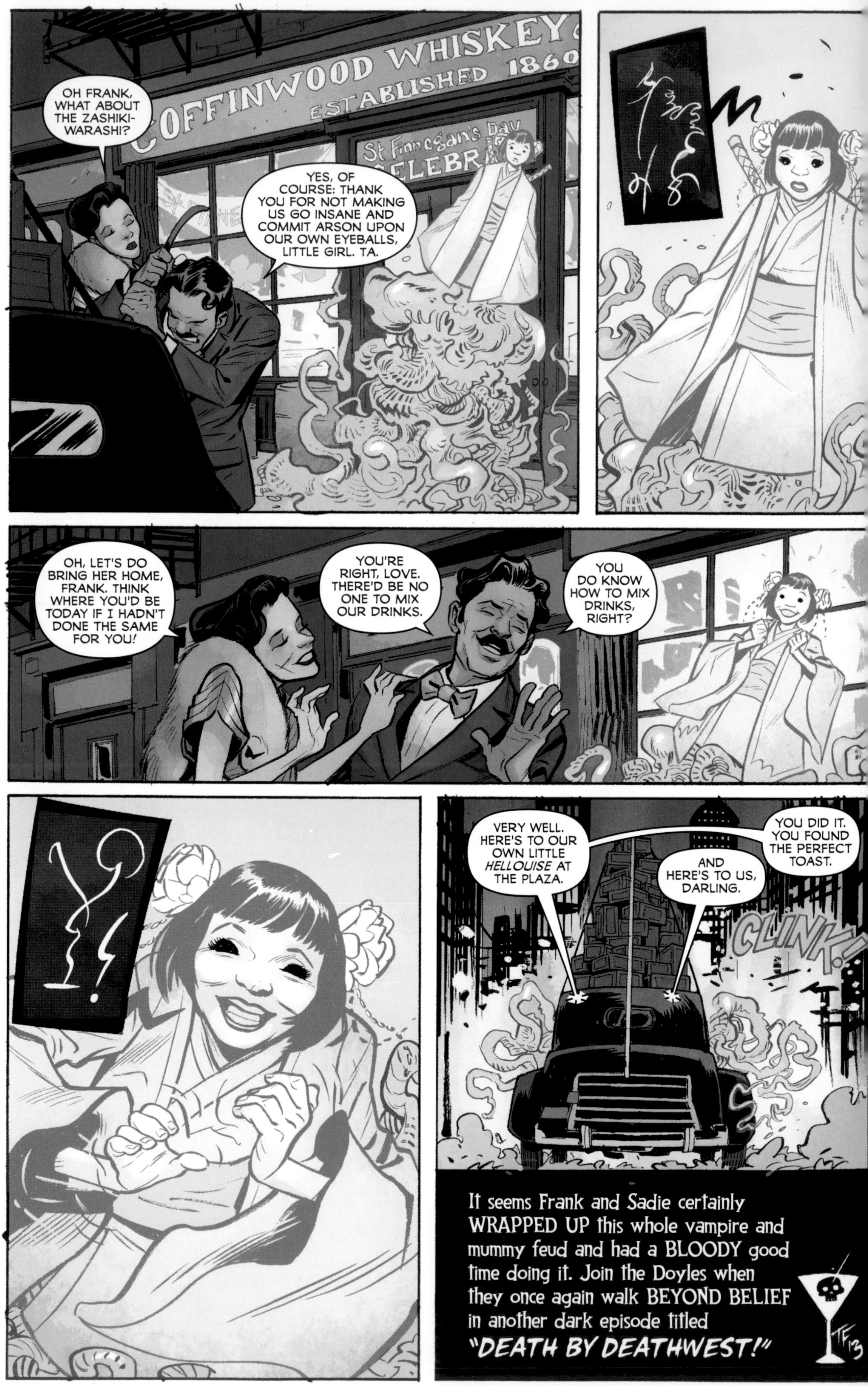
COFFINWOOD WHISKEY
ESTABLISHED 1860
St Finnegan's Day CELEBR
OH FRANK, WHAT ABOUT THE ZASHIKI-WARASHI?
YES, OF COURSE: THANK YOU FOR NOT MAKING US GO INSANE AND COMMIT ARSON UPON OUR OWN EYEBALLS, LITTLE GIRL. TA.
OH, LET'S DO BRING HER HOME, FRANK. THINK WHERE YOU'D BE TODAY IF I HADN'T DONE THE SAME FOR YOU!
YOU'RE RIGHT, LOVE. THERE'D BE NO ONE TO MIX OUR DRINKS.
YOU DO KNOW HOW TO MIX DRINKS, RIGHT?
VERY WELL. HERE'S TO OUR OWN LITTLE *HELLOUISE* AT THE PLAZA.
AND HERE'S TO US, DARLING.
YOU DID IT. YOU FOUND THE PERFECT TOAST.
CLINK!
It seems Frank and Sadie certainly WRAPPED UP this whole vampire and mummy feud and had a BLOODY good time doing it. Join the Doyles when they once again walk BEYOND BELIEF in another dark episode titled
*"DEATH BY DEATHWEST!"*
TF '13

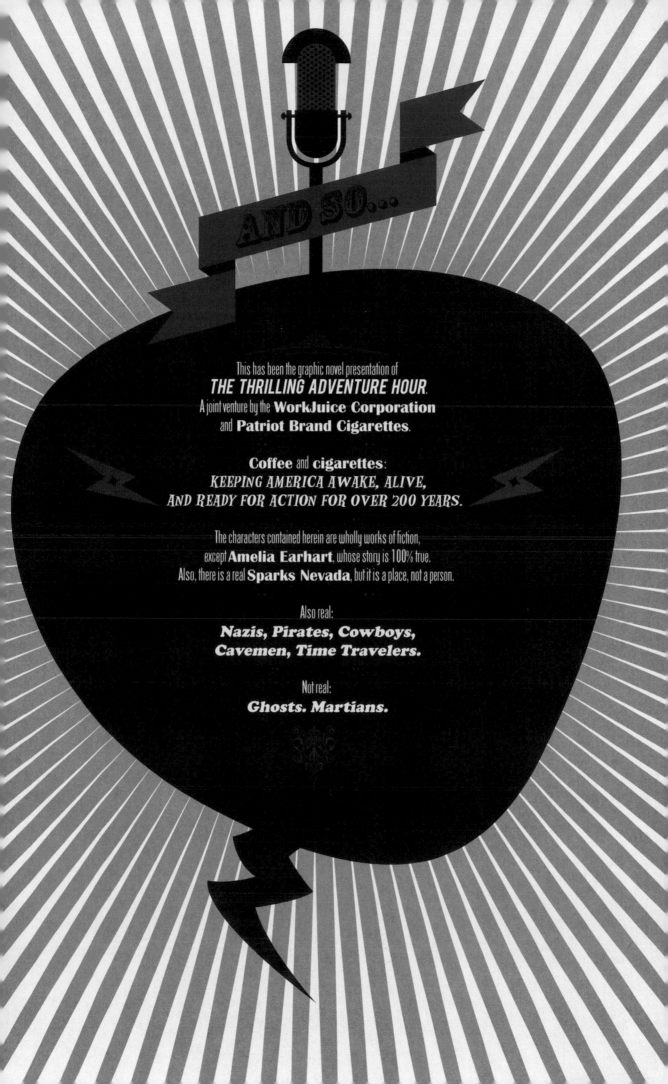

**AND SO...**

This has been the graphic novel presentation of
*THE THRILLING ADVENTURE HOUR.*
A joint venture by the **WorkJuice Corporation**
and **Patriot Brand Cigarettes**.

**Coffee** and **cigarettes**:
*KEEPING AMERICA AWAKE, ALIVE,
AND READY FOR ACTION FOR OVER 200 YEARS.*

The characters contained herein are wholly works of fiction,
except **Amelia Earhart**, whose story is 100% true.
Also, there is a real **Sparks Nevada**, but it is a place, not a person.

Also real:
*Nazis, Pirates, Cowboys,
Cavemen, Time Travelers.*

Not real:
*Ghosts. Martians.*

# ABOUT THE CREATORS

### Vagrants, Scoundrels, and Thieves

## BEN ACKER & BEN BLACKER

Ben Acker & Ben Blacker are the creators of *The Thrilling Adventure Hour*. *TAH* has provided Acker & Blacker with exciting opportunities in entertainment. They sold several sketches to Fox late night television, developed the segment "Sparks Nevada, Marshal on Mars" as an animated cartoon for Nickelodeon, and a pilot for a primetime animated comedy with 20th Century Fox Studios. In 2010, they wrote two pilots for the USA network—an hour and a half-hour—as well as a half-hour comedy for Spike. They have written episodes of Nickelodeon's *Supah Ninjas* and CW's *Supernatural* (where they were on the writing staff).

## HEIDI ARNHOLD

Heidi Arnhold is a comic artist living in Atlanta, GA who has worked on a multitude of projects involving such properties as *The Dark Crystal*, *Fraggle Rock*, and *Star Trek*. She has three rabbits, one husband, and a constant desire for donuts. Seek out more of her work by searching for "heidiarnhold" on most things, like deviantart, tumblr, and her own .com.

## JORDIE BELLAIRE

Jordie Bellaire is a comic book colorist living in Ireland. Her current projects include *Manhattan Projects*, *Nowhere Men*, *The Massive*, *Captain Marvel*, *Rocketeer: The Spirit*, and *Quantum & Woody* with frequent collaborator, Tom Fowler. She enjoys watching Twin Peaks and listening to Stephen King audiobooks with her cat Buffy.

## RANDY BISHOP

Randy Bishop is a freelance illustrator and character designer living in eastern Idaho with his wife and two sons. He's been a lifetime comic book and cartoon fan, movie enthusiast, and an avid reader. As an artist, he looks forward to many many years working in the entertainment and publishing industry doing what he loves. You can see some of his work at www.randybishopart.com.

## CASEY CROWE

Casey Crowe is an illustrator and storyboard artist who has previously done work for the likes of Disney, Nike, Universal Pictures and Nickelodeon among others. He lives in Los Angeles with his wife and dog. Wanna see more of his stuff? Cool, mosey on over to www.caseycrowe.com.

## LAR DESOUZA

Lar deSouza was born to humble surroundings on a Hallowe'en night many years ago. Fortunately his monumental ego was able to overcome the humble bits. He is the artist half of Sohmer & Lar, producing the online comics *Least I Could Do* and *Looking for Group*. He has no idea what to write for bios and suggestions are welcome. The Hallowe'en bit is true. You can see his online work at www.leasticoulddo.com, www.lfgcomic.com, and www.lartist.com.

## JOANNA ESTEP

Joanna Estep is an artist, a writer, and an accomplished whateverist. She has illustrated such titles as *Fraggle Rock*, *Reflection* (winner of the S.P.A.C.E. Prize), and her self-penned story *Happy Birthday, Michael Mitchell*. She is currently unraveling in Madison, WI where she hones her skills as an amateur taxidermist, watches all the horror movies she can stand, and nurtures a veritable cornucopia of vice. To see more of her work, visit www.joannaestep.com.

## BILLY FOWLER

Billy Fowler is a freelance illustrator and comic artist from North Carolina. He acquired a passion for comic related art since he was a kid watching cartoons in the early 80's and has been drawing them ever since. You can find his work on his website www.billyfowlerart.com.

## TOM FOWLER

Cartoonist and illustrator Tom Fowler has worked in comics, advertising, and film and game design. Past clients include Disney, Simon & Schuster, Wizards of the Coast, Hasbro, MAD, Valiant, Marvel, and DC Comics. His best known comics work include ***Venom***, ***Hulk Season One***, ***Quantum & Woody***, the critically acclaimed ***Mysterius the Unfathomable*** with writer Jeff Parker, and the ***MAD Magazine*** feature ***Monroe***. Tom eats only raw meat, stands 13 feet tall, and shoots lasers from his eyes.

## EVAN LARSON

Evan Larson is an illustrator, animator and former faculty member at The Rhode Island School of Design and Montserrat College of Art. His work has been showcased in Best American Comics 2008 and American Illustration among others. He lives in Hillsboro, OR with his wife and is currently working at Laika, Inc. He drew this story in the wee hours of the night while listening to Oneida's "Sheets of Easter" on repeat.

## JOE LEFAVI

Joe LeFavi is an obnoxiously passionate, hyper, silly person. When he first saw ***The Thrilling Adventure Hour***, he swore to someday make a graphic novel of that world. Years later, he is now the editor of this very book and helped to orchestrate the Kickstarter campaign that funded its creation. A veritable hat rack of titles (transmedia producer, publishing packager, consultant, writer, aspiring ninja), Joe finds purpose as an ambassador of awesome storytellers and ideas destined to thrive in all facets of entertainment. Share in his latest quests at **www.quixotictransmedia.com**.

## ANDRÉ MAY

André May is a comic colorist from Brazil who doesn't really have an interesting story to write about. He is a perfectionist and strives to bring inks to life with his colors. If you liked his work and want to see more, be sure to check **saerus-coloring.deviantart.com**, if that URL, and the internet, still exists as you're reading this.

## CHRIS MORENO

Chris Moreno encounters adventure every day, whether it's crossing against a green light, stretching the boundaries of the "five-second rule", or creating a zombie comic at the height of the zombie bubble. But his greatest adventure started over 10 years ago, and continues to this day – a career in illustration. Comics, games, storyboards, concept art and design – he's conquered and survived them all. Follow the chronicles of his adventures at **www.chrismoreno.org**, **chrismoreno.deviantart.com**, and **www.zombiedickheads.com**.

## SCOTT NEWMAN

Scott Newman is an award-winning graphic designer who has worked in production, illustration, and graphic design for over ten years. A two-time graduate of the University of Southern California, he has worked with CBS, The Recording Academy, Hasbro, American Rag Cie, and Top Cow Productions. As Archaia Entertainment's Production Manager he has designed and packaged numerous graphic novels including ***Moon Lake***, ***Sharaz-De: Tales from the Arabian Nights***, ***Spera***, and ***Last Days of an Immortal***.

## NATALIE NOURIGAT

Natalie "Tally" Nourigat can't believe she gets paid to do things like this. Her days consist of drawing comics at Periscope Studio, studying French, and taste-testing every plate of nachos in Portland, OR. You might enjoy her comic autobiography (***Between Gears***) or her movie review comics. Visit **www.NatalieNourigat.com** for more of Natalie's work!

## JOEL PRIDDY

Joel Priddy doodles and teaches doodling. Previous works include ***Pulpatoon: Pilgrimage***, ***The Preposterous Voyages of IronHide Tom***, and an adaptation of O. Henry's ***The Gift of the Magi***.

## EVAN "DOC" SHANER

Evan "Doc" Shaner has drawn books for Archaia, Dynamite, and Dark Horse Comics. He lives in Colorado with his wife, their daughter, and their dog. Doc is wild as a cactoid but has yet to become King of the Martian Frontier.

## JEFF STOKELY

CONGRATULATIONS! You've made it to Jeff Stokely's biography!!! Well... There really isn't much to say about him. He likes to draw comics, eat pizza and drink coffee, sometimes all at once... but then really, who doesn't?! You can see more of his work in Archaia's ***The Reason for Dragons*** and BOOM! Studios' ***Six Gun Gorilla***. That is of course, if you live to do so...

PREPARE
YOURSELF
FOR MORE!

**We're Not Done Yet**

The industrious Acker & Blacker, along with your friends at the WorkJuice Corporation, ask your indulgence as they commend the many supporters of ***THE THRILLING ADVENTURE HOUR***.

# OUTRODUCTION

From Ben Acker & Ben Blacker

For those of you reading the book backwards -
**WELCOME!**

It would be falsely humble to begin this outroduction with something like, "When we created ***The Thrilling Adventure Hour*** over eight years ago, we never imagined it would be a comic book..." Because, see, we always imagined it would be a comic book. And not just a comic book, but television programs, feature films, web-series, and any other media you care to invent. ***The Thrilling Adventure Hour*** was always meant to be an incubator for our ideas. Somewhere along the line we were just having too much fun playing in the worlds of ***Sparks Nevada***, ***Beyond Belief***, and the rest to do much more than write and produce the stage show (still going strong every month in Los Angeles!). With the stage show, we were given the opportunity to tell stories completely unfettered by outside interference. We also got the chance to collaborate with some of the best actors around; collectively known as the WorkJuice Players, they deserve as much credit as we do for breathing life into these characters. We cannot thank them enough for helping to make the show—and thus everything that has spun out of the show, including this book—what it is.

This book should serve as a jumping off point for you to explore the show, available as a podcast on the Nerdist network. Jump in anywhere. ***Sparks Nevada, Marshal on Mars*** is particularly rewarding if you listen in order, as it's the most serialized, but we try to keep the stories accessible for newcomers and longtime fans alike.

And speaking of those fans... When we created ***The Thrilling Adventure Hour***, we never imagined we'd sell out a 250-seat theater every month, play to packed crowds in New York and San Francisco, have 150,000 monthly downloads of the podcast, and be the subject of interest in the ***Hollywood Reporter*** and NPR's ***All Things Considered***. We are so thankful to the fans of the show for their support and for legitimizing a thing that started out playing in a 100-seat supper club where we knew every person in the audience.

Eight years later, this book was funded entirely by one of the most successful comics campaigns on Kickstarter with over 2,500 backers worldwide. One of the rewards available was a "special thanks" in this, the Special Thanks Section of the book. It's flattering seeing so many familiar names on this list, both real-life friends and collaborators and fans whom we meet at the shows or interact with online.

Some of you have been with us for all eight years. Some are joining us for the first time with this anthology. Whomever you are, we couldn't be more excited to have you aboard for this, which we see as just the beginning of a long thrilling adventure.

**Ben Acker & Ben Blacker**
LOS ANGELES, CA, AMERICA
2013

## Original Graphic Novel Plus Backers

A very special thanks to those whose generous support made this graphic novel possible.

**Aaron Ginsburg**
**Albert Camacho Jr.**
**Alexander Erik McGill**
**André T. Parrish**
**Andrew J. Connelly**
**Andrew Franks**
**Andrew Miller**
**Ashley Nikole Schrader**
**Aviva Lorelei Cooley**
**Becca Gurney**
**Benjamin Hendy**
**Blane A. Elferdink**
**Bradley Bowen**
**Brian Carroll**
**Charles Lucas Douros**
**Charlie Fonville**
**Chris McGowan**
**Christina Sullivan**
**Christopher O'Neal**
**Cindie Flannigan**
**Damon Hines**
**Daniel Figg**
**Darren Prewer**
**David Tai**
**Denitt Perez**
**Dennis Kelly**
**Don Spiro**
**Doug Hanke**
**The Family Dunn**
**Eduardo Herrera**
**Eric S Reardon**
**Fran-Bob Malina**
**Gideon Cohen**
**Graham and Joyce Orndorff**
**Indiana Ford-Mar**
**Jamie Latta**
**Jason Dietz**
**Jennifer Toshiko Frey**
**Jessica Howard**
**John A Craig**
**John Smith**
**Jon Schnepp**
**Jonathan Bresman**
**Kat Neall**
**Katherine Shearon**
**Keiran Courville**
**Kristie Leach**
**Liam James Callen**
**Lucas Wilson**
**Lukas Bergstrom**
**M. Elizabeth Hughes**
**Marcia L. Gaines**
**Mark S. Wallace**
**Mathieu Doublet**
**Michelle Biloon**
**Natalie Poluha**
**Nate Martin**
**Nick Strann**
**Nicole Denae Stolpa**
**Paul Guyot**
**Paul Sweeney**
**Paula Lynn Hoffman**
**Peter Lin**
**Phil Caron**
**Rachel Sklar**
**Ralph G. Bittelari**
**Rizwan Kassim**
**Rob Hansen**
**Robert J. Wagstaff**
**Rosalyn Foster**
**Steve Treadwell**
**Tammy Golden**
**Thomas Leong**
**William G. Wu**

The Special Thanks section is brought to you by
**Patriot Brand Cigarettes**
*"They're Good For Your Constitution!"*

## SPECIAL THANKS

We couldn't have picked a better group of
like-minded individuals to publish this book than

### Archaia Entertainment

Jack Cummins      Rebecca Taylor
Mel Caylo      Scott Newman
Mike Kennedy      Stephen Christy

Likewise, **Nerdist Industries**
gets us. We're proud to be under the Nerdist banner.

Chris Fealy      Katie Levine
Chris Hardwick      Peter Levin
James Miller      Seth Laderman

### The Work Juice Players

were their usual giving, supportive selves during and for the Kickstarter campaign.
Whether they offered up Skype chats, meet-and-greets, tweets, or humored us when
we granted backstage visits to guests, we owe them more than we can ever repay.

Annie Savage      John DiMaggio
Autumn Reeser      John Ennis
Busy Philipps      Joshua Malina
Craig Cackowski      Marc Evan Jackson
Dave (Gruber) Allen      Mark Gagliardi
Hal Lublin      Paget Brewster
James Urbaniak      Paul F. Tompkins

We're lucky in that, through the show, we've made some **Great Friends**
Some of them have attended, others have guest starred, some have even guest-written episodes;
some are folks we've worked with in other capacities, but all are folks whose company we enjoy.
All of these people were kind enough to donate rewards to the campaign
or otherwise prove themselves instrumental in its success:

Andy Paley      Jackson Publick
Adam Busch      Jane Espenson
Adam Rogers      Jeff Greenstein
Amber Benson      Jonathan Dinerstein
Barre Duryea      Maarten DeBoer
Brian Stack      Mark Flanagan and everyone at Largo
Brian Tatosky      Nathan Fillion
Ben Edlund      Nick Kroll
Chris Storer      Paul Pape
David Fury      Patton Oswalt
David Nadelberg (Mortified)      Yael Zinkow

From the
**Oral Tradition**
to the
**Aural Tradition**
and **Beyond,**
this exemplary literary achievement
has been another
**FINE DISTINCTION**
from your friends at
**WorkJuice Corporation**
and
**Patriot Brand Cigarettes.**

Finally, a few people had to put up with a solid two months of strategizing,
minute-by-minute updates, setbacks and, ultimately, successes.
They are the people **Most Dear to Us**
and there aren't words for the gratitude we feel.
Thank you doesn't begin to express it.

Julie Lacouture      The Acker Family
Todd Cooper and Sara Watkins      The Blacker Family
Aaron Ginsburg, again      The Lacouture Family
The LeFunkel Family

And we'd be remiss not to mention our
editor, producer, transmedia guru, and friend,
**Joe LeFavi**
Joe was instrumental to pulling this book together.
Anything you like in it is because of him.

The WorkJuice Coporation presents...

# THE SHAPE OF THINGS TO COME!

**FLYING CARS!**
**MEALS HELD IN TEENY TINY PILLS!**
**ROBOT BUTLERS!**

**And in the past, everything that we have now was something that would exist in the future.**

**SHIRTS!**
**TAXI CABS!**
**REGULAR BUTLERS THAT AREN'T ROBOTS!**

**Yes, everything from shirts to butlers, including taxi cabs, were invented by inventors fueled by WorkJuice Coffee.**

WORKJUICE™ *"Filled to the Brim With Zip and Vim!"*

This message was brought to you by your friends at the WorkJuice Coporation.

*Experience Coffee Brewed for the Fairer Sex*

## WorkJuice *Femme*

**Blend for Her**

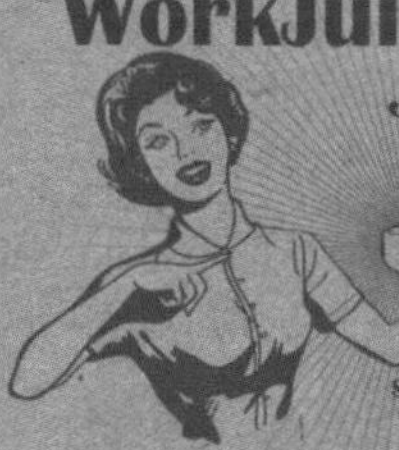

**Beans Specially Selected to Interact with a Woman's Female Biology**

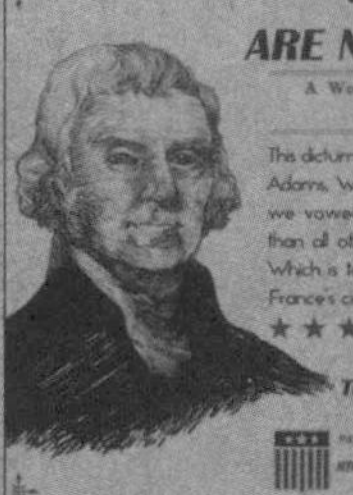

## "ALL CIGARETTES ARE NOT CREATED EQUA

A Word from the Third President of the United States
★ THOMAS JEFFERSON ★

This dictum isn't in the Constitution, but it may as well be. Wh
Adams, Washington and I got together to found Big Tobac
we vowed that Patriot Brand Cigarettes would be as bet
than all other cigarettes as America is than all other natio
Which is to say 'all the way better.' And they are. Ever tr
France's cigarettes? Like smoking what came out of your d

★ ★ ★ ★ ★ ★ ★ ★ ★ ★ ★ ★ ★ ★

**Try Patriot Brand Cigarettes**
***They're Good for Your Constitution!***

## ★ ★ ★ ★ ★ A MESSAGE FROM ★ ★ ★ ★ ★
# A PRESIDENT OF THE UNITED STATES

~ on behalf of ~
**Patriot Brand Cigarettes**

My fellow Americans.

Since taking office, I've been given a special phone line. I use it and I get whatever I want. If I want a panda sandwich, I pick up the phone, press six, and I tell them *"panda sandwich."* 20 minutes later, the tenderest, most endangered sandwich you've ever tasted. I'll tell you what though. Every hour or so, I pick up that phone, I hit six, and I order me up some Patriot Brand Cigarettes.

They're tastier than a hummingbird salad, which is delicious and goes down fast. Panda meat is tender and surprisingly smoky. But nowhere near as flavorful as a Patriot Brand Cigarette.

God bless America.
And God Bless **Patriot Brand Cigarettes.**

PATRIOT BRAND CIGARETTES IS PLEASED TO BRING YOU JEFFERSON REID: ACE AMERICAN A THRILLING ADVENTURE HOUR PRODUCTION

"THEY'RE GOOD... PATRIOT BRAND CIGARETTES ...FOR YOUR CONSTITUTION!"

**Don't Forget!**
**Collect Patriot Points for Exciting Rewards!**

" The best thing in the world **JUST GOT BETTER**. Rejoice, fellow Adventurekateers! Our time is now at hand! Things like this are why we beat the Russians. "

**MATT FRACTION**

{ Eisner Award-winning writer of *The Invincible Iron Man, The Immortal Iron Fist, Uncanny X-Men,* and *Casanova* }

THE THRILLING ADVENTURE HOUR

" Ladies and Gentlemen, it is me, **JOHN HODGMAN**, who offers this testimonial. It has been only 21 months since I first encountered ***THE THRILLING ADVENTURE HOUR***, and my life has not been the same since. Beyond being the best staged episodic radio comedy of the 21st century, ***THRILLING*** is also and more plainly just wonderful: one of the most joyously and smartly written entertainments that I have encountered. Acker, Blacker, and the WorkJuice Players just make me happy. And also I am generally more alert and my eczema has cleared up. So it is extra exciting to welcome THRILLING to the funny pages, thus merging two great marginal American art forms into one, and eliminating the need for all those human actors and singers, who are generally longwinded jerks. Myself most of all. "

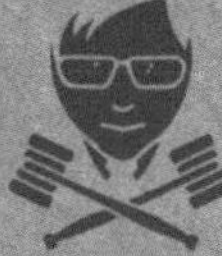

John Hodgman
Author of the trilogy of *Complete World Knowledge*, humorist, frequent contributor to *The Daily Show*

**TUNE-IN AND JOIN THE ACE AMERICAN ON HIS LATEST ADVENTURE!**

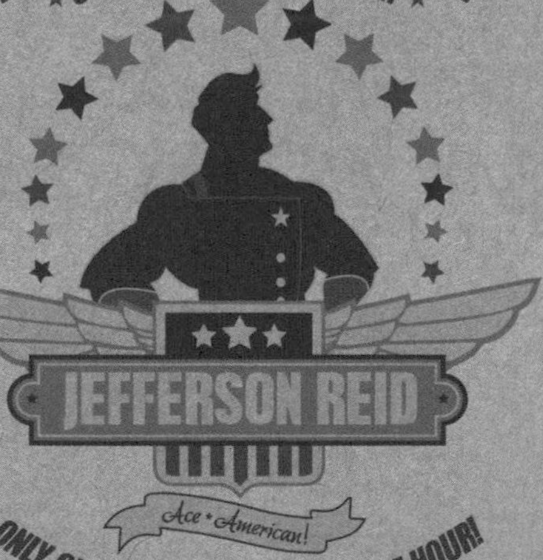
JEFFERSON REID
Ace • American!

**ONLY ON THE THRILLING ADVENTURE HOUR!**

★ *SPONSORED BY* **PATRIOT BRAND CIGARETTES** ★
"THEY'RE GOOD FOR YOUR CONSTITUTION."

*The*

# ROYAL CHRONO PATROL

*Quality Time Pieces*

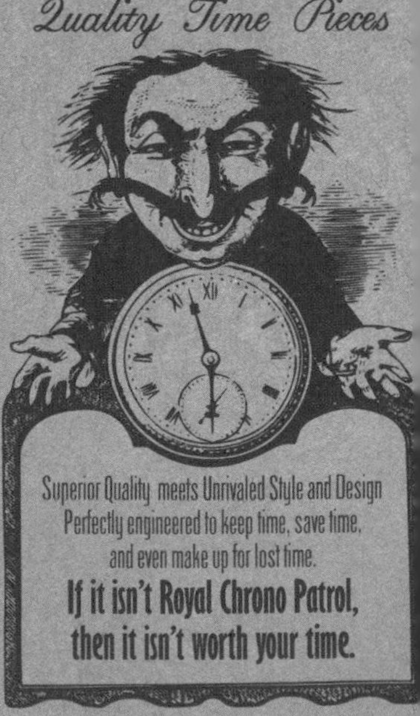

Superior Quality meets Unrivaled Style and Design
Perfectly engineered to keep time, save time, and even make up for lost time.

**If it isn't Royal Chrono Patrol, then it isn't worth your time.**

**MAKE HISTORY HAPPEN... ON TIME!**

Stand Sentry Over the Century and Enjoy Colonel Tick-Tock
Only on The Thrilling Adventure Hour

*Now in Print and Available from Fine Retailers of Goods for Women*

# THE THRILLING ADVENTURE HOUR

**Original Graphic Novel**

*Ladies Edition*

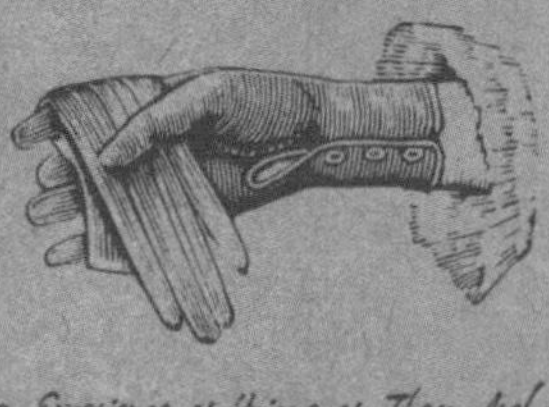

✦ *Specially Designed, Formulated, and Printed for Women Who Enjoy a Reading Experience as Unique as They Are!* ✦

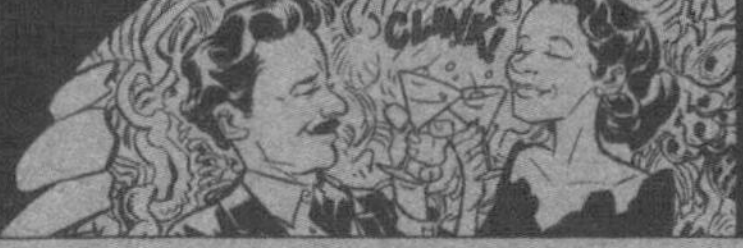
CLINK!

**Are You Losing Your Pep While You Rea**
Nothing Goes Better with a WorkJuice Comic than a Cu
**WORKJUICE BRAND COFF**
**Stimulate Your Reading Experience!**